Praise for

POLISH FOLK MAGIC

Ancestral Lore & Traditions of the West Slavs

"As a first-generation Serbian-American raised in folk Orthodoxy, the Byzantine-derived equivalent of the folk Catholicism described in *Polish Folk Magic's* pages, I found so many areas of overlap with my own culture's beliefs and practices—right down to the particularities of terminology in several instances—that I found myself cheering with delight quite audibly as I read. Truly, besides being a treasure trove of lore and spell craft, Tarnawska's excellent book ultimately serves as an ancestral summons: one that gathers us home again in its pages."

—Anna Urošević Applegate, author of *Slava! Slavic Paganism and Dual-Faith Folk Ways*

"In much of the Western world, the deep folk traditions of countries like Poland have long been overshadowed by dominant religions. As a native Greek priestess practicing my own ancestral traditions, I know how difficult it can be to find and keep one's voice in such a landscape. Joanna Tarnawska has not only kept her voice, but amplified it, selflessly, voicing—for the first time in an English language book—the depths of Polish folk magic. In doing so, she has offered a gift not only to the Slavic diaspora, but also to those in Poland working to revive and carry forward their ancestral practices. *Polish Folk Magic* deserves a place on the shelf of every serious folk magic practitioner."

—Elyse Welles, author of *Sacred Wild: An Invitation to Connect to Spirits of the Land*

"*Polish Folk Magic* opens a doorway into the enchanted heart of Poland, where ancestors, spirits, and land still speak. Joanna Tarnawska weaves myth, ritual, and memory into a living tapestry of fire, water, forests, and stars. Written with reverence and clarity, *Polish Folk Magic* shares the practices and spirits that sustained generations of Polish people through hardship and change. It is a guide for those who long to reconnect with ancestral ways and find magic in the everyday."

—Vlasta Pilot, author of *Gentle Hearts Unite Zine*

"If there is one thing you can expect from Joanna and her work it is absolute honesty, no sugarcoating, no whitewashing or watering down to make people feel more comfortable—it is raw, unadulterated and wonderfully real. For those interested in Polish folk traditions and Slavic folklore, this is an absolute treasure trove that engages the mind and soul. This book feels alive. A book many, myself included, have yearned for, truly a first of its kind. Written by a native, who is genuinely immersed in the culture that she is writing about and generously passing on to all those who want to step into the world of the creepy, bizarre and beautiful Polish-Slavic folk traditions."

—Ella Harrison, author of *The Book of Spells,* BA in Social and Cultural Anthropology

"What Joanna Tarnawska delivers in this written work is a treasure trove of Polish folk magic and traditions, ideal for readers looking to connect with their ancestral heritage. Whether you're part of the diaspora or local, *Polish Folk Magic* will quickly become your favored resource for understanding regional folkloric spirits, seasonal practices and holidays, and traditional remedies. Tarnawska writes methodically, making the material easy to digest due to her wealth of knowledge as a firsthand account of the region. This book is bound to become a favored addition to your personal library!"

—Leah Middleton, author of *Magic from the Hilltops and Hollers*

"High praises for *Polish Folk Magic: Ancestral Lore and Traditions of the West Slavs!* Joanna demonstrates how one's practice of these traditions can remain culturally relevant while staying true to the bioregionalism of the lands on which one is currently residing. She has woven a robust tapestry of the people, lore, history, and the living tradition of Polish folk ways and bound it together with personal experience! *Polish Folk Magic* is a Baba-approved guide for living in communion with nature, aligning with spirit, and tapping into the liminal space which forms and informs the practice of a Slavic (or Slavic-hybrid) folk witch. For English speakers yearning to learn the ways of our ancestors in the diaspora, our wait is over!"

—Caireann V., Slavic diaspora content creator at *Hearth and Besom*

"*Polish Folk Magic* is a gorgeous culmination of a lifetime of learning, dedication to community, and listening to the land and the earth spirits. This book creates an altar where the reader can commune with the stories, histories, and lessons of this lifelong dedication—a meeting place on the page. Joanna Tarnawska has written a necessary book, one for the wild and wandering magic maker, that honors folk magic in its divine multiplicity. Her skill of writing at the crossroads of poetic magic and academic research creates an artifact and an invitation that deftly takes the reader on a journey to a deeper understanding of folk magic rooted in Polish ancestry, the elements, spirits, spells, and Poland itself. This book is for anyone longing to cultivate a profound sense of and connection to Polish folk magic, and it will be one I return to again and again."

—Kate Belew, author of *Word Witch, How to Call Upon and Cultivate the Creative Magic Within You*

"This book is an unapologetic statement on the nature of Slavic witchcraft and the path of the old ways. An informative yet pragmatic approach to folkcraft which inspires and encourages the reader to delve deeper into their craft. A must read for the student of Slavic and other folk practices alike."

—Elwynn Green, teacher and creator at *The Antlered Crown*

"What a delight Joanna Tarnawska's book is. She skilfully guides the reader through Slavic conceptions of folk magic in a clear and straightforward manner, introducing the culture, perceptions of the spirit world, and the significance of fire and water in the work of the folk magic practitioner. It offers information I haven't encountered in other books of this kind and truly resonated with me. In her straightforward, accessible writing style, she introduces the reader to how she conceives of folk magic working and guides the reader through *Zamawianie* and the words used in folk magical practice to effect change, exploring cleansing, protection and the evil eye, *Uroki* in more detail, along with other areas folk practitioners will be familiar with. What Tarnawska has given us here is such a solid, generous introduction to important ideas, practices, philosophies, and approaches that, until now, we haven't had in the English language. Joanna has truly blazed a trail with this work, opening the door wide for others to follow, and I hope there's plenty more to come."

—Scott Richardson-Read (Cailleach's Herbarium), author of *Mill Dust and Dreaming Bread*

"*Polish Folk Magic: Ancestral Lore & Traditions of the West Slavs* stands as an indispensable resource—an encyclopedic work that interweaves history, ethnography, and spiritual practice. Joanna Tarnawska, widely known as "The Polish Folk Witch", writes from her lived experience as a practicing folk witch in Poland, bringing rare authenticity and authority to her work. The result is a meticulously detailed account of folklore and customs that preserves a cultural inheritance scholars and practitioners alike will return to again and again."

—Mary-Grace Fahrun, author of *Italian Folk Magic* and *Living Folk Magic*

POLISH FOLK MAGIC

Ancestral Lore & Traditions of the West Slavs

ABOUT THE AUTHOR

Joanna Tarnawska is an animist, folk practitioner, writer, and psychologist residing in the mountains of Lower Silesia, Poland. Joanna's work is rooted in the bioregional traditions and folklore of the area, drawing upon the historical practices of the early modern period, as well as anthropological and ethnographic studies of both pre- and post-Christian West Slavic customs. She aims to promote and educate about Polish folk culture and heritage through *Polish Folk Witch*—a community-focused platform offering articles, courses, and group studies on Polish folk magic, animism, and traditional folkloric withcraft. Tarnawska has been published in *Femme Occulte* magazine, and *Mandragora Digital Bulletin* by Mandragora Foundation.

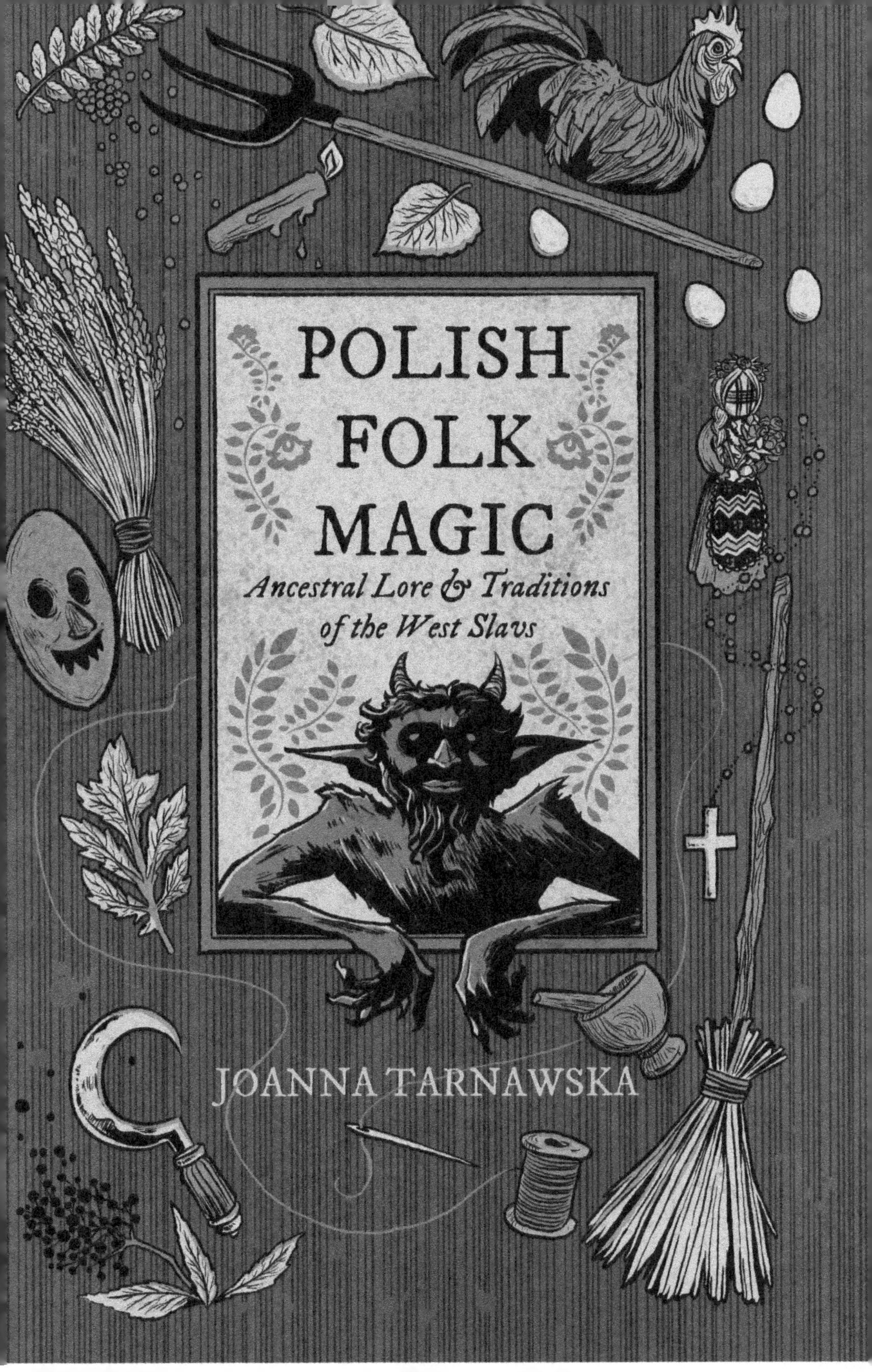
POLISH
FOLK
MAGIC
Ancestral Lore & Traditions
of the West Slavs
JOANNA TARNAWSKA

Paperback ISBN: 978-1-964537-54-2
Hardcover ISBN: 978-1-964537-63-4
eBook ISBN: 978-1-968185-43-5

Library of Congress Control Number on file.

Published by:
Crossed Crow Books, LLC
518 Davis St, Suite 205
Evanston, IL 60201
www.crossedcrowbooks.com

Printed in the United States of America.
IBI

ACKNOWLEDGEMENTS

I wish to express the depths of my gratitude to the ancestors first and foremost. If it wasn't for your resilience, determination, and deep-rooted love for the stories sung by the land, none of this could be preserved and shared forth for the world to be nourished by. To my beloved grandmothers Danusia and Czesia, I continue to do this work in your name and miss you dearly.

To my parents who, despite hardships, raised me to be so deeply in love with the lore, the land, and the ecology around us through art, poetry, and hikes. Mom, for never giving up your strength despite the ancestral burdens, you're a legend! Dad, I hope you do write that book about the rural folk life and stories you grew up around—they are indescribably precious and worth preserving for future generations!

To my beloved husband, Tymoteusz, for being my rock at sea; for your patience, encouragement, care, and continued support during the writing process—thank you. For always being right by my side in eternal appreciation for wilderness, deep creativity, and hermitage. I love you.

To all the amazing friends and folks of my online community who continue to support my work, cheer me on, and root for me no matter what—I couldn't have done any of this without you. You folks showed me that I have this book in me, and that it might be worth writing. I never felt so lovingly held by a community of people before.

Last but not least, I wish to extend my heartfelt thanks to the amazing crew at Crossed Crow Books, who continue to have exceptional, genuine ethics and values, and hold fast to them. For all your fantastic hard work and care, for believing in platforming the voices of locals across the globe, for being continuously anti-AI and inclusive. Thank you!

ACKNOWLEDGMENTS

TABLE OF CONTENTS

Part Two:
Polish Folk Magic in Theory

Part Three:
Polish Folk Magic in Practice

Part Four:
Spirits and Allies

Part Five:
Agrarian Traditions and Polish Folkloric Year

INTRODUCTION

The book you hold in your hands is a labor of love. It is dedicated to the Polish ancestors who kept our old folkloric traditions alive the best they could throughout centuries of hardship, displacement, serfdom, partitions, occupations, regimes, and war. Through this publication, I wish to give an authentic, local voice to the spirit of this land and its inhabitants. While there is no one correct way to observe, interpret, and cultivate these traditions, what follows is the way that I have been taught by my grandmothers, by the folks in my communities, and by the land spirits themselves. It is a testament to a lived experience of folk tradition as perceived through the eyes of a practitioner of the folk ways. This tome is steeped in the holy and the heretical; equally guided by historical sources, legends, and dreams—ultimately subjective, yet expressed as genuinely and from the heart as was possible within the limitations of a written piece of work. Although much regrettably had to remain beyond the scope of this work, such as the vast traditions of Polish folk herbalism or the depths of our native folk demonology, this work should nevertheless equip the reader with a solid foundation for incorporating our ancestral traditions into one's daily life and practice. As the first publication of its kind, it should pave the way for future (hopefully more detailed and niche) works of fellow Polish practitioners and enthusiasts of our folkloric traditions.

WHO IS THIS BOOK MEANT FOR?

The original intent for writing this book was to provide a solid, well-sourced publication for folks of the Slavic diaspora worldwide. I also welcome any Polish and Slavic culture enthusiasts who don't speak our languages, thus having diminished access to the lived experience of locals and authentic sources about Polish and Slavic folk magic. It has also been my humble intention to blaze the trail for future publications by fellow local practitioners—the world needs to hear your voices.

To all the folks who have been feeling somewhat rootless, longing to reconnect with the traditions and beliefs of their ancestors, this book is for you. May it help you find the red thread of connection to the old ways of our forebears, and with it, the realization that they have always been there for you—no matter how close or far you find yourself from their original homeland—and that you belong.

LIMITATIONS OF THE BOOK

Any attempt to package the heritage of an entire culture within a single book is bound to have its limitations. The sheer scope of the information that should be included to paint a somewhat complete and satisfactory picture of Polish folk magic, realistically, would necessitate several tomes, especially when much of it deserves proper attention to detail in its explanation, not to whitewash or entirely lose the cultural nuance. Therefore, during the process of writing this publication, I was repeatedly faced with impossible decisions in terms of what to include and what to exclude to match its parameters. Ultimately, I hope I have arrived at a structure that serves as an introductory, yet still comprehensive, foundation for those who wish to engage with our cultural practices of folk magic. I am confident that perceptive readers will notice how certain aspects have been left out, and I hope that they can be expanded upon in future works.

It should also be noted that this book does not attempt to offer a comparative dive into *Rodnovery* (Slavic native faith) or Slavic neo-pagan traditions present in today's Poland. As I do not identify as pagan or a Rodnover, it is not my place to write about this movement and its traditions. Out of respect for my Rodnover friends, I do not wish to speak in their place, nor introduce their faith as an outsider. To remain authentic toward Polish folk practices as they've been preserved in our culture, while also respecting the religious practices of contemporary pagans, Slavic pagan reconstruction and religion remain outside of the scope of this publication, in favor of approaches recognized in rural dual faith practices. This means that wherever pre-Christian elements have survived relatively untouched to this day, they are openly presented as such, and apparent syncretisms are pointed out. However, the elements that have been syncretized or Christianized, respectively, shall not be synthetically stripped back to their pre-Christian forms to be presented as pagan.

REGARDING ACADEMIC RIGOR

It has been essential for me to base all the information I am presenting in this publication on the foundation of legitimate sources, all of which are either academic or properly sourced, and to quote and attribute said sources in accordance with academic rigor to the best of my ability. It was my ambition only to include the works of Polish scholars and researchers, rather than those from abroad, to avoid an "outsider gaze" and maintain a local understanding of the presented source material. Scarce exceptions include scholars of European traditions whose scope of work bears a close resemblance to that of our own. That said, this book should not be mistaken for an academic work, nor expected to adhere to the rules and rigor of academia entirely and without flaw. As an author, I claim no professional scholarship in related fields (folkloric studies, ethnography, anthropology, and such), and thus have no right to claim academic rigor. Moreover, the sourced material is presented from the perspective of an active practitioner of traditional folkloric magic and animism, interwoven with personal anecdotes of lived experience, and ultimately, interpreted subjectively through my own eyes as a local who grew up and continues to live in the Polish culture. It is expected of the reader to adjust the expectations and not mistake this publication for an academic one. However, for those academically inclined, the included bibliography is a treasure trove of sources that adhere to academic rigor and are better suited for scholars and researchers interested in the topic.

PART ONE

POLISH FOLKLORIC AND MYTHIC PERCEPTION OF THE WORLD

CHAPTER ONE

WHAT IS POLISH FOLK MAGIC?

Before we can properly dive into the actual practices of Polish folk magic, it is imperative to explain what folk magic is and what it certainly isn't. While every modern practitioner will have their own ideas and practices, often a unique mixture catering to their needs and the land where they live, a kind of folk craft also exists outside the context of the individual, and instead originates from the collective.

Polish folk magic is a practice rooted in a syncretic combination of things, as are all folk magics, of all cultures. Firstly, and most importantly, Polish folk magic is not an inherently religious practice—it exists at the intersection of all cultural, religious, and socio-political components present among the people living in the land of its origin. Thus, Polish folk magic is neither a pagan practice, with ancient unbroken lines of transmission, nor is it a Catholic practice, despite Polish folk magic practioners shamelessly using aspects of this religion. When we speak of authentic practices of Polish folk magic, we do not speak of a religion or faith—we speak of a craft that is firmly set in its living cultural context, including the language, knowledge, beliefs, arts, laws, customs, capabilities, and habits of its people.

Therefore, an aspiring folk practitioner should care to learn of the local folklore, history, pre-Christian and post-Christian mythos, beliefs, and customs of the common folk; traditional ways of tending to the land, the taboos and sacrums of the people; and the legends and stories of local spirits and sacred land features. Aspiring practitioners should also consider how the folk have traditionally formed relationships with the living ecology of plants, animals, land, spirits, and ancestors around them.

Folk magic is the magic of the people. It is for every person, of any social class, religious belief, identity, (dis)ability, and life circumstance. Polish folk magic welcomes everyone who feels kinship with our people. We do not—and will not—exclude you based on your ancestry, or where you live now. If you or your ancestors moved to Poland and you want to partake in our cultural practices, or if your Polish ancestors were displaced abroad many generations ago, or you were adopted or married into a Polish family, you are equally welcome.

Historically, Polish folk magic has always been utilized by practitioners and non-practitioners alike, meaning that everyone brings elements of folk magic into their daily lives as a means of survival and bettering their circumstances. Back in the day—and in some respects, even today—every household would be actively practicing apotropaic magic, healing magic, reversal magic, love magic, fortune telling, and ancestral veneration, among other magical workings. Working with plants and herbs for medicinal and magical purposes was once a common occurrence. Leaving offerings for the dead and household spirits, or treating certain natural forces as divine beings, was a staple in every Slavic household. Folk magic embedded in common folks' lives can be traced back to our animistic roots, ages before Christianization, predating even our pantheons and many of the pre-Christian pagan practices that developed among our people after the agrarian revolution. However, despite the ever-changing religious and political climate of a culture, both animism and folk magic always found a way to blend in and remain relevant as the unchangeable foundations of authentic folk spirituality. Whether it's pagan gods or the Christian God and Devil, we continue to make it work and coexist alongside the local forces and spirits, no matter how their names may change or how the masks they bear might transform based on who's in power.

In Slavic culture, this dynamic is embedded in the very myth of the creation of the world. The core symbolism and values conveyed by the myth remain unchanged. Still, the names of spirits and various lesser components may have changed and evolved in a syncretic manner to remain tolerable under any political and religious climate. In various iterations of this myth, the world is always created by light and dark forces: God and the Devil, together. The pre-Christian version may have originally involved Perun instead of God, and Weles instead of the Devil. However, the names and faces are not as important as the primary forces dwelling underneath them. And thus, no matter their accepted names and masks, they both work within their unchangeable spheres of influence: God/Perun in the heavens and the Devil/Weles in the depths of waters and underground. Such details are relevant for the folk practitioner, for a wise witch knows that they cannot ask a spirit to aid them in something that is outside of their sphere of influence. Such is the nature of practices that stem from animism; we do not pick sides, we embrace the full spectrum of existence, outside of religion and modern black-and-white morality, in tune with the laws of nature. This is why, in folk magic, you may witness people working with seemingly opposing spirits and forces. As we say, *"Bogu świeczka, a diabłu ogarek"* ("A candle for God, and a wick for the Devil"), meaning that a wise practitioner cultivates right relations with all sides, not just one. If one needs help with formal learning, they can ask the spirits of the upper worlds who deal with matters of intellect. If one needs help with money or health, they can ask the chthonic spirits who guard access to the riches of the land. While it may seem unacceptable to some, there is nothing impractical or illogical about the folkloric perception of the forces that be. It simply works the way it is.

The amazing thing about practices rooted in animism, such as folk magic, is that once one begins to live and breathe the animistic, folkloric perception of the world, one loses the need to follow the more anthropocentric rules of working one's craft. One understands that magic has only two rules: the rule of sympathy and the rule of contagion (to be explored in further chapters). One understands that the spirit world is not ruled by man-made hierarchies, but instead by the living ecology around them, and thus, one needs to cultivate right relations with all surrounding spheres of influence to have a good, balanced life. Things click into place, and human authorities on the subject cease to have any real impact on the practitioner. This is why folk magic is inherently heretical, as it frees the individual from replicating man-made hierarchies in their relations with the world of spirit and the ecology around them.

An aspiring Polish folk witch should not expect to be forced into a tight box of prescribed rules and hierarchies or have all their questions answered by some omniscient authority. The act of practicing folk magic is an act of taking one's power back from human authorities and returning it to the land, to oneself, and one's spirit allies. The practice of folk magic is an act of returning to a world of interconnectedness and community, of being fully present in this world and standing one's ground in it. A folk witch is never alone and never works just for their own gain. A folk witch becomes one with the land upon which they stand, tending to its inhabitants, traversing the otherworlds for mutual aid and vision, rewilding and giving back to the soil, and becoming a good ancestor for the future folk of their *Ród* (family lineage).

CHAPTER TWO

CULTURAL REGIONALITY AND BIOREGIONALITY IN FOLK MAGIC

Polish folk magic falls under the umbrella of Slavic folk practices. However, one cannot (and should not) equate all Slavic practices, nor pick and choose from different groups of Slavs at whim. In the broader, especially Western world, the Slavs are often perceived as one homogenous group, usually stereotypically equated with East Slavic culture. We observe this in Western pop culture and various Western sources, where the terms "Russian" and "Slavic" are frequently used interchangeably. This may reinforce the stereotype that we're all the same people with no differences among us. This is, frankly, rather ignorant and will not take you far in terms of accessing the authentic aspects of our cultures, as well as traditional magical practices.

The Slavic peoples are generally divided into three distinct groups:

- West Slavs: Poles, Czechs, Slovaks, and Sorbs
- East Slavs: Ukrainians, Belarusians, Russians, and Rusyns
- South Slavs: Bosniaks, Bulgarians, Croats, Macedonians, Montenegrins, Serbs, and Slovenes

To equate us all is to erase our unique cultural heritages, languages, customs, beliefs, and thus, our unique folk magics. While it is undeniably true that we share a strong common core, each group of Slavs is significantly distinct from the others.

One such distinct characteristic that makes a difference in the context of folk magic practices is our religious beliefs: The majority of West Slavs are considered Catholic; East Slavs, Orthodox; and South Slavs are considered Muslim, Orthodox, and Catholic. While the Slavs shared some common beliefs (for example, ontological myths, the importance of ancestral veneration, or names of a select few deities or spirits), they were still very diverse in terms of their pagan beliefs. Their pantheons differed, as did the local land spirits and demons. Therefore, a seeker interested in researching and reclaiming their Slavic heritage while living abroad can focus on a country of origin as a good first step. For individuals who already reside in a country of ancestral origin, researching the lore, legends, and traditions of the region where you live, as well as the region(s) where your ancestors lived, can further enrich your practice.

Slavic culture is like a *matryoshka* doll: once you start opening it up, it turns out there is more and more inside. Learning about the culture is the gift that keeps on giving! Likewise, the cultural differences do not stop with specific geographical regions, nor with the countries. Every Slavic country consists of smaller regions, each with a unique history and often surprisingly stark differences in folklore, myth, legends, dialects, beliefs, and folk practices (including folk magic). Although it is outside the scope of this book (as well as my knowledge and expertise) to cover all of the countries and their regions, I would like to offer some basic layman's insights into the most important aspects of this within Poland to illustrate how crucial it is to get to the bottom of things and search for clues in regions of interest.

It all began in the early tribal times, long before the country of Poland was even on the map. Our origins remain somewhat shrouded in mystery and new research continues to actualize our understanding. We know that the Proto-Slavic people were possibly already active on the territory of today's Poland at least as early as 1500 BCE, with some research tracing the Slavic roots in these lands to the indigenous tribes living here during the Iron Age. However, we shall focus on a much better documented period prior to the tenth century, just before the Slavic tribes of these regions were united under the country of Poland in 966. At that time, the biggest Polish tribes were: *Pomorzanie* (Pomeranians), *Polanie* (Polans), *Ślężanie* (Silesians), *Mazowszanie* (Masovians), *Wiślanie* (Vistulans), and *Lędzianie* (Lendians). Each tribe had its distinct tribal culture, customs, and beliefs. The historical regions of Poland were later formed from these tribes.

POMORZE (POMERANIA)

The region of Pomorze was named after the tribe Pomorzanie. The name itself comes from the fact that this region is located in the north, by the Baltic Sea (*morze* = sea). Kashubians, an ethnic group native to Pomerania, are direct descendants of the Pomeranian tribes. With their distinct language, rich folkloric tradition, and culture, their folk practices can, at times, differ significantly from those of the other groups. Kashubian folk art is well-known across Poland, especially for its unique ceramics and embroidery. A subgroup of Kashubians known as Slovincians is now nearly extinct. Pomeranians are the people of the sea.

WIELKOPOLSKA (GREATER POLAND)

This region's name could be translated to mean "big Poland," as it is located on the vast plains of the western-central part of the country. It was originally inhabited by the Polanie tribe. The name most likely comes from the fields (*pole* = field; *polanie* = field people) around which their tribal communities were organized. The Piast dynasty, which was the first ruling dynasty of Poland after its inception, comes from this tribe of Slavs. Polans are the people of fields and plains.

ŚLĄSK (SILESIA)

Located in southwestern Poland, this region is named after the Ślężanie tribe, whose name is derived from *Ślęża*, a holy mountain and a place of worship for our pre-Christian ancestors, where I happen to hail from. Śląsk's past is historically complicated, having changed hands over the centuries, belonging to Poland, the Czechs, and the Germans. Ultimately, however, it is the original homeland of *Ślązacy* (Silesians), the autochthons of this region with a distinct language and folkloric traditions, often with mixed roots of Polish, Czech, and German origin. Silesians are the people of foggy hills and rich mines.

MAZOWSZE (MASOVIA)

Mazowsze is a region located in the eastern-central part of the country, in the central reaches of the Vistula River, named after the tribe Mazowszanie. Today's inhabitants, historically known as both Masurians (older) and Masovians (current), descend from the tribe and speak their distinct dialect. Subgroups of Masovians, such as Łowiczans, Poborzans, and Podlachians, are known for their beautiful traditional folk clothing, as well as *wycinanki*, a form of traditional papercut folk art. Masovians are the people of lush, swampy forests.

MAŁOPOLSKA (LESSER POLAND)

Located in southeastern Poland and formerly inhabited by the Wiślanie tribe, this region is rich in mountainous terrains, including the Carpathian Mountains and the Tatra Mountain Range. Here, you will encounter *górale* (highlanders), who speak a unique dialect and cultivate distinct folkloric traditions and arts. Much of their folk art is recognized worldwide, similarly to Masovians. Some of the most interesting folk magical traditions have been preserved among the highlanders to this day. Vistulans are the people of the Vistula River and the high mountains.

RUŚ CZERWONA (RED RUTHENIA)

This historical region's first known inhabitants were the tribe Lędzianie. Now, Red Ruthenia is located both in Poland and Ukraine, and therefore, is no longer formally recognized under this name. The part within Polish borders is in the very southeastern corner of the country, with the magical Bieszczady Mountains, a well-known travel destination for those who enjoy solitude. Ruthenians are the people of remote mountains and forests.

While these are the biggest and most broadly documented Slavic tribes indigenous to the lands of today's Poland, each of the regions was originally inhabited by many smaller tribes over the centuries. The tribes intermingled with each other, as well as with tribes of neighboring ethnic groups. They exchanged goods, customs, skills, and language, married into each other's families, and spread myths, tales, and legends of gods, spirits, and deeds. The northern tribes traded with Scandinavians, the western ones with Germanic tribes, while the eastern and southern ones traded with other groups of Slavs. Much of this is reflected in today's distinct traditions and legends of each region in Poland, with many additional influences accumulated and developed over the centuries of wars, conflicts, partitions, occupations, displacements, and resettlements.

BIOREGIONALITY AND ANIMISM IN FOLK MAGIC

An equally, if not more important factor in the shaping of the culture, lore, and traditions of a people is bioregionality—the features of the landscape, the fauna and flora, the unique microclimate, ecology, and seasonal peculiarities. A major portion of the rich lore and legends of a people is born out of their relationship with the natural world around them. Over the centuries, generations upon generations who inhabit any given area have learned to observe and listen to the land, to speak its unique language, and to channel its songs and stories into the wealth of oral tradition: Tales of holy mountains, sacred springs, dangerous valleys, and cursed crossroads; legends of the magical and healing properties of plants that grow in the area; stories of kinship with animals and insects who aid or oppose human efforts; and songs of spirits and gods blessing or cursing the community with an abundance of crops or natural disasters. All this tradition arose from the foundations of cultivating a relationship with the world around us for the purposes of mutual aid and survival.

Many such stories are unique to the region because they emerge directly from the landscape, whispered or relayed in dreams and visions to the most open-hearted, humble folks, who work intimately with the land and tend to their communities. Some regions are known for Bald Mountains where witches traveled to the sabbath to partake in feasts and orgies. Other regions are rich in stories of sacred springs and water spirits who protect their people from floods and hunger. Yet other places cultivate legends of forest devils guarding the wildlife, feasting on cruel humans, and signing pacts with those who sought their aid. While similarities or even overlap often exist between neighbors, the names of spirits, details of the customs, plants employed in the work, or places involved remain distinctive to the landscape of a particular region.

As an example, the place where I live is steeped in legends about the Ślęża mountain and how it was created. Hordes of devils and angels threw boulders at each other from the peaks of two nearby mountains until Ślęża was formed, sealing an entrance to hell at its base. To this day, the devils who remain locked out of their portal to hell are believed to roam these woods and mountains in search of opportunity. The mountains are known as places of cult and pilgrimages at least since the Bronze Age, with remains of old cult walls, sacred springs, ancient stone statues, and burial mounds of early Slavic settlements. Despite the region's history filled with resettlements and displacements over the centuries, the legends have remained strong as a testament to their origin in the land itself, rather than the people.

The bioregionality of folklore emerges from its animist foundation, acknowledging that the landscape is alive. Animism is a way of life recognizing that the ecology around us is inhabited by countless beings, all of whom possess personhood and should be respected as equally important members of the local community. As one of humanity's oldest ways of relating to the world around us, animism stands at the very foundations of all the folkloric traditions we cultivate to this day. While modern human civilization remains steeped in anthropocentrism and brutal disregard for the broader ecology around us, old folklore remedies this by maintaining stories of local land spirits and the ways our ancestors cultivated relationships with them through land-based customs and agrarian traditions, thus preserving the fragile balance of the local ecology for centuries.

The most important and distinct aspects of the cultural regionality and bioregionality of the Polish Slavs, in the context of folk magic practices, will be explored in more detail throughout this publication, providing a foundation for anyone willing to engage with this heritage in ways that remain true to local traditions. It is my sincere hope that this heartfelt introduction to the living traditions of my people offers insight and guidance toward making one's craft as bioregionally and culturally relevant as possible, wherever we may live. While this may appear to be less accessible to folks connecting with their Slavic heritage from abroad compared to those living here, I believe it is important to recognize that authentic traditions are never cultivated in a vacuum, and the circumstances are rarely ever straightforward when ancestry is concerned. Therefore, it is most beneficial to combine our immersion in ancestral traditions with authentic land connectedness wherever we find ourselves in the world.

Instead of romanticizing a landscape far away, our attention is better invested in tending to the land beneath our feet. You certainly don't have to live in a place of ancestral origin to cultivate the worldview of stewardship and reverence for the natural world around you, or to engage in traditional customs and activities of your people. You can get quite far by researching where your ancestors came from, which region their surname is most popular in, which dishes or traditional folk art were relevant to the place of their origin, and which features of their local landscape were regarded as special, or perhaps even revered. Often, our ancestors won't be coming from just one place, but several across the country. It is also important to keep in mind that the culture of your ancestors did not cease to evolve the moment your forebears emigrated across the pond. Cultures and their diasporas continue to evolve and intermingle with their neighbors, making the research and immersion in our heritage all the more exciting and the repertoire of folkloric elements to include significantly richer and more alive.

CHAPTER THREE

THE FOLKLORIC PERCEPTION OF THE WORLD:

ONTOLOGY, THE WORLD TREE, AND THE OTHERWORLDS

Before diving into the practical aspects of engaging with the cultural traditions and folk magic of the Slavs, it is essential to acquire a basic understanding of the folkloric perception of the world cultivated by its people. Unsurprisingly, folk practices, along with their rules and taboos, are rooted in the foundation of an ontology—the myth of world creation, and everything that came after.

Whether we look at pre-Christian reconstructions of the creation myth or their much later, folkloric versions, what stands out is the apparent dualism present in the stories. A single force from the heavens did not create the world; rather, both the heavenly and chthonic forces tirelessly collaborated and competed during the creation process. While they primarily govern and dwell in their respective realms, both have an equal influence over the middle world inhabited by beings of the flesh.

In Slavic mythos, the world as we know it revolves around the World Tree. In some Proto-Slavic cultures, such as the Lusatians *(Łużyczanie)* and Pomeranians *(Pomorzanie)*, conifers—like spruce, fir, or pine—were most often perceived as representations of the World Tree. However, as our culture, and thus our mythos, evolved over the centuries, the World Tree became more commonly identified as an oak tree—still considered to be one of the most sacred trees of the Slavic people to this day.

Oak trees played an important role in Slavic pre-Christian cults and magic. They were believed to be sacred to the god Perun, bringing strength and healing. They were often used in folk medicine and spells, especially infusions of oak leaves and bark, for cleansing baths or to rinse the throat. Oak groves were also places where oaths and prayers were spoken. If an oak grove grew on a hilltop, it was commonly recognized to be a place of witches' sabbats, known as *Łysa Góra* (Bald Mountain).

While alternative versions of the ontological myth exist, such as the one where the world sprang from a single egg existing in a void, one of the most archaic myths of the Slavs tells a tale of the creation of the Cosmic Tree and the three worlds. A folkloric version of this myth weaves a story of how God and the Devil created the world together.

At the beginning, there were only the skies and waters. God sailed through the endless waters in a boat when he stumbled upon the Devil, whom he invited aboard. Together, they decided to create land upon which one could stand. Thus, God ordered the Devil to swim to the bottom of the vast waters and bring a handful of sand in God's name. And so, the Devil dove into the depths and seized the sand, but instead of doing so in God's name, he did so in his own. Upon returning to the surface, however, he discovered that his hand was empty. He tried again, this time seizing the handful of sand in both his and God's name. He managed to bring a single grain of sand to the surface, and from this grain, land was created. As they walked the land, God created good, beautiful fauna and flora, while the Devil created beasts and poisonous plants. Eventually, they realized that wherever they walk, the land expands, thus covering more and more of the waters. To prevent the land from covering all waters, God took up a staff and thrust it into the soil, stopping it from further expansion and designating the center of this world and the four directions. From the staff, the World Tree grew up into the heavens and down into the underworld, splitting the world into the upper, middle, and lower worlds. The heavens were the domain of God, while the underworld, with its vast waters, was the domain of the Devil.

The sky, imagined as a giant dome, was believed to be supported by an enormous tree trunk that grows all the way up to the Pole Star. The tree trunk of the World Tree was recognized by many names, some of which include *stożar, gwózd,* and *przypór*—while hard to translate, all these words refer to its function as a pillar, a nail that holds up the skies. The observable movement of the stars in the night sky throughout the year supported this theory enough for our ancestors to cultivate this vision for many centuries.

The upper branches of the Tree were believed to be inhabited by the heavenly (uranian) spirits and deities who watched over the world from above. The tree trunk was believed to be inhabited by humans and other living creatures. The roots of the Tree were believed to be inhabited by the dead, the ancestors, and chthonic (telluric) deities and spirits. This vision of the Three Worlds has been artistically represented in a statue known as *Światowid ze Zbrucza* (The Zbruch Idol)—a sculpture likely dating back to the eleventh century, dressed in carvings of four figures in the Upper World, humans in the Middle World, and ancestors in the Lower World.

THE UPPER WORLD: PRAWIA

Prawia (read: Pravia) comes from the word *prawo,* meaning law. The word itself is a modern reconstruction, sometimes used interchangeably with the older name *Wyraj* (read: Vyray). The crown of the World Tree is inhabited by spirits and deities of heavenly attributes. The Zbrucz idol depicts four beings representing patronage over four aspects of nature and life—two male and two female-presenting figures. It cannot be definitively concluded which deities or beings we're looking at, however, there are some theories. One of the theories, often favored by Rodnovers, is that the four main deities are: Perun (god of thunder and patron of warriors), Dadźbóg (the solar god of abundance), Mokosh (Earth goddess and matron of women), and Łada (goddess of family and marriage). However, new theories and more accurate research may still shift these interpretations in the future.

Prawia or Wyraj was commonly imagined as a sacred grove island or green pastures in the Upper World located beyond the *Zabyt Reka,* or "river of oblivion," where trees (usually oaks and lindens) grow. Alternatively, Wyraj is also seen as green pastures where spirits of the dead reside, transformed into birds, such as geese. This vision of the otherworlds is reflected in the beliefs surrounding the annual bird migration patterns, as birds were believed to carry the spirits of the dead to Wyraj for the dark half of the year, and then carry them back to reincarnate as they return in spring.

As mentioned earlier, the skies were also imagined as a giant dome of darkness, behind which lay the world of the gods, filled with divine light. The dome of the firmament itself was believed to be made of stone or metal and operated on giant hinges that opened it during the day and closed it by night. Therefore, the stars in the night sky were believed to be little holes through which the gods watch over us. Our ancestors were often afraid of the heavens, unable to comprehend how they continued to be held up. One commonly documented fear of our ancestors was that the sky would eventually collapse onto the earth when the pillar could hold it no longer, resulting in the end of our world as we know it.

Post-Christianisation, Wyraj became syncretically linked and eventually replaced with *Raj* (paradise) - a place where people would continue to live after death - thus gradually diminishing the cultural relevance of the belief in reincarnation.

THE MIDDLE WORLD: JAWIA

Jawia (read: Yavia) comes from the word *jawny,* which means "visible" or "apparent." The Middle World encompasses everything that we can perceive and know. It revolves around the trunk of the World Tree. In the Zbrucz Idol, we can see four people carved around the trunk, forming a circle of community. The circle is sometimes also interpreted as folks gathering around the Sacred Fire in devotion. Many of the Slavic rites are conducted around the Fire, believed to be a link between our world and the otherworlds. Back in the day, people commonly believed that as long as we continue to uphold the cosmic order by heeding the taboos, tending to the hearth fire, and cultivating our agrarian traditions, the natural order of things will continue, thus upkeeping our world as we know it. Through mutual support and devotion, the human community stays safe, ensuring shared prosperity, and well-being.

While the Middle World of Jawia was generally believed to be separated from the other worlds, it was believed that at certain points of the agrarian cycle (such as the times of intensified ancestral veneration in spring and autumn), the boundaries between the worlds become more open, allowing us to commune with the ancestors, but also making us more vulnerable to the influences of malicious spirits.

Naturally, the world of Jawia is inhabited by all the creations of God and the Devil and is always equally influenced by both heavenly and chthonic forces. The inhabitants of the Middle World—beings of flesh, the plant world, mountain ranges, sacred springs and rivers, countless land spirits, demons and devils, and other beings bound to this Earth—coexist in a shared ecology. Some beings may share a stronger inclination and longing toward the chthonic realms, while others may have a longing to the heavens above. After all, some have been shaped by God and others by the Devil. Humans, as the ones wielding the power of intricate speech, exist in a particular mutable state in between. Depending on an individual's needs and inclinations, one may choose to align themselves with forces of either realm, thus expressing the cunning ability of humanity toward securing the survival of our species at all costs.

THE LOWER WORLD: NAWIA

Nawia (read: Navia) originates from the Proto-Slavic word *navь*, meaning corpse. *Nawie* is also one of the terms used to describe the souls of the dead. The Lower World rests within the roots of the World Tree, guarded by *Żmij* (The Serpent)—a zoomorphic form of the god Weles.

In the bottom portion of the Zbrucz Idol, we observe three figures who appear to be sitting or kneeling, with their arms outstretched, as if carrying the rest of the world with the sheer strength of their muscles. This beautifully illustrates the key importance of acknowledging all the work and hardships our ancestors endured to provide a future for us. One may say that the very earth that we walk upon is upheld by those who came before us. The figures present at the bottom of the idol are commonly interpreted as the ancestors, or as a representation of the chthonic god Weles.

Traditionally, Nawia was sometimes believed to be a place that is empty and dark, with no sun, warmth, food, or drink. Other times, it was imagined as endless underworld pastures and lands filled with unimaginable riches, guarded by Weles as the shepherd of souls, who takes care of the dead transformed into cattle. This is where a part of our soul comes to rest after we die—the part of us that becomes one with the ancestors.

The souls who reside in Nawia are sometimes capable of haunting the Earth as invisible beings carried by the winds; other times giving wise counsel and protecting the living folk of their Ród from beyond. This vision of the underworld is directly reflected in the elaborate traditions of feeding, bathing, and taking care of spirits of the dead during *Dziady* (Forefathers) and other ancestral celebrations.

Post-Christianisation, Nawia would gradually become syncretically replaced with the belief in *piekło* (hell) and *czyściec* (purgatory), which further complicated the folkloric understanding of the otherworlds, as well as demonized the perceptions of spirits of the dead.

The Zbrucz Idol provides the basic information we need to understand how the world was perceived and believed to be structured in the old times. The Upper World, inhabited by the spirits of heavenly and mutable nature, remained the most alien and inconceivable for the common folk. It was seen as equally awe-inspiring and terrifying, reminding people to remain humble in the face of that which remains unknowable. The Middle World was seen as residing at the very center of creation, a threshold between the Upper and Lower worlds, the place where beings of flesh live and die. At the core of all creation resides the Lower World—the foundation rooted in the old traditions, and the ancestors—a source of timeless wisdom, protection, and unimaginable riches. After all, no tree can exist without the support of its roots. The beliefs surrounding the Three Worlds directly shaped our ancestors' beliefs, not only in regards to the perception of the tangible world itself, but also the human soul and the afterlife. This will be further explored in the following chapter.

CHAPTER FOUR

VISIONS OF SPIRITS, HYPNAGOGIA, AND LIFE BEYOND DEATH

So far, we have covered the ontology, the folkloric perception of creation, the structure of the world, and the three Slavic worlds of Nawia, Jawia, and Prawia. Now, we are ready for a deeper exploration of the beliefs surrounding matters of life, death, the altered states in between, and how they shaped the perceptions of the spirit world and Slavic demonology. These understandings will come in handy when engaging with the theory and practice of the folkloric magic of our predecessors.

AFTERLIFE

There is no one homogenous version of belief surrounding the Slavic afterlife. Sources point to a few possible choices, all of which make perfect sense in the context of the cosmogonic myths of the Slavic people. However, they seem to have been developed independently and regionally, sometimes even coexisting in the same region.

In pre-Christian times, the Slavs burned their dead, a practice deeply rooted in the cult of Living Fire (detailed in the following chapter) and the belief that fire is a sacred portal between the worlds, capable of freeing the souls of the deceased from their flesh and allowing them to depart. Afterward, the ashes and remaining bones were placed in urns and put to final rest in burial mounds, sometimes with accompanying objects that may prove useful in life beyond death.

There are several aspects of belief surrounding the afterlife present in the sources, some of which may be mutually exclusive. While some folks seemed not to have believed in the afterlife at all—or at least that is how outside observers and chroniclers described them—the general consensus seems to be the belief in some form of reincarnation, accompanied by beliefs of what happens to the soul and the kinds of transformations it can undergo *post-mortem.*

Łowmiański expounds in *Religia Słowian i jej upadek* (The religion of Slavs and its Downfall) how the beliefs of life after death are tied to the ontological myths, based on examples of folk beliefs:

"As God washed himself in baths, he sweated and wiped himself with a wisp and threw it upon the earth from the heavens; and the devil argued with God which one of them shall create the first human from the wisp. And so the devil created the human, and God placed a soul within him. This is why, when a human dies, the body goes into the soil [to the devil] and the soul goes to God" (Łowmiański, 1986, p. 189).

After death, the human spirit is believed to roam the earth for 40 days, after which it moves on to the otherworlds. During these 40 days, they can attend to all unfinished business and care for their grieving family and community. Once the time is up, the soul is believed to split: one part transforms into a migratory bird and travels with them to Wyraj (Upper World), while the other settles into the Earth, making its way to Nawia (Lower World). The part of the soul in the Upper World eventually reincarnates back into the Ród (family bloodline) or an animal. The part in the Lower World dwells there among the ancestors. The caveat is that those who died tragic or taboo deaths (such as suicide) are believed to transform into a demon specific to their type of death, rather than move on, and continue to roam the Earth in spirit form.

Although some of these beliefs may seem inconsistent or mutually exclusive, they often coexisted and were honored interchangeably depending on context, time of year, or region. Some of these beliefs may have also been more connected with certain psychopomps or chthonic deities and spirits than others, which suggests that, depending on which deity's cult was favored in the region, the accompanying beliefs would also be more prominent there.

BIPHASIC SLEEP, DREAMWORK, AND SPIRIT ENCOUNTERS

When speaking of life beyond death, ghosts, and spirits, we can't omit one of the crucial factors that shaped the perception of our ancestors regarding what's out there, beyond the seen. Substantial evidence points to the fact that our preindustrial ancestors' sleep cycles were different from our own. Unlike the average modern humans who sleep in a single block of approximately eight hours per night, people used to sleep in two blocks: first falling asleep sometime after dusk for around four hours, then waking up for an hour or two around midnight, to finally fall back asleep until dawn. Researchers have speculated that biphasic sleep and other forms of polyphasic sleep are the natural ancestral sleep patterns of most mammals.

When electricity entered the picture in the Industrial Revolution era, human lifestyle underwent significant changes in terms of wakefulness and sleep patterns—sleeping in complete darkness and staying awake to the accompaniment of light, be it natural or artificial. In Poland, these changes occurred much later than in the West. In 1950, only about 10% of Polish villages had access to electricity, so many of our grandparents grew up without it.

So, what does this have to do with folk tradition and practices of magic and witchcraft? It appears that the key to understanding the folkloric stories of nighttime encounters with ghosts, spirits, and demons, as well as acts of spirit flight, is this short period of wakefulness in the middle of the night.

Historian Emma Wilby explains: "Anthropological studies have revealed that in cultures where visionary experience is highly valued, it is considered to be as real as the perceptions of normal waking life. Indeed, as anthropologist Jackson Lincoln has observed, in some cases it is regarded 'as having a greater reality value than actual experience'" (Wilby, *The Visions of Isobel Gowdie: Magic, Witchcraft and Dark Shamanism in Seventeenth-Century Scotland,* 2011, p. 250).

We modern humans seem to enjoy when everything can be neatly explained, rationalized, tamed, and controlled. We dislike surprises, and we certainly dislike being afraid. Hence, the things we experience in dreams or during altered states of consciousness, we tend to rationalize as "just a dream," rather than a real experience.

Our ancestors spent significantly more time than us in darkness or in the low light of a candle. Times of wakefulness in the middle of the night were often spent pondering one's dreams, doing simple repetitive chores, having a snack, or engaging in folk practices. This all occurred in a somewhat altered state of hypnagogia—the transition between sleep and wakefulness—enhanced by the low light of a candle, or no light at all. In such conditions, the experiential value of dreams and altered states of mind remained more fluid than our own. What occurred in dreams and spontaneous liminal states of ecstasis, hypnagogia, or trance was perceived to be just as real as that which occurred in the normative consciousness of waking life.

Today, we know that hypnagogic states resemble trance states in a lot of ways. Our perception can be significantly shifted, the body deeply relaxed to the point where we may feel it change shape, the eyes and ears appear to play tricks on us, and we may be prone to seeing things out of the corner of our eye or hearing the entire house come alive with the creaking of the old floors as the winds creep in. In other words, folks would take advantage, sometimes purposefully, other times spontaneously, of the hypnagogia and trance states that naturally occurred in this period of wakefulness that enabled them to experience varied visionary states, spirit encounters, and leaving the physical body. This is why so many folkloric stories of encounters with spirits and demons describe them as occurring in the middle of the night, or during dusk and dawn, when our perception is altered.

HYPNAGOGIA AND SLEEP PARALYSIS DEMONS

One example of a folkloric demon encounter speaks of beings capable of leaving their body at night and going forth to haunt or even kill unsuspecting victims in their sleep—the *Mara* or *Zmora.* The name of the demon alone points to an existing connection with the Slavic goddess Marzanna, who, other than being the goddess of agriculture and death, is also associated with dreams and nightmares. The name Mara means "nightmare," but it is also used to describe the demon who haunts people (especially women) at night by sitting on their chest and suffocating them. Mara demons were generally believed to be the souls of dead sinners. However, a more sinister form of Mara, known as Zmora, was believed to be a living female witch whose soul left her body at night and suffocated people the same way Mara did.

Some folks say that Zmora is a woman born with two souls who only received one name at her baptism, thus allowing the other soul to remain unnamed, untamed, and dangerous. Others say that a child born of a difficult delivery—where its mother called upon the devil in desperation—is doomed to become one. Zmory were often unaware of what they did at night, unless they actively practiced witchcraft and developed their skills to be able to control their second soul. Growing up in 1990s rural Poland, I still vividly remember folks gossiping about an older woman who was believed to be a Zmora in our village. Such stories of Zmora are cognate with other similar accounts describing witches' shapeshifting abilities into animals at night, and then traveling to the Bald Mountain to attend the sabbath, fly by night, surveil other people, or perform other sorcerous deeds, leaning on the enhanced abilities of their animal body.

Today, it is broadly recognized that being on the receiving end of a visit from Mara or Zmora is how sleep paralysis can unfold. Sleep paralysis is a state that can occur as part of the hypnagogia, thus pointing at a clear connection with the abilities of spirit flight, shapeshifting, dream work, and achieving trance states. Sleep paralysis, therefore, could be perceived as an involuntary altered state, of moving beyond the veil while simultaneously being trapped in the body and unable to control the experience.

SPIRITS AND DEMONOLOGY

The word "demonology" might hold negative connotations for modern people. But in the context of Polish demonology, it is understood as a field classifying the forces and spirits present in the ecology around us, rather than "demons" in the negative religious sense of the word.

Folk demonology is a direct reflection of the animistic beliefs of our ancestors. In the animistic worldview, everything that exists possesses personhood, including the invisible forces that influenced our ancestors' well-being and survival. These forces are responsible for illnesses and talents, misfortunes and good luck, curses and blessings, sudden deaths and miraculous recoveries, failure and abundance of crops, natural disasters and wonders, and countless other phenomena.

Our predecessors understood that nothing happens in a vacuum, which means that whenever a problem arises, somewhere there must be a reason—a force, an entity, or an intelligence responsible for it. Recognizing and establishing contact with said force—while understanding their function, their reasoning, and their needs—is the key to finding the answer, solution, or cure. For our ancestors, this manifested in the form of deep reverence for the natural forces, as well as highly developed everyday demonology. Hundreds, if not thousands, of nature spirits, devils, ghosts, and mythical beings existed at the heart of every place, every natural and unnatural phenomenon, every illness, and every blessing. Notably, while our ancestors may have perceived some spirits as more powerful or relevant than others, it was not necessarily perceived through the lens of anthropocentric hierarchies—at least not until deities became involved.

Spirits and demons were generally divided into categories of those with human and non-human origin. Many of the especially hostile spirits were formerly humans who died tragic or taboo deaths, and thus were unable to fully move on from this Earth, instead transforming into various types of wraiths that continued to haunt the community of the living.

Some of the most well-known categories of spirits of human origin include:

- Vampires and other blood-sucking spirits
- Mares and spirits that choke people at night
- Spirits of drowned humans
- Spirits of suicide victims
- Spirits of prematurely deceased children
- Devils of human origin (usually those who signed a pact and became a devil posthumously)
- White Ladies *(Biała Pani)* and spirits haunting castles and buildings
- Ancestors and protective family spirits

A plethora of spirits and demons were regarded as those of other origin, including:

- **Spirits of the land:** Trees and forests, plants, water reservoirs and shores, rocks and mountains, caves, underground areas, crossroads, fields, boundaries and thresholds, and more.
- **Spirits of atmospheric phenomena and seasons:** Wind, rain, clouds, snow, storms, thunder, times of day, seasonal shifts, and more.
- **Spirits of illnesses:** A subcategory of beings who could dwell in or corrupt the above realms, causing illness.
- **Spirits of inhabited spaces and families:** Household spirits, farm spirits, spirits of fate, spirits stealing children, and more.
- **Devils and familiars:** A subcategory of beings who possessed powers and could be bargained with.
- **Spirits of celestial bodies:** Moon, Sun, Venus, Pole Star, and a few observable constellations.
- **Deities:** Spirits of greater renown, whose cult was more widespread across regions, often with more developed roles and dominion over matters of both the natural world and the human societal and political roles, such as deities of agriculture, war, or various crafts and trades. Later syncretized with figures of demons, folkloric Devils, Marys, and saints.

SPIRIT SYNCRETISMS

When authentic practices of Polish folk magic are concerned, perhaps surprisingly to some, the cult of Slavic pagan deities does not play a central role in spirit work unless the practitioner actively identifies as pagan, polytheist, or Rodnover. Folk magic is inherently neither pagan nor Christian. It is a living tradition that adapts to and changes with its environment, absorbing living cultural elements into itself. Therefore, an average folk practitioner works primarily with the ancestors, as well as spirits that are still actively recognized in their unique local lore, community, and ecology. Thus, local spirits of the land, household and natural phenomena, spirits of the dead, folkloric Marys, Devils, and saints would be the primary allies and familiars.

As contemporary research progresses and people grow more interested in the ancient beliefs of their ancestors, we also grow more aware of the syncretisms that have been occurring with pre-Christian deities. We recognize the older being underneath the figure of a Saint or Mary and honor this being to the core, while still retaining the syncretized elements. Meanwhile, deity worship as a religious practice remains more prominent among people who choose to identify as polytheists, pagans, and Rodnovers, rather than folk practitioners *per se.* The most important spirits and allies will be properly introduced in later chapters.

CHAPTER FIVE

LIVING FIRE: THE CULT OF FIRE IN SLAVIC FOLK TRADITION

Fire plays a central role in Slavic tradition—both for pre-Christian and syncretic folk traditions that developed later. When we take a closer look at the customs surrounding all the major agrarian celebrations of the seasons (see more in: "Agrarian Traditions and Polish Folkloric Year"), most of them involve elements of fire cult, be it in the form of a bonfire or hearth fire, the thunder candle *Gromnica,* the burning of an effigy of *Marzanna* in spring, or votive candles used around *Dziady* and *Zaduszki,* or "Forefathers" and "All Souls Day," respectively. Fire has been and continues to be sacred to the Slavic peoples.

In Celtic, Germanic, and Norse traditions, sacred fire is usually known as the Need-Fire, but in Slavic traditions, it is most commonly known as *Żywy Ogień,* or "Living Fire."

What distinguishes Living Fire from other fires is how it is traditionally obtained—by rubbing two pieces of wood (oak, alder, hazel, or aspen) against each other, or with flint and tinder. This way of kindling the ritual fire is common throughout most of Europe, including the Slavs. Post-Christianization, this evolved into obtaining blessed fire for the hearth directly from the church.

SWAROŻYC'S FIRE AND RITES OF PASSAGE

According to reconstructionists, *Swaróg* is one of the most prominent deities of the Slavic pantheon. He is the heavenly blacksmith and father to two sons, *Swarożyc,* "the sacred flame" and *Dadźbóg,* "the Sun."

The bonfire kindled using the traditional ways represents Swarożyc, the son of Swaróg. This Living Fire is called *Ogień Swarożycowy,* "Swarożyc's Fire," and it is believed to be a living portal and an intermediary between the worlds—a direct link between the earthly reality of the living and the realms of the ancestors, as well as the divine realms of the gods. On a symbolic level, this sacred flame becomes a pillar connecting the three worlds of Jawia (middle world), Nawia (underworld), and Prawia (upper world).

Living Fire is a crucial part of all the solar celebrations around the agrarian cycle. In ceremony, offerings of bread, beer, and mead are placed in the Living Fire to ensure that the gods and spirits receive them. When kindled for ritual purposes, it is often encouraged by the participants with a song:

"Gore gore jasno, żeby nie zagasło."
"[Fire] Burns, burns bright, so it doesn't fade away."

During celebrations of the coming of spring, all old fires are extinguished, and a new Living Fire is kindled and carried home to mark the beginning of a new year. During *Kupała Night* (Summer Solstice), participants jump through the fire to gain the blessings of strength, health, and fertility. During Dziady (Forefathers), we light our votive candles or torches to bring the Living Fire back home, and with it, invite the ancestors to dine with us. The same pattern is repeated in April (the first Thursday after Easter) for the celebration of *Dziady Wiosenne* (Spring Forefathers).

Apart from agrarian rituals and celebrations, fire played an important role in rites of passage and funerary rites. Living Fire, other than carrying offerings into the otherworlds, was also believed to help carry the souls of the dead to their afterlife. This is why the Slavs traditionally practiced rites of cremation until it was forbidden post-Christianization. Building funeral pyres and then kindling them in traditional ways ensured that the soul would be released from the body and move on. The general belief was that the soul would still be present in the local community for forty days after death, and the soul could use this time to tie all loose strings and finish their earthly business. After that initial period, the ashes would be laid to rest in an urn or burial mound, and the soul would depart into the otherworlds. Oftentimes, flint and tinder were added into the mounds, suggesting that the dead might still need to possess the means to kindle Living Flame in the afterlife.

LIVING FIRE IN THE HEARTH

Other than the rites of passage and the grand seasonal celebrations, Living Flame was also crucial in the household, as a sacred guest. This is best evidenced in traditional prayers and ways of addressing fire upon kindling it in the household:

"Ogieńku mój kochany
Od Boga przysłany."

"Fire, my beloved
Godsent."

"Witam cię, gościu
w czerwonym płaszczu,
nie szerz się szeroko,
tylko wysoko."

"Welcome, our guest,
clad in a red coat,
may you grow high,
but never spread wide."

"Ogieńku święty, skarbicku boży
Nie dejże nas też nigdy zubożyć."

"Sacred fire, treasure of the gods
Won't you ever allow us to be impoverished."

Fire, revered as a sacred substance and a living being, was to be treated with the utmost respect. The fire of the hearth was always kindled either from the local ritual fires or by the head of the family (usually the father) using traditional ways. Once kindled, it was carefully looked after to make sure that it never went out—apart from specific times of the year when new Living Fire was brought home from the seasonal rituals. It was also possible to kindle the hearth from the flame of one's parents' hearth (for example, if a son moved out, he would receive the embers from his father to bring to his new home). Should the flame accidentally go out, it was still possible to rekindle it by borrowing some from a neighbor. However, it wasn't recommended, and there were taboos around how this should be done (if at all)—it had to be during the night or in the wee hours of the morning before dawn. When carrying these borrowed embers from the neighbor, one should never say the customary greeting *"Bywajcie zdrowi,"* "Be well," or else their house would burn down.

Still, it was considered bad luck to be generous in this regard. It was believed that lending fire to neighbors could cause poverty. This likely stems from the old belief that fire is a generous, wealthy god, bogacz. In Polish, *bogacz* means "rich man." Interestingly, this word comes from the word *bóg*, meaning "god." While this may seem confusing and complicated, it is directly related to Swaróg and his two sons: Swarożyc (the Sacred Flame) and Dadźbóg (the Sun). While Swarożyc is a diminutive of Swaróg, pointing at him being the earthly manifestation of the powerful blacksmith god Swaróg, *Dadźbóg* means "the giving god" or "the generous god" (*Dadź* meaning "giving" and *bóg* meaning "god"). All this reinforces how the element of fire and the Sun were both revered as good, generous gods.

Back in the day, every household had a large *piec* (stove) in the living area, where most of the family life occurred, where all meals were cooked, illnesses were cured, issues were tended to, herbs and mushrooms were dried, and where humans and animals slept (in the *zapiecek*, "behind-stove"). The stove was the center of the household—the heart and soul of the home, a sacred altar. The stove is where the family's Living Fire dwelt, thus also marking it a place between the worlds, where the ancestors and household spirits could be contacted or messages could be sent to the otherworlds. It offered protection and survival to the members of the family, as well as the survival and continuity of the Ród (bloodline). This further explains why folks weren't too eager to share their Living Fire with neighbors—it was considered sacred to the family.

REMNANTS OF THE CULT OF FIRE IN FOLK BELIEFS

The Living Fire that resided in the hearth was treated as a living being, possessing personhood. It was considered an offense to spit or pee in the fire or pour dirty liquids in it. It was believed to be dangerous to disrespect the fire by drying diapers by the hearth flame, as it could take revenge on the child. People would also avoid using sharp objects around the fire so as not to wound it. Sometimes, it was even inappropriate to turn one's back to the hearth fire.

There are countless folk stories of neighboring hearth flames communicating with each other. One such story speaks of how the flames consulted with each other to compare how their owners treated them. One flame would complain to the other about his matron, saying, "She never sweeps me, she never makes the sign of the cross above me, she just leaves me untended. I'll burn her." The other flame would reply, "Burn her! Mine always sweeps me nicely and makes the sign of the cross."

The tale sheds some light on how the Living Fire in the hearth should be treated with special care. During the day, it was carefully tended to, ensuring that it never went out. It was never to be extinguished with water, under the threat of revenge (usually equivalent to burning the household down).

In the evening, the scattered ashes that accumulated throughout the day needed to be respectfully swept onto the embers, creating a neat little mound, sometimes also covering it with a brick. Then, the sign of the cross should be made above it to ensure safety from fire-related accidents. The matron who takes care of this should say:

"Święty Wawrzyńcze przebłogosławiony, tobie oddaję ogieniaszek sławiony, pod najświętszą twoją opiekę."

"Saint Laurentius, O blessed one, to you I give the blessed flame, under your saintly protection."

Tucked in this way, it could still be easily rekindled the next morning, ensuring its continuity. Another safety precaution so that the flame "doesn't walk out of the fireplace," was to ensure that when the fire is being rekindled anew in the morning, the person doing it should be silent and never look behind their back, no matter what they hear.

Gesturing the sign of the cross was also an important—and most likely ancient—part of the fire cult. It was customary to make the sign of the cross when rekindling the fire in the morning, as well as when tucking it away in the evening. It served the purpose of greeting it in the morning and then bidding it goodnight in the evening, as well as expressing deep reverence for this otherworldly substance. This proves the utmost sacred nature of fire, for the only other beings that were greeted and similarly bid farewell were the waters, the sun, the moon, and the *Zorze.*

Moreover, whenever a candle or lamp was brought into a room, everyone would greet the light. The original pre-Christian words of greeting did not survive; however, we know that post-Christianization, it shifted toward, *"Niech będzie pochwalony Jezus Chrystus,"* or "Praised be Jesus Christ!"

FIRE AS PROTECTOR AND DESTRUCTOR

In folk tradition, Living Fire was a powerful weapon against evil forces: It cleansed and protected the household from all evil, witchcraft, sickness, bad luck, etc. It was essential to tend to the hearth around the birth of a new child, as children were considered to be especially helpless against the attacks of dark forces. Meanwhile, the thunder candle *Gromnica* had a very similar purpose as it was thought to be especially effective as protection from storms and wolves, as well as possessing healing properties.

Living Fire was also helpful in protecting the fields from witchcraft and thus ensuring a bountiful harvest. Pieces of burned straw from the Marzanna effigy were scattered around the fields for that purpose. Ashes from ritual fires were also scattered around the fields and pastures to protect the crops and the animals from witchcraft and dark forces. Sometimes, the coals from ritual fires would also be added to animal fodder to heal them.

During Dziady (Forefathers), torches or votive candles lit from the ritual Living Fire would be placed at the crossroads and in windows to help guide the souls of the dead and ancestors to visit the living, as well as find their way beyond the veil afterwards.

In some regions of Poland, people believed that one could encounter two kinds of flames, male and female. Male flames were supposedly much easier to control, and should a male fire break out, one could use a spell to stop it from spreading. The spell was "*ustanowytsia,*" which could be very roughly translated to mean "stop" or "get a grip" (although there is no one correct translation that I know of, as the word seems to be a slang combination of Polish and Ukrainian). If the fire was female, there was no way of stopping her from spreading and wreaking utter destruction. Therefore, it was safer to step away and allow the fire to unleash her rage.

KEEPING THE FLAME ALIVE

Over the centuries, what began as an ancient cult of Sacred Fire and the sun shifted more and more toward tending to the tamed (albeit still sacred) fire—our source of warmth, cooked food, light, and safety. Post-Christianization, the figures of fire-wielding deities and spirits became syncretized with the patron saints of fire. Despite that, the humble respect, reverence, and cult of fire endured in small yet significant ways.

Living Fire remains an intrinsic part of both the sacrum and the everyday life of the Slavic people. Treated as a sacred, living being, a manifestation of the solar principle, it bestows the powers of cleansing, healing, and protection to all those who cultivate the sacred flame.

CHAPTER SIX

SACRED WATERS: THE CULT OF WATER IN SLAVIC FOLK TRADITION

Fire and water are the two elements that play equally important—albeit very different—roles in Slavic folklore, animistic practices, and syncretic folk magic of our people. Similarly to fire, the element of water is present in all agrarian seasonal celebrations, as well as family traditions related to healing, blessing, birth, and death, marking important life transitions and thresholds. Simple folk respect and venerate water as an essential component of life, both physically and spiritually. Water is regarded as the primary carrier of life force; thus, the absence of moisture is equivalent to death. In the face of disasters, when our very survival is threatened, it is believed that the most basic needs are water and fire, to provide hydration and warmth. Similarly to how fire was treated with respect, similar taboos were present toward the element of water: It was forbidden and a sign of disrespect to spit, urinate, or throw trash into the water.

As an essential life-sustaining element, the lore surrounding water is rich with guidance on how to best interact with it, when to gather it for specific purposes, which water reservoirs to avoid, how to use it for healing and blasting, and which spirits can be expected to inhabit bodies of water.

In Polish folklore, waters tend to be divided into two primary kinds:

1. ***Żywa Woda* (Living Water):** This type of water is often believed to possess miraculous healing properties. It comes from springs, streams, wells, rain, or other sources of clean water that don't freeze in winter but remain in motion all year round. Żywa woda can be used in blessing, healing, and protection magic.
2. ***Martwa Woda* (Dead Water):** This type of water is believed to house evil water spirits, devils, and demons and can cause illness

or death. It comes from still reservoirs of water that freeze during winter, such as dark and stagnant ponds, bogs, and swamps, as well as other sources of water that have been corrupted by someone dying in or near them. Martwa woda can be used in baneful magic.

On a pragmatic level, this contrast could also be seen as a way of distinguishing safe sources of clean drinking water from sources that were unclean and thus unfit for safe consumption. After all, the magical always goes hand in hand with the practical.

Other than the apparent dual symbolism, there are a few other ways to categorize natural sources of water:

- **Heavenly waters:** These waters come from rain and dew and they possess fertilizing and rejuvenating powers. In a folkloric perception of the world, the sky covers the Earth and impregnates it with rain, whereas dew is directly linked to youth, abundance, health, and beauty.
- **Underground waters:** These waters are spring and well waters that flow directly from the depths of the Earth. They possess purifying, detoxing, healing, and regenerative powers. Despite their powerful qualities, wells were especially respected due to their chthonic nature, extending deep into the darkness of the Earth, they could be dangerous when trifled with.
- **Rivers:** These waters cut through the land, dividing and separating it, thus creating liminal space. Metaphorically, rivers correspond with the separation between this world and the afterlife. After all, the Slavic otherworlds are believed to exist *za rzeką* (beyond the river). In a folkloric perception of the world, rivers tend to mark the boundary between that which is known and that which lies beyond, which is unknown.

Polish folklore is filled with regional stories and legends about sacred springs, miraculous waters, water demons, river spirits, wells dedicated to Mother Mary or various saints, and a plethora of other local water-related beings and phenomena, wondrous and terrifying, life-giving and deadly alike. This dual symbolism—of life and death—is very prominent in all water-related folklore and magic.

WATER SYMBOLISM IN SEASONAL RITES

Slavic culture's myth and lore are largely built on the foundations of agrarian cycles (see more in: "Agrarian Traditions and Polish Folkloric Year"). Spring is the beginning of the folkloric year, and water plays a central role in its myth and symbolism.

God and the Devil (syncretized with Perun and Weles), the two adversaries who perpetually fight each other around the yearly solar cycle, fight over waters. When Weles wins the fight in autumn, thus bringing about the dark half of the year, he "binds the waters," freezing them and taking control over them. As Perun defeats Weles and brings about spring, he helps release the waters that were previously bound, thus moistening the earth and starting a new season of vegetation.

Because water is the symbol of life returning in spring, it plays a central role in folklore and ritual practices of this time of year. Other than the ritual drowning of a Marzanna effigy during the spring equinox—re-creating the mythical departure of Lady Winter from the land—there are plenty of water-related practices that survived in Polish folklore of the Easter time.

On Maundy Thursday and Good Friday, those who wash themselves in a river are believed to be granted good health and beauty. The act of washing oneself in a source of fresh Living Water helps magically wash away all sickness, curses, or evil charms that accumulated in and around oneself during winter.

Holy Saturday is when the miraculous healing qualities of water become most potent. To take advantage of the healing waters, one must acquire it from a spring or a river before sunrise, and then bring it to church to be consecrated by the priest. Such water is believed to stay clean and fresh for much longer than usual, have miraculous healing properties, and bring extraordinary beauty.

In the evening of Holy Saturday, this consecrated water is then used to sprinkle the house, both inside and around, to protect it from evil charms, curses, and witchcraft. The remaining consecrated water is kept safe throughout the year for its healing and cleansing properties, to be used whenever needed.

Around midnight between Holy Saturday and Easter Sunday, all waters are believed to possess magical qualities. It was considered wise to bottle some of this magical water to bring home and use it to consecrate things around the household. It could also be used for washing the eyes to enhance vision and heal infections, as well as add to healing baths to make them more potent.

The second day of Easter is also known as *Śmigus Dyngus* or *Lany Poniedziałek* (Wet Monday). On this day, it is customary to playfully whip each other with birch twigs and pour fresh, cold water on each other. This custom symbolizes washing away winter sickness and fatigue, and replacing them with new vitality, fertility, and lust for life.

HOLY WATER

Other than the spring rites, where water-related magic is at its peak, there are several other occasions throughout the year when obtaining *woda święcona* (holy water) is especially sought after for purposes of magic and healing.

Epiphany (January 6) is when one could obtain *woda trzochkrólowa* (Three Kings Water), which is especially potent for apotropaic purposes, as well as undoing and nullifying magical attacks.

St. Agatha's feast day (February 5), holy water is helpful for extinguishing fires and purifying wells.

Holy water was also used on the Eve of St. Lucia's feast day (December 12). Together with blessed herbs, it was added to the batter for a special bread that was fed to cattle to protect them from witchcraft.

However, the most potent holy water available was one consecrated in multiple churches—usually at least three, but even up to nine. The more churches it was blessed in, the more powerful it became.

WATER IN POLISH FOLK MAGIC AND HEALING

Due to water's vast, miraculous, magical, and healing properties, the cult of water naturally made its way into folk magic and healing, becoming one of the most important components used by witches, cunning folk, herbalists, healers, and priests alike. Folk practitioners use water in the diagnosis of curses, as well as *zamawianie,* a type of spoken charms that can help cure illnesses, banish bad habits, and get rid of curses, the evil eye, evil charms, and other negative consequences of malicious witchcraft. In this form of magic, water is often charged with specific prayers, words of power, and charms, and then either drunk, used for washing, bathing and cleaning, or sprinkled on the person or place targeted by the spell. Oftentimes, the water used in such practices would be gathered against the current from rivers or come from trusted wells or sacred springs. Other times, the working required a very specific kind of water, or water collected and blessed on a specific day.

The practice of *kropienie* or *pokropiny* (asperging, sprinkling) remains very prominent in our culture to this day. As can be expected, in present times, it is mostly the local priests who perform services of blessing with holy water for their community. In Poland, they are still invited to all openings—be it a new shopping mall, bridge, road, a new statue, new school year, or a new sowing season—the priest is there with his holy water, ready to asperge it and thus bless the new endeavor. As our society changes and fewer people are religious, it is sometimes perceived as old-fashioned or unnecessary. However, when recognized from a folkloric rather than a religious perspective, it echoes the old practices of blessing and healing with water and shows how deeply ingrained these practices always were in our customs.

Back in the day, priests weren't as involved in matters outside of the church, which means that, unlike today, common folk still performed many of these services for the family and community. Folks would customarily mark the start of any important work with asperging Living Water as a blessing for the process. Examples of this include pouring water on a wagon before it set off to start field work in the spring, pouring water on a calf to ensure it would bring a lot of milk when it grew up, pouring water on the wheels of a wagon carrying newlyweds, and sprinkling water on family members on Christmas Eve to bless them with health and abundance in the coming year.

Obmywanie (washing) has been an equally important type of water magic and healing. As will be further explained in "The Rules of Polish Folk Magic," to heal, cleanse, cure, or otherwise restore someone's lifeforce back to balance, moisture must be reapplied into their body through washing and healing baths. Washing with specific types of water, be it infused with materia or obtained on certain days, could achieve a plethora of beneficial results. For example, water with coins placed in it could be used to bestow good *dola* (fate) and physical endurance upon those who wash their face and hands with it. A newborn's first bath must be prepared with water gathered with the current of the river and not against it. After the bath, such water must be disposed of backwards and poured between the legs in a place where nobody walks, to ensure that nobody can steal the child's good fortune. In death, the last bath was also ritualized—the water for such a bath wasn't to be taken from a spring, lest it spoil it. It also couldn't be disposed of into any living source of water afterwards, as it was believed that it would kill all the lifeforce residing in it. A similar taboo was present around sources of water where someone died—it irreversibly changed the properties of the water in that place from *Żywa Woda* (Living Water) to *Martwa Woda* (Dead Water).

WATER SPIRITS AND DEMONS OF POLISH FOLKLORE

In the Slavic animistic perception of the world, every source of water—be it a spring, lake or river—has its own local spirit. For example, the spirit of river Warta was often seen by local farmers walking the shores of Warta. The spirit of river Odra, named Viadrus, is still commemorated with statues in several places along the river's course. In addition to local spirits specific to a water source, plenty of spirits and demons lived in or near water, many of whom originated as spirits of the dead who drowned, died near water, or were sacrificed to the water as an offering to protect the community from the wrath of water spirits.

Here are some of the most important and commonly recognized water spirits.

Rusałka

Known under many names, some of which include *brzeginia, bogunka, wodiana,* and *baba wodna.* Depending on regional beliefs, Rusałki were sometimes recognized as the souls of girls and women who died at a young age, other times as personifications of non-human water spirits who feed on moonlight. Rusałki take up the form of beautiful women, dancing naked by the shores of lakes or rivers on the night of a full moon. Some others, like Brzeginie, who live near mountain streams, have green hair and are believed to guard treasures. Baba wodna, on the other hand, is an older, more experienced type of Rusałka, appearing as a crone. Some say they spend the winter underwater and emerge on the shores during summer, luring men to their death. These feminine demons or spirits can be playful but also terrifying and merciless.

A local type of Rusałki living specifically and only by the Bug River basin are known as *Bogunki.* They are seen wearing green wreaths, and, unlike other Rusałki who feed on moonlight, they prefer consuming dew and salt. Some compare their songs to the morning screams of cattle. However, their otherworldly beauty still made it easy for them to lure men to their death.

Carrying a sprig of wormwood helps protect oneself from Rusałki.

Utopiec

These water demons are believed to be the souls of humans who committed suicide by drowning, or the souls of miscarried fetuses. They live in rivers, lakes, ponds, wells and other inland water reservoirs, where someone might've ended their life or drowned. They appear as a tall, skinny creature with green, slimy skin and a big head with large dark eyes. Utopiec is an ambivalent creature—sometimes being hostile towards humans and dragging them to their death, while other times aiding them in exchange for payment or playing riddles. Some tales describe them as capable of enchanting people, similarly to sirens, and compelling them to drown themselves. Other tales speak of them competing with local peasants, or engaging in local dramas. These spirits have a peculiar relationship with the moon, revering it while also being afraid of it, begging the moon not to punish them. Because of their strength, they were rather avoided and seen as extremely dangerous, which meant that some folks avoided aiding drowning people out of the fear of Utopiec.

To protect oneself from Utopiec (which wasn't considered very effective, but still better than nothing), one should carry a rosary, or a piece of consecrated chalk."

Wodnik

Sometimes also referred to as *diabły wodne* ("water devils"), these old water spirits are known for dwelling in and protecting inland water reservoirs, such as lakes, ponds, or even old wells. Often imagined as a fish-eyed, short old man, with unnaturally long membranous fingers, and long tangled hair. Some of them may enjoy spending their time on the banks of their reservoirs, or even luring children with shiny things. Folks were rather scared of *wodniki* (plural), for they could easily drown those who came too close or dared to pollute their home. At the same time, the spirit was equally respected and revered for their protective function, crucial to the local ecosystem, ensuring access to safe drinking water, or healthy fish. Wodnik is among the water spirits who used to receive regular offerings from local communities to appease him. The offerings usually consisted of a sacrificial farm animal, which would be given into the waters with seasonal or annual regularity. In exchange for proper care, respect, and offerings, Wodnik would guarantee that the local community wouldn't suffer from floods, drownings, water poisonings, and such.

PART TWO

POLISH FOLK MAGIC IN THEORY

CHAPTER SEVEN

HOW DOES POLISH FOLK MAGIC WORK?

One thing that is often omitted in witchcraft books and resources is a simple explanation of how and why it all works. No matter how well-researched and well-sourced your average resource is, an author often assumes that everybody already knows the underlying mechanisms of it all. As countless—supposedly traditional—examples of workings, spells, or recipes are listed, the instructions on navigating them are lacking. There is rarely mention of how crucial it is to form a bond with the spirits of materia and the allies, without whom all this would be but an act. Some may say it is a way of witchcraft gatekeeping itself from being abused. However, I believe that it is symptomatic of the general state of our modern society's dismissal of and oblivion to our animistic roots and their foundational importance in working one's craft. Plenty of modern theories of magic exist, and are undoubtedly useful when dealing with contemporary models and paradigms. However, folk magic—as a historically much more archaic expression of the craft, firmly rooted in animism and the spirit model—is best described within the frameworks of the history and anthropology of magic and religion, as well as the history, culture, and language of a people.

When sourcing folk magic or witchcraft practices, such as folkloric spells or traditional rituals, no matter how historical or modern they are, it is not the impeccable reconstruction of step-by-step instructions regarding the setting, ingredients, words, and gestures that make the working work. What does is the recognition of and direct involvement with the undercurrent of presence of the local ecology and land-dwelling forces whom we invite into our work: the spirit of the plant, the familiar ensouling a tool, the spirits of place who grant or deny permission to hold space, the powers who are being petitioned or pacted with for aid, and so on. Should the spirit connection be absent, the working itself remains dead, functioning as spiritual psychodrama at best and violating the local ecology and customs at worst.

Folk magic is never about the individual, and it does not exist in a vacuum. Any given act of magic is performed within a living cultural ecosystem and is witnessed by the powers around us. When the practitioner truly understands this, suddenly all historical practices—no matter how vaguely preserved—begin to make sense and become infinitely more enriching and meaningful. I want you to keep this in mind as you read, especially when going through the practical section of this book. All the practices, spoken formulas, and such that I source for you directly from my culture come to life when practiced with the acknowledgment and active inclusion of the spirits, forces, and virtues being worked with. This is how our animistic ancestors perceived the world around them, and thus how they practiced. Recognizing that the land around them is alive, ensouled, and inhabited by countless beings possessing personhood, they actively communed and communicated with the spirits of plants, places, objects, illnesses, natural phenomena, and such. Each time a witch speaks a *zamawianie* (spoken charm), it is an act of speaking directly to the very soul of the recipient of the enchantment, human and non-human alike. This shall be further explored in the practical section of this book.

SYMPATHETIC AND CONTAGIOUS MAGIC

It should come as no surprise that the core of Polish folk magic, similarly to most other folk practices around the globe, stems from sympathetic magic. As Frazer puts it in *Golden Bough:*

"If we analyze the principles of thought on which magic is based, they will probably be found to resolve themselves into two: first, that like produces like, or that an effect resembles its cause; and, second, that things which have once been in contact with each other continue to act on each other at a distance after the physical contact has been severed. The former principle may be called the Law of Similarity, the latter the Law of Contact or Contagion. From the first of these principles, namely the Law of Similarity, the magician infers that he can produce any effect he desires merely by imitating it; from the second he infers that whatever he does to a material object will affect equally the person with whom the object was once in contact, whether it formed part of his body or not" (Frazer, 2009, p. 36).

One of the commonly observed ways animism is believed to have survived in the folk magical practices of traditional societies worldwide, including

Polish folk magic, is the prevalence of the rules of sympathy and contagion in historical spoken formulas and practices of the common folk. The two always occur in conjunction, where components such as objects, ingredients, words of power, and symbolic gestures are combined and worked with to enact desired change.

The rule of sympathy is seen in formulas where the practitioner imitates or enacts the desired outcome through ritual (symbolic) actions, thus causing the outcome to occur outside of the ritual setting. Sympathy means that "like causes like"—by imitating what is to happen in ritual, the same is bound to occur outside of ritual. For example, if one wishes to cause harm to their neighbor, they may enact what is to happen to the neighbor via gestures and words of power directed at a symbolic representation of the neighbor.

The rule of contagion means that if an object was in direct contact with the subject of the working, the practitioner can cause an analogous effect upon the subject by dealing it directly to the object. This is often seen in formulas where an object is used to represent a person or animal: their belonging, a piece of hair, or even their footprint in the dirt can be used to cause them harm or blessing. To continue the example of affecting a neighbor, the practitioner may procure their hair and use it as a focal point for the working. Because the hair belongs to the neighbor, the two are connected, and thus, by working magic on the hair, it is, by extension, affecting the neighbor.

CORRESPONDENCE

An additional component often employed in folk magic practices is the law of correspondence, which is based on the belief that a direct resemblance of one thing to another creates a correspondence or link between the two. This is especially often seen in Polish folk medicine, where a plant's medicinal (and magical) properties are deduced based on the visual or behavioral similarity to the subject. For example, some plants may resemble certain bodily organs in shape, while others may produce flowers or fruits in the color of a bodily fluid and thus be used in healing or strengthening the corresponding body part. The same proves to be true for correspondence in a broader plethora of magical applications: plants with sharp thorns may be used to wound or harm, talismans made of certain animal parts can imbue the wearer with the perceived strengths and abilities of the animal, and so on.

FOLKLORE AND ORAL TRADITION

Other than the rules of sympathy and contagion, as well as observable correspondences, folk practitioners rely heavily on local legends, stories, and folklore of places, plants, animals, and spirits to inform their work. This local cultural component was orally transmitted from generation to generation and was only known to folks in their region. As explored in previous chapters about cultural regionality and bioregionality, the customs, lore, and beliefs largely inform the regional expressions of traditions and rituals of a people. This is of notable importance for practitioners who wish to engage with unique local spirits, sacred land features, and regionally relevant observances.

PRACTICAL AIM AND SURVIVAL

Unlike the ceremonial or theurgical practices of the privileged sphere, folk magic always aimed to be—above all—useful and practical, supporting the common folk in their everyday struggles and giving hope and agency in situations that were otherwise impossible to control due to factors related to facing unpredictable natural phenomena or matters of privilege, wealth, freedom, and fundamental human rights. Historically, the peasantry of Poland had it rather rough compared to other parts of Europe. In some regions, even up until the modern period of the late nineteenth century, people lived in poverty and were owned by their landlord or semi-free under "*pańszczyzna*" serfdom, owning very little of their own, if anything, often sharing their huts with farm animals, with limited access to medicine or education, and child labor in herding and farming being the norm. In such conditions, folks relied on folk medicine and folk magic for survival. Therefore, three primary types of magic were commonly practiced: produce magic, protection magic, and baneful magic.

Produce magic would be the equivalent of modern-day prosperity magic practices, focusing on bringing in an abundance of crops, hunting, animal produce, various crafts, and trade.

Protection magic includes practices related to warding off evil and bad luck, preventing and healing illnesses, and ensuring safety from the ill intent of others and the unpredictable natural phenomena or wild animals.

Baneful magic was historically practiced as a way of taking back one's power, taking revenge, escaping punishment, stealing away someone else's profit, or otherwise, as a last resort when one's survival was being threatened.

How Does Polish Folk Magic Work?

The simple practices of everyday folk magic helped our ancestors feel less hopeless in the face of living in a hostile, rough reality, where danger and death lurked from all sides, and they were given very little agency or privilege to face these challenges. While our modern struggles may seem very different to those of our forebears, depending on where we live, it is thanks to their resilience, determination, and hard work that we get to experience and carry on their legacy into the future, and to apply their wisdom into surviving through the crises of global scale climate change, the collapse of societal values, late stage capitalism, and short-termism of modernity.

CHAPTER EIGHT

THE RULES OF POLISH FOLK MAGIC

Broadly speaking, folk magic is usually characterized by the common descriptors explored in the previous section. However, specific cultural folk magic of a people will have its unique local rules and beliefs surrounding the intricacies of the craft, stemming from the peculiarities of the people's language, history, and customs. In Polish folk magic, this is notably characterized by elements of dual-faith practices, the unique grammatical structure of spoken charms, and rules stemming from the folkloric perception of the world, such as the rule of moisture and dryness.

DUAL FAITH AND HERESY

Traditional folk magic practices largely survived the process of Christianization thanks to people adapting elements of dual faith into their beliefs and worldviews, which has been the case for most Slavic peoples, regardless of region. Dual faith is characterized by the religious syncretisms adapted by common folk, whereby the old pre-Christian beliefs and agrarian land-based traditions remain at the foundations of a people's worldview, with Christian beliefs and holy days then being retrofitted over them, equated, and coordinated with each other over time, thus creating an inseparable amalgam of both. In the case of Poland, which has always been predominantly Catholic, it took up the form of Folk Catholicism.

From the very beginning, the process of Christianization of the Slavic peoples was not very successful as the moral, educational, socioeconomic, and sometimes even cultural differences between the church officials and the common folk, as well as the language barrier (Roman Catholic Mass was led exclusively in Latin until the second half of the twentieth century), made basic Christian theology rather inaccessible for the Polish people. This led to a very surface-level conversion and indoctrination, as well as folks filling in the holes with their own pre-Christian understandings and syncretisms that stemmed from preserved elements of old belief and the folkloric-animist perception of the world.

In practice, this means that many figures of Catholic saints have been syncretized with land spirits and older deities. The wayside shrines dedicated to folkloric Marys, so commonly present in our landscape of rural crossroads, hedges, and places of power, still remind us of their prior function as focal points for communion and making pacts with local spirits. Ancestor veneration and agrarian traditions have been linked to certain holy and feast days for convenience. Certain symbols and tools evolved to better fit in with the dominant religion, but the core remained. This is why, unlike neo-pagans who prefer to sterilize the post-Christian additions, traditional folk witches often embrace the dual faith elements and don't mind the syncretisms, understanding that the surface-level Catholic symbolism has only aided in the survival of our folkloric land-based practices through all the religious and cultural transformations over the centuries.

While some folk witches choose to embrace the Catholic faith, some of us choose to remain non-religious or to follow a more heretical path. We draw upon the cultural and folkloric, rather than religious elements of the Catholic faith, and make the practice appear quite acceptable on the surface, when truly functioning on the furthest threshold from the acceptable, where the folkloric devils are dearer to us than the monotheist God. This is clearly observable in the records of the Polish Witch Trials, where heretical practices of using the rosary, stealing the host, or practicing magic in churchyards, while also partaking in spirit flight and sabbatic rituals at the Bald Mountain are rather commonly reported.

THE STRUCTURE OF POLISH SPOKEN CHARMS

Most Polish historical formulas recorded during the witch trial period and later share a similar sentence structure, which can be very illuminating in terms of the kind of magic that was historically used most often, both by practitioners and the common folk who also engaged in basic protection and healing magic on a daily basis.

Sympathetic magic, with its core laws of similarity and contagion, is clearly present in the examples of Polish spells I'm about to share with you. Like many of our best-preserved historical formulas, they come from the records of Polish witch trials. I'm presenting them to you as translated into English by the scholar Michael Ostling in *Between the Devil and the Host: Imagining Witchcraft in Early Modern Poland* (Ostling, 2011, p. 120). The original Polish words of the formulas have been sourced from *Procesy Czarownic w Polsce w XVII i XVIII wieku* by Bohdan Baranowski (2021, p. 191-232).

- **Love formula:** *"Just as I cannot live without my blood, so you christened and called [name], cannot live without me".*

Original Polish words of the spell: *"Jako ja nie mogę przez swojej krwie, tak ty krczony, mianowany [imię], nie możesz być beze mnie..."*

This spoken formula would be accompanied by pricking one's finger and sneaking a drop of one's blood into a drink, which would then be served to one's target.

- **Love formula:** *"Just as it is hard for a dove without his mate, so you christened and called [name], cannot live without me [name]".*

Original Polish words of the spell: *"Jako nie może gołąb bez gołąbice, tak ty krczony, mianowany abyś nie mógł, Janie, beze mnie krczonej, mianowanej Zofiej."*

This spoken formula was recited during a ritual bath where one would mix water with the hearts of doves, wash oneself in it, then served the water to one's target.

- **Court case success formula:** *"Just as people crowd around the Most Holy Sacrament, in the same way let their graces the lord deputies of the court show favor in our cases".*

Original Polish words of the spell: *"Jak wielka ciżba do komunii bywa, tak żeby cały trybunał był łaskaw na panią moją."*

This spoken formula would be recited while mixing the batter for pancakes made with a stolen Eucharist wafer, to be later fed to the judges.

- **House destruction formula:** *"Just as the soil has toppled over, so will these houses topple over".*

Original Polish words of the spell: *"Jak to się wywróciło, tak się one wywrócą."*

This spoken formula would be recited while sprinkling the soil or dust from a whirlwind at a building that is to be destroyed.

- **Crops destruction formula:** *"Place two chicken eggs on the field border, so that the fields will be as bare as those eggs, and roll the eggs in ashes, so that the grain will be destroyed, as the eggs are destroyed in the ash".*

Original Polish words of the formula: *"[...] położyć dwa jaja kokoszę na miedzy, aby rola była tak goła jak te jaje, a jaja otocz w popiele, aby zboże zniszczało, jak niszczeje w popiele jaje te."*

This formula is purely instructional, describing the acts that one must perform to achieve the destruction of a field's fertility. Despite this not being a spoken formula per se, it still retains the familiar structure in its retelling.

As is evident from the above examples, all these formulas conform to a uniform structure, which could be described as follows: *"Just like [symbolic object] affects [symbolic target], so shall [object] affect [target]"* or *"Just like [object] causes [change], so shall [target] experience [change]."* The sympathetic aspect is conveyed through the use of correspondences, such as doves representing love, blood representing life force, ashes representing destruction, and so on. The contagion aspect comes from connecting these correspondences to a situation, a place, or a person that is supposed to be affected by the formula. This is achieved by means of declaring the desired outcome verbally, as well as reinforcing it through ritual actions. Therefore, by calling upon a true correspondence that exists in nature, it is transferred by the powers of magic in accordance with the witch's will.

According to Ostling, "magical analogies are rhetorical: they do not proceed by finding similarity but by finding difference, and 'evoking' or 'arguing for' or exhorting' similarity. [...] A relation of similarity is not found but asserted, in the hope that it will come to be" (Ostling, 2011, p. 121). While the researcher's conclusions might be correct in regards to the importance of actively asserting the similarities and how they are expected to interact with the target, as a non-practitioner, he certainly missed out on the relevance and potency of the symbolic correspondences employed in these formulas. By extension, he missed out on the relevance of the similarities present between the object used and the purpose that it is to serve in the working. These factors are far from accidental, but rather deeply rooted in folklore and more apparent to those with a working understanding of sympathetic magic.

THE BALANCE OF MOISTURE AND DRYNESS

Another prominent feature present in Polish folk magic are the rules surrounding moisture and dryness, which are directly related to the prominence of the cult of Sacred Waters and Living Fire in Polish and Slavic old beliefs. These two elements, regarded as powerful forces present in most Slavic rites, are reflected in the archaic rules of the flow of life force in all living things. To give moisture is to heal and bless. To steal moisture, or worse, to dry someone up, is to curse and kill.

The presence of **moisture** could be generally perceived as proof of life. On a micro scale, as living creatures we are carriers of blood, sweat and fat, and are dependent on water and nutrients to survive. The moist substances within our bodies circulate and distribute nutrients, as well as expel toxins. The same is observed on a macro scale, where the well-being of the entire ecosystem relies on the circulation of rain and water to grow and thrive. Thus, moisture was seen as a carrier of life and applied as needed to restore health and vitality. Practicing beneficial magic or folk healing was often done by applying moisture into the body: rubbing dew into the skin, soaking in herbal baths, washing oneself in sacred springs and rivers, drinking medicinal brews, drinking animal blood to embody the creature's strengths, pouring wax into water over one's head, egg rolling, and such. Blessing was commonly done by asperging water, washing or anointing. Conversely, theft of moisture was employed as a form of *maleficia*–stealing dew from the fields or milk from the cows to take away the vitality and fertility of a place or animal.

Dryness, on the other hand, was considered a sign of illness and death, and seen as a lack of life force. Unlike the living whose bodies are filled with moisture, the dead are "dried up" – their bodies devoid of liquids, decomposed down to a dry bone, or burnt to ash. Therefore, as a way of mimicking this diminishing of life force, traditional baneful workings often include spoken charms that curse the subject to "dry up". An example of such a formula goes as follows: *"Waszą chałupę podleję z trupich kości wódką, tedy wszyscy poschniecie"* ("I'll drench your hut in dead man's bones vodka, and you shall all dry up"). Bones and graveyard soil, as objects coming from the dead, and thus devoid of life, were commonly employed in baneful work, or spirit contact. Dried up footprints in the mud would be used as a taglock base for a curse. Burning objects to ash and using such ash to cause harm was also quite common in historical formulas – sprinkled over the threshold, blown on the wind in the direction of the target, or added to one's drink. However, graveyard soil, ash or bones, as *materia* devoid of moisture, were also used to absorb or suck out illnesses or curses from the body, or worn as protective agents against the restless dead (the wearer is camouflaged by the dry substance and thus becomes indistinguishable from the dead).

In nature, the balance of moisture and dryness fundamentally dictates our living conditions. Just as an unexpected period of drought could ruin an entire supply of crops for the season, so could the same disaster be caused by a sudden flood. Neither dew nor parched bone is an ally when abused, and too much of a good thing always ends up biting us in the tail. The imbalance of these forces in any direction could have dire consequences for the survival of a people. Our ancestors knew that the odds were too often against them, and that the way they themselves contributed to this balance would not go unnoticed by the local spirits. If you don't work hard for your share and don't contribute to the well-being of your community, you may not have enough resources to survive. Therefore, to remain safe, it was important to cultivate a mindset rooted in mutual aid and right relations with the community, the land and the ecology around us. Just as an individual depended on the community for support, the community as a whole depended on the spirits' benevolence. After all, it was within the spirits' power to regulate moisture and dryness through atmospheric phenomena as they see fit. When treated right, they could send just the right amount of rain and sunshine to make the crops grow strong. When mistreated or disrespected, they could just as easily cause a flood or withhold all the rain, thus causing a drought.

Outcasts and individuals existing on the outskirts of a community were often the first suspects when things weren't going so well in this regard. After all, if the spirits are punishing the community, somebody must be responsible for this. This is where the common accusations of witches stealing the milk of their neighbor's cows comes from. However, it appears that even when stealing something by means of magic, folks would commonly employ a formula that maintained the overall balance of forces, ensuring that they don't anger the spirits by taking too much. The formula is known as *"Biorę pożytek, ale nie wszytek"* ("I take the excess, and leave everything else"), meaning that they would, at best, "borrow" the overflow or excess of the thing, leaving the rest untouched. In this way, respect for the spirits and the community's long-term prosperity was maintained, ensuring that nobody would be illegitimately stripped bare and left entirely resourceless. One could say that the resources were merely redistributed so that those who had more than they needed would share with those who didn't have enough, thus maintaining the overall well-being of the community.

As becomes evident in the symbolic role of balancing of moisture and dryness, our ancestors understood that the stability of the world hangs on a delicate thread, that access to resources isn't limitless and nothing is given freely; everything has its cost and takes time to replenish, forces of nature are ultimately unpredictable and impossible to control, and the laws of nature don't cater to nor particularly favor the human kind. This stands in stark contrast to contemporary capitalist thought, and the popular belief present in modern spirituality, whereby everyone has unlimited access to "abundance" awaiting to be "manifested," and that we can infinitely consume and exploit the earth's resources. Such an approach, ultimately stemming from upper class privilege, is fundamentally incompatible with the kind of worldview that informs the practice of Polish folk magic.

CHAPTER NINE

WITCH LORE PRESERVED IN POLISH WITCH TRIALS

The Polish Witch Trials culminated in the seventeenth and eighteenth centuries, which could be considered rather late compared with the rest of Europe. The last witch in Europe to be on official trial and burned at the stake in 1811 was Barbara Zdunk from Reszel, a village in the present-day Warmia region of Poland (back then belonging to the Protestant Duchy of Prussia), accused of arson caused by witchcraft. As for the last known victim of such accusations in Poland outside of trial, Krystyna Ceynowa was lynched to death in 1836 by her neighbors who accused her of witchcraft but were refused the trial, as the offence of witchcraft was no longer recognized by law at that point.

Witch trial records remain among the richest sources of witch lore today, allowing access to an absolute wealth of information about the folkloric vision of the world, as well as deepening our understanding of magic and witchcraft local to the trials. While the records of witch trials in Western countries have been serving as inspiration for traditional witches and folk practitioners for decades now, it seems that the Eastern European records, including Polish, haven't yet gained their spotlight in this regard.

When studying witch trial records, it is important to first address the common questions: Weren't a lot of the confessions coerced out of the accused through torture? And, if so, aren't they inauthentic and useless? The answer to this would be yes and no. At the time of the witch trials in Poland, the country was in a unique sociopolitical situation, which caused the trials to be less harsh compared to Western Europe. At the time, the Catholic Church in Poland had been actively competing with Protestantism, which was creeping in from the West, for dominion over the country. While Protestants were the ones known for their deep hatred for witches and championing the number of witch hunts and trials conducted in Western countries, the Catholic Church understood that it wasn't in their best interest to turn the society against them by persecuting witches. Instead, it focused more on demonizing the Protestants, thus, ironically, allowing the practices of folk magic to remain unchallenged. Without going into too much detail about the sociopolitical issues of that time, the result was that Poland had seen significantly fewer severe witch trials than the West, and the results of the trials themselves weren't as often concluding in the deaths of the accused.

Another significant aspect of this is the confessions and what they tell us about the practices recorded therein. While it may be true that not every accused person was indeed a witch, it is undeniable that many of the confessed practices on record adhere to the rules of Polish folk magic, thus remaining cohesive with a broadly recognized system of how folk magic should be practiced. In a twisted way, the coherence and repetitiveness of the recorded practices prove how widespread these practices were among the common folk, and how everyone had access to the basic know-how of how to say zamawiania (spoken charms), which herbs to use for *okadzanie* (fumigation), how to cast an *urok* (enchantment), or where to look for a spirit to pact with for profit. On top of this, folks confessing their otherworldly encounters with devils and spirits, flying to the sabbat, or indulging in intercourse with unholy forces, often described experiences that may have occurred in altered states of consciousness or their sleep (as discussed in "Visions of Spirits, Hypnagogia and Life Beyond Death"), which shed crucial context on the authenticity of these experiences. This perspective too often remains unexplored in research due to the lack of a working understanding of the nature of altered states, and the common perception of them before the Industrial Revolution and the age of the worship of hard science. Our predecessors did not consider their sleep or altered states as any less real than waking experience, nor should a practitioner.

I firmly believe that the Eastern European Witch Trial records contain a unique and priceless insight into the common folk perceptions of magic, offering crucial nuance helpful in developing an understanding of other aspects of Slavic culture, such as folklore, myths, and legends, and pre-Christian origins of Slavic animism and land-based practices. While it is outside the scope of this book to cover everything, I have chosen to showcase the most important takeaways from witch trial lore, providing a foundation for understanding what Polish folk magic looked like during the late medieval and early modern periods.

PACTS WITH THE DEVIL

One of the most common accusations in witch trials was that of consorting with the Devil. In Polish trials, confessions don't shy away from calling out the Devil's involvement, although he isn't always mentioned directly. This stems from the peculiarities of the Polish rural culture itself, favoring local folkloric names for various devils and spirits. Despite the persecutors' apparent attempts at forcing certain pre-established scenarios or language into the accused's confessions, Polish folks naturally favoured their local understandings of spirits and witchcraft, which is why their confessions still serve as an invaluable reservoir of authentic folklore and beliefs of our people. Some confessions describe the accused's relationship with their Devil familiar in much depth, listing the name of the spirit, what they looked like, how long they've been working together, as well as the kinds of powers or gifts the Devil granted to them. It is important to note that the trial confessions come from simple village folk, often underprivileged, poor, and neglected by the system. In such dire circumstances, one of the main observed causes for accepting a deal with the Devil seems to have been the promise of being lifted out of poverty or receiving gifts of food and money from the spirits. This is significantly different from the kind of pacts with the Devil signed by men of noble standing, who willingly approached the Devil to bargain for wealth, power and privilege in exchange for their soul. In witch trial records, it is predominantly peasant females who are approached for pacts, and who would rarely seek it out themselves.

A commonly recurring motif reported in the pact-related confessions is that a Devil presenting as a young and handsome man would pay a visit to the woman while she was preoccupied with chores, such as cooking, working in the garden, or milking her cows. He would introduce himself with either a common male name, like Janek or Paweł, or a strange and exotic name, such as Chorainiczi or Tebus. Oftentimes, his looks would be ambiguous, so that it wasn't entirely clear whether he was a human or a spirit. The suspicious looks align with the common folkloric characteristics of Polish folk devils, such as him having no nose, speaking in a strange muffled voice, being hooved, smelling of tar, disguising horns in his thick hair, as well as his phallus being ice cold during intercourse.

The pact itself was a rather simple agreement or transaction— a commitment to an ongoing mutual exchange of goods and services, which consisted of regular sex, and providing each other with gifts and aid. The Devil would provide gifts of money, alcohol, fatty foods, or dairy products, while the woman would give him specific kinds of meat, or steal the Eucharist wafer for him.

As a result of the pact, both parties would remain involved in a mutual relationship, and the woman would be invited to partake in sabbatic feasts on the Bald Mountain several times a year. The witch's sabbat lore will be explored shortly.

DEVIL'S BAPTISM

Another interesting theme in witch trial confessions includes the witch being initiated into a relationship with the Devil by receiving a heretical "baptism" or otherwise denouncing God as a means of dedicating oneself to the spirit. While the witch trial confessions often portray these experiences as spontaneous, involuntary or even forced upon the accused witch, we also know of instances preserved in folklore, where a candidate for a practitioner would perform such acts out of their own free will, as a means of self-initiation. Let us explore some of the most prominent themes of Devil's "baptism" present in trial records and folklore.

Interestingly, the "baptisms" would unfold somewhat similarly to the aforementioned pacts, except it appeared to be more formalised. The Devil, presenting as a young and handsome man, would visit the woman while she was preoccupied with everyday chores, or resting alone at home. He would introduce himself with a popular male name, such as Janek, Daniel, or Kacperek, and appear interested in the woman romantically. His ambiguous looks would make it unclear whether he was a human or a spirit.

After the initial interaction, the Devil would begin to bargain with the woman, offering to become a provider of goods, such as money, fatty foods, healing herbs, in exchange for the woman undergoing the "baptism", denouncing God and agreeing to a sexual relationship in return. Should she refuse the offer, the spirit would turn unpleasant or even violent, threatening. Should they strike an agreement, the Devil would proceed with the anointing of his new accomplice. The initiation itself usually consisted of the woman speaking the baptism prayer or *Paternoster* prayer in reverse, and denouncing God. Then, she would be marked by the spirit with a dark substance resembling tar, and receive a new name, such as Zofia or Łucja.

The "baptism" was then concluded and consummated with intercourse between the Devil and the initiate. According to reports, the sex itself wasn't the most pleasant, the Devil's phallus was ice cold, and his overall presentation may have appeared changed from that of a young handsome man to a strange hybrid being—possessing animal-like features, such as bull legs, or hooves, concealing horns under his thick hair or stinking of sulfur. From that point on, the sexual relationship would continue on a regular basis, and the Devil would bring the promised gifts and payment in return. Despite the ongoing sex, the women never got pregnant, however they sometimes got violently sick from it. In such instances, the spirit would care for them and help them heal by providing herbal medicine.

THE BALD MOUNTAIN AND THE WITCHES' SABBAT

In Polish witch lore, the most commonly documented sabbat spots were places of old pre-Christian cults, as well as locations known for being haunted and steeped in legends, such as certain mountain tops, meadows, crossroads, abandoned old ruins, secluded places in wilderness. Any hill or mountain that was known as a place of sabbats would be called *Łysa Góra* (Bald Mountain). A few examples of such historical sabbatic mountains in Poland include: Łysa Góra (Łysica) in the Świętokrzyskie Mountains, Ślęża and Radunia Mountains near Sobótka (Sabath), Babia Góra with her highest peak known as Diablak (Devil's Top), Góra Milczenia (Mountain of Silence) in Świętokrzyskie. Many more hills and mountains like this exist, and the easiest way to recognize them is by the old cult walls forming a circle around the top of the mountain. These cult walls, however, were not built by medieval witches themselves. They date back hundreds or thousands of years, hinting at the continuous significance of old, pre-Christian places of cult and worship. A good example of this is the cult walls around Ślęża, dating back to the Iron Age.

On certain nights of the year—such as Maundy Thursday, Pentecost, May Eve, St. John's Eve, or St. Lucia's Eve—witches met at the sabbat to feast and dance. The sabbatic dates would differ depending on region, however they coincided with the eves of significant celebrations marking seasonal changes, being associated with lore of liminality, times when the dead were more active, or when God was thought to be preoccupied and thus unable to see the heretical acts performed during the sabbatic feasts.

The witches' sabbats usually unfolded according to a particular, somewhat predictable, structure. First, the witch would either be transported spontaneously by her familiar Devil, or travel to the sabbat herself with the help of a flying ointment. The details of the flight itself will be described below.

Upon arrival at the spot—a mountain top, a castle under the mountain, or a meadow—they would be greeted with a feast consisting of the most desirable drinks and food, as well as their familiar Devils already waiting for them. Those who attended for the first time, would sometimes undergo their pact or "baptism" at the sabbat, before enjoying the celebration. The sabbat itself always consisted of a delicious feast, dancing and sleeping with one's spirit. Trial records detail how the attendants would enjoy all the food and drink, especially since most of them lacked such luxuries in daily life. They mention drinking alcohol out of eggshells, enjoying high quality meats and delicious fruit. Everyone, no matter their social status in daily life, was treated fairly and received gifts of money, food, alcohol, fresh clothes, and such, from their Devils.

One of the most iconic aspects of witches' sabbats on the Bald Mountain was the witches' dance, likely for its naturally trance-inducing properties, lending itself to ecstatic practices of witchcraft and heresy. At the sabbat, there was always music—either played by the Devil, by various spirits, or by peasant men who were transported to the feast together with the witches. It is important to note that in medieval times, dance was considered an impure and deranged activity, supposedly causing people to stray from the "good path." An odd, yet often-repeated confession is that of the aforementioned peasant men being employed to play music at the sabbats. Interestingly, the instruments they used were often not actual musical instruments, but farming tools and implements such as harrows, listers, sickles, or hooks. In trial records, we can encounter scarce confessions of men who claimed to have been kidnapped to play at the sabbat, despite having no prior involvement with such things. On the other hand, the attending women confessed to recognising some of the participants—detailing that their neighbors or known local individuals were present as fellow witches, that they recognised some of the peasant men hired as musicians, or that local thieves and criminals were seen frequenting these feasts.

The sabbats were said to end before the first crow of a rooster, before dawn. While the participants may have remembered how they arrived at the sabbat, almost none of them could recall making their way back home. Singular confessions detail the familiar spirit saying a particular word, such as *"hei"*, resulting in the person being instantly teleported home. More commonly, folks would report waking up in their bed in the morning, with a vague recollection of last night's celebrations. Trial confessions additionally detail that the gifts received at the sabbat would transform into useless items, or that they would disappear altogether the next morning, thus leaving them with nothing. Some of the accused would even openly voice their disappointment and feelings of betrayal at this deception. The disappearance of gifts given at the sabbat is a common motif repeating in trial records.

SPIRIT FLIGHT

No witch lore exploration would be complete without the tales of spirit flight to the sabbat. While the witch's broom is thought to be the most popular and stereotypical witch's tool today, trial records point at a plethora of other bizarre means of transport that were utilised for spirit flight. Naturally, brooms and similar everyday tools with long handles were featured, although not as prominently as one might think.

The flight usually appears to be facilitated by some means of transport organised by the spirits—be it an animal, a cart, or a devilish familiar in person. Documented examples include folks confessing to flying to the sabbat by holding onto a cow's tail, or mounted on a black dog, a goat, an owl, or other "devilish" animals. Some reported being personally carried in the arms or on the back of their Devil or familiar spirit. Cases of being instantly teleported, or having no recollection of the process are also common. For those who knew how to facilitate the flight themselves, keyholes, thresholds and chimneys were preferred as portals to slip through in spirit. For those who had a chimney, it served as a liminal space, believed to be a doorway used by witches and spirits to come in and out of the household, mimicking the pathways of smoke—which is likely why it was a preferred gate for spirit flight. In more modest houses that weren't equipped with a chimney, slipping through a window, a wall crack, under the door, or through a keyhole served the same purpose.

Similar to other European witches, Polish witches also used the infamous flying ointments for the purpose of flight. The documented historical recipes commonly called for animal components as bonding agents or carrier fats for the ointment: the ash of a burned toad, blood of frogs and toads, fat of frog spawn, or baby fat. Other miscellaneous ingredients included a stolen Eucharist wafer, powdered human bones, human secretions, or other taboo, heretical items. As can be expected, psychoactive and poisonous plants were also mentioned—mugwort, wormwood, henbane, datura, deadly nightshade, opium poppy, bryony, monkshood, black nightshade, poison hemlock—all native to the region. One may also speculate the use of native psychoactive mushrooms, such as the *amanitas*, or those of the *psilocybe* family. Incidentally, the latter share a peculiar familiarity with the name of the place of the sabbat itself: *łysiczka (psilocybe)* and *Łysica* (Bald Mountain).

In Polish witch trial records, whenever an ointment is mentioned, the accused confess to acquiring it through unexplained means, or directly from spirits. They describe smearing their bodies with it—especially the armpits, feet, pulse points, as well as the objects used as means for "flying". Some would mark the sign of the cross with an ointment on the chimney they escaped through, others would rub it into their pitchfork handle. Interestingly, the ointment itself was reported to stain its users black, thus hinting at an apparent shared characteristic with the aforementioned dark substance used by the Devil to anoint his initiates. Could it be one and the same substance? Although we may never know for certain, this would certainly explain the common reports of witches receiving it directly from spirits.

While we merely dipped our toes into the witch lore preserved in Polish witch trial records, it is my hope that the above helps illustrate how the trial confessions serve as an exceptionally interesting direction of studies for seasoned practitioners, offering entry points for deeper immersion into spirit-led practices of witchcraft. By tapping directly into the kind of craft that the witches in one's region practiced in medieval and early modern periods, one can discover a new (yet old) route of relating to local land and the currents of magic residing therein. It is a way that is still somewhat ancestral and yet predominantly arising from and motivated by the primal need for adaptation and survival, rather than purely focused on the cultural or otherwise anthropocentric aspects. Equipped with this simple, yet rich and priceless historical knowledge of Polish witch lore, one can easily recognise elements of it present in one's craft, or adapt more of them in practice. The most prominent aspects of historical craft have always been right there, in records of witch trials and folkloric practices, waiting for practitioners of magic and witchcraft to filter through the syncretic, to tap into something older lurking underneath.

PART THREE

POLISH FOLK MAGIC IN PRACTICE

CHAPTER TEN

ZAMAWIANIE AND SPOKEN FORMULAS

Zamawianie is the practice of spoken charms, consistently present under various names in traditional cultures across the world. Our ancient ancestors believed that the spoken word possesses the power to make that which is expressed verbally to happen by means of sympathy and contagion. *Zamawiać* (verb) means to order, to enchant, and to speak over. An effective *zamawianie* (noun) is an act of communicating with or narrating the world around us in such a way that directly addresses and instructs the matter or being to whom we are calling. From an animistic perspective, the world is inhabited by human and non-human persons, all of whom are worthy of proper acknowledgment and respect. As folk practitioners, we do not wish to dominate, subdue, or extort from the world around us, but instead treat other beings as equals with whom we can form bonds of mutual aid for the benefit of all. To form an allyship with a being, they need to be addressed appropriately so that they may feel inclined to listen to us and respond. While this may not apply in the same way to beings who are openly hostile toward humans, boundaries, and careful respect remain at the forefront of all spirit relations.

Whenever a practitioner wishes to call upon an ally, such as a plant, spirit of place, a being, or phenomenon, they address them as a living spirit. They call upon their virtues, giving them compliments, reminding them of their powers, coaxing them with promises of reward (which must be fulfilled!), and kindly asking for aid. On the other hand, when addressing malicious powers, such as spirits of illness or harmful beings, the witch may use profanities, attempt to offend and intimidate the spirit, and threaten it with dire consequences should it refuse to cooperate. The basic rule of thumb is you give what you get.

As explained in "The Rules of Polish Folk Magic," the short form zamawiania and spoken formulas that can be easily crafted on the spot have their own unique structure of *"Just like [symbolic object] affects [symbolic target], so shall [object] affect [target]"* or *"Just like [object] causes [change], so shall [target] experience [change]."* However, rhyme, prayer, and storytelling components play an equally important role when weaving an effective charm. Such formulas are known as narrative charms or *historiolae.* In this type of formula, figures of spirits, saints, Mary, God, or Jesus were often called upon, retelling stories of how the chosen figure once found themselves in this very situation and what they did to remedy it. Sometimes, the zamawianie may even include another formula within it, spoken by the being in the narrative. In this way, through the weaving of a narrative, the practitioner is instructed on how to perform a working (by imitating the being in the story), while inviting the mentioned spirit into the process, thus identifying oneself with them via a sympathetic link and opening oneself up to being guided by their powers.

As Nordblom eloquently explains in *Historiola: The Power of Narrative Charms:*

"It is the very narrative itself that helps create the dynamism of the spell, enabling a direct 'movement' of the ritual procedure which is sometimes difficult to access otherwise. The narrative [...] defines a procedure of magical action and at the same time executes it. Without having to summon high powers and ask/beg/bargain/threaten them to do your bidding, one is instead immediately granted access to their power" (Nordblom, 2021, p. 23).

Many recorded formulas resemble little poems, prayers, or folk songs, with simple rhyme structures that are easy to remember and repetitive in form. Naturally, for folks who were largely illiterate, this served as a great aid in remembering the formulas and incorporating them into little chants and songs, which made them easier to pass on through oral tradition.

There are numerous historical formulas that survived in records to this day, a selection of which will be offered below for the practitioner to adapt to their own work. While such formulas are known for being used repeatedly by many healers and practitioners over the years, they were not the only way of speaking zamawiania. It is important to note that zamawiania can also be spoken spontaneously—addressing the forces from the heart and speaking to them in a way that is deeply felt in the body and resonates through the vocal cords with conviction—often including elements of the aforementioned bargaining, begging, or threatening, which naturally reflect the practitioner's emotional state. While it may be helpful to adapt the existing formulas or even create ones closely following the historical structure, one should never underestimate the power of viscerally felt communication that arises from the depths of one's dire need, thus allowing for heartfelt communion with the forces that are being addressed. This shall always prove more powerful than any historical formula when spoken with no heart present in it.

Below, I offer a selection of traditional, historically documented examples of Polish zamawiania, spoken formulas and prayers for a plethora of needs, including weather magic, healing, protection, addressing the natural forces, and more. Each is offered in its original form (often in dialects), with an English translation below. For folks who can speak the Polish language, even if this isn't your first language, speaking the original formula can add extra strength to your workings, so don't be shy! However, the translations have also been carefully curated to bear as much of the original impact as possible and are suitable for incorporating into anyone's folk practice. Alternatively, one may choose a hybrid approach of speaking them in English and adding the original Polish formulas written on parchment into one's working. Importantly, wherever the original formula has been recorded along with additional instructions or context, they are explained just below the title of each formula. Additional formulas are scattered throughout the book in chapters relevant to their context.

Zamawianie to Chase Away Storms and Invite the Sun

"A idźcie-z ta, chmury,
Na tatarskie góry.
Gdzie Talary siadają,
Krople wody żądają.
My jej nie żądamy,
Bo jej dosyć mamy;
Cebrzykami, konewkami
Za plac wylewamy,
Kamycki zbieramy,
Na kościół frygamy;
A z kościoła na wodę,
By dał Pan pogodę.
Zaświec-ze mi słoneczko,
Dam ci białe jajeczko.
Położę ci na łące,
Wezmą ci je zające,
Położę ci na dębie,

Wezmą ci je gołębie.
Położę ci je na grusce,
Wezmą ci je chrabósce.
Położę ci na śliwie,
Dadzą ci je sczęśliwie."

"Ah begone, clouds,
To the Tatar mountains.
Where the thalers sit,
Demanding drops of water.
We do not demand it,
For we have enough;
With buckets, watering cans
We pour it behind the square,
We collect pebbles,
We throw them on the church;
And from the church onto the water,
So that Lord gives good weather.
Shine on me, little sun,
I will give you a white egg.
I will put it for you in the meadow,
The hares will take it for you,
I will put it for you in the oak tree,
The pigeons will take it for you.
I will put it for you in the pear tree,
The maybugs will take it for you.
I will put it for you in the plum tree,
They will give it to you happily."

Another Zamawianie to Chase Away Storms

"Idźcie, chmury!
Na lasy,
Na góry,
Gdzie pastuszkowie siadają,
Kapki wody nie żądają.
My jej mamy dosyć

Garnuszeczkiem nosić."
"Go, clouds!
To the forests,
To the mountains,
Where shepherds sit around,
Not asking for even a drop of water.
We have enough
Of carrying it in little pots."

Greeting the Morning Sun

This greeting is traditionally spoken while facing the East.

"Dzień dobry Ci, jasne słoneczko
Ty święte, ty jasne-przekrasne
Ty czyste, wspaniałe i szanowne
Ty oświecasz góry i doliny
I wysokie kurhany
Oświeć mnie, przed całym światem
Dobrocią, krasą, wdziękami i miłością
Jakie Ty jesteś jasne
Wspaniałe, przekrasne
Żebym i ja była taka jasna
Wspaniała, przekrasna."

"Good morning to you, bright sun
You holy, you bright and wonderful
You pure, wonderful and respectable
You illuminate the mountains and valleys
And high burial mounds
Enlighten me, before the whole world
With kindness, beauty, grace, and love
How bright you are
Wonderful, beautiful
May I be this bright
Wonderful, beautiful."

Folk Prayer to the Midday Sun, So It May Shine for the Dead in the Otherworlds

"Słoneczko jasne na niebie
wzejdź w ich ciemnice nieprzejrzane
choć jednym promykiem jasnym
choć jednym cienkim włoskiem złociutkim
kropelką rosy płonącej
ogniem twym świętym
choć robaczkiem świętojańskim."

"Sun, bright in the sky
descend into their impenetrable darkness
with at least one bright ray
at least one thin golden hair
with a drop of burning dew
with your holy fire
or at least a firefly."

A Folk Calling of Field Workers to the Sun

"Żebyś ty słonecko,
na wyrobku było,
tobyś ty, słonecko,
prędzej zachodziło.
Ale ty, słonecko,
nie wies, co wyrobek,
chodzis se po niebie
kiej biały gołąbek."

"If you, dear sun,
were working the fields,
then you would, dear sun,

hurry to set.
But you, dear sun,
don't know field labor,
you stroll through the sky
like a white dove."

Greeting the Morning Zorya

This greeting is traditionally spoken while facing the East.

"Witajcie Zorze
Witaj gwiazdo poranna."

"Welcome, Zoryas
Welcome, Morning Star."

Morning Prayer to the Waters

This prayer is traditionally spoken on the morning of the Summer Solstice, accompanied by offerings of bread.

"Dzień dobry, wódeczko, najstarsza caryczko!
Obmywasz góry, korzenie, kamienie
Obmyj i mię z wszelkiego plugastwa
Ażebym była tak wspaniałą jak wiosna
Ażebym była tak piękną jak zorza jasna
Ażebym była nasyconą jak jesień
A bogatą jak ziemia."

"Good morning, water, the eldest tsarina [queen]!
You wash over mountains, roots, stones
Wash me also from all filthiness
May I be as wonderful as spring
May I be as beautiful as the bright Zorya
May I be as satisfied as autumn

And as rich as the earth."

Calling to the Waxing Moon

This zamawianie is spoken at the crossroads by the light of the waxing moon, while looking directly into the moon.

"To co widzę, niech przybywa,
To czego nie widzę, niech ubywa."

"Let what I see come,
Let what I do not see diminish."

Chant for Flight to the Bald Mountain

This chant may be repeatedly whispered or sung to achieve a trance state, leading up to spirit flight.

"Płot nie płot,
Las nie las,
Wieś nie wieś,
Biesie nieś!"

"A fence is not a fence,
A forest is not a forest,
A village is not a village,
Bies, carry me!"

Protective Prayer to the Guardian Angel

This formula is a close equivalent to various Paternosters present in other European cultures' protective prayers. It should be spoken before sleep.

"Idę jo se spać, ni mom se co posłać.

Pościele se święto wanielijo,
Świętem się krzyżem przyodzieje,
Ciebie się, szatanie, nie boję!
Ustępujcie wszyscy źli
Ze śtyrech kątów, piątych drzwi!
Bo tu będzie Przenajświętsza Panienecka spocywała
Ze siedmioma krzyżeńkoma,
Ze dwunastoma aniołkami.
Aniele Boży, stróżu mój.
Rano, wieczór, we dnie, w nocy,
Bądź mi zawsze do pomocy!
Nie dej mi umrzyć!
Dej mi zyjrzyć święto Annę,
Co porodziła Najświętsze Pannę.
Święta Anno,
Strzeż duszy moji, ciała mojego
Do żywota wiecznego!"

"I go to sleep, I have nothing to make the bed.
I'll make my bed with holy gospel,
I'll put on the holy cross as my duvet,
I'm not afraid of you, Satan!
Begone, all evil ones
From the four corners, from the fifth door!
For here the Most Holy Virgin will rest
With seven little crosses,
With twelve little angels.
Angel of God, my guardian.
Morning, evening, day, night,
Be always to my aid!
Do not let me die!
Let me see Saint Anne,
Who gave birth to the Most Holy Virgin.
Holy Anne,
Guard my soul, my body
Unto eternal life!"

Zamawianie to Acquire a Good Husband

This should be repeated every day at dawn and dusk.

"Zorze, zorzeczeńki!
Wszystkieśta moje siostruczeńki!
Siadajta na konia wronego
I jedźta po towarzysza mojego.
Żeby on nie mógł beze mnie
ni spać, ni jeść,
ni siadać, ni gadać.
Żeby ja mu się spodobała we stanie, w robocie, w ochocie.
Żeby ja była wdzięczna i przyjemna Bogu i ludziom,
i temu towarzyszowi mojemu."

"Zoryas, little zoryas!
You all are my little sisters!
Sit on a black horse
And go fetch my companion.
So that he could not without me
neither sleep, nor eat,
nor sit, nor speak.
So that he likes me in standstill, in work, in desire.
So that I would be graceful and pleasing to God and men,
and to my companion."

Sickle Zamawianie for Eye Inflammation

For this formula, one requires a sickle. As the formula is spoken, the sickle is gently touched to the eyes and guided down thrice, as if cutting the illness away.

"Sierpiku, sierpiku,
Zegnałeś (z pola) oźminę, jarzynę,
Spędź z oka uraz!"

"Sickle, sickle,
As you harvested winter grains and vegetables (from the field),
Remove injury from the eye!"

Zamawianie for Pain Relief

"O mój bólu, o mój piękny, mój najpiękniejszy, mój najśliczniejszy,
proszę cię imieniem Panny Marii,
proszę cię imieniem Krystusa, Ducha świętego, Świętej Trójcy nierozdzielnej ze wszystkimi świętymi,
żeliś ból kołtunowy, zastrzałowy albo różowy,
upatrz se miejsce na Szklanej Górze, na Perzowej Górze i na Włoszczowej Górze.
Jak się wanielija rozchodzi po kościołach,
tak się i ty, bólu, rozeiść po gałęziach,
po tarninach, po kamieniach, po korzeniach.
Wyjdź z ciała i kości,
proszę cię do Boskiej miłości."

"Oh my pain, oh my beautiful, my most beautiful,
I am asking you in the name of the Virgin Mary,
I am asking you in the name of Christ, the Holy Spirit, the Holy Trinity inseparable and
all the Saints,
if you come from tangle, or strut or rose,
look for a place on Szklana Góra [Glass Mountain], on Perzowa Góra [Grass Mountain] and on Włoszczowa Góra [Vloshchova Mountain].
As the gospel spreads through the churches,
so you too, pain, spread among the branches,
on sloes, on stones, on roots.
Come out of flesh and bones,
I am asking you in the name of Divine love."

Headache Relief Zamawianie to the Waxing Moon

"Witaj, miesiączku nowy,
żeby nas nie bolały głowy."

"Welcome, young moon,
may our heads not hurt."

Zamawianie to the Moon for a Toothache

During this zamawianie, one is supposed to touch the aching tooth. After the below formula is spoken, it should be followed by reciting "Our Father" three or seven times.

"Księzycu, widzę cię z dwoma rogami,
Proszę cię, aby mię nie bolały zęby,
Póki cię nie zobaczę z trzema rogami,
Tego chciej!"

"Moon, I see you with two horns,
Please make my teeth stop hurting,
Until I see you with three horns,
May you want this!"

Zamawianie to the Waning Moon to Cure Lichen

This formula is spoken to the waning moon (old moon) on a Friday by a child born on a Sunday, while standing by a willow tree and rubbing the lichen with a belt until it bleeds.

"Liszaj!
Z wiatrem znikaj!"

"Lichen!
Disappear with the wind!"

Zamawianie to the New Moon to Cure Warts

This zamawianie is to be spoken while riding a pig during the New Moon.

"Miesiącu! daj mi jajeczka,
A ja ci dam brodaweczki."

"Moon! Give me little eggs,
And I will give you little warts."

Healing Formula for Rheumatism and All Illnesses

This formula has been popular in traditional folk magic across Europe, including Poland. To cure illness, the formula should be worn on the body, and every day, one letter of the formula should be taken away until no letters remain. As the length of the formula is diminished, so is the illness.

Abracadabra
Abracadabr
Abracadab
Abracada
Abracad
Abraca
Abrac
Abra
Abr
Ab
A

Healing Formula for a Snake Bite

"Wymawiam was Bożą mocą,
Pana Boga pomocą
Węże, wężyce, żmije, żmiice,
Padalce i padalczyce,
i wszelki robaku!

Z rozkwituś się urodził,
diabeł cię stworzył,
Pan Jezus w cię ducha włożył,
A nie dał ci żadnego jadu ani mocy,
Przez Pana Boga moc,
Syna Bożego i Ducha Świętego pomoc,
Jako ta woda opływa,
Niechże i to ciało opływa.
W imieniu Boga Ojca i Syna, i Ducha Świętego."

"I order you with God's power,
With Gods's help
Snakes, female snakes, vipers, female vipers,
Slowworms and female slowworms,
And every worm!
You were born from the bloom,
The devil created you
The Lord Jesus put his spirit in you,
And he has given you neither venom nor power.
Through God's power,
The Son of God and the Holy Spirit's help,
As water flows around,
Let it also flow around this body.
In the name of God the Father and the Son, and the Holy Spirit."

Formula for Rabies

For this formula, a Catholic wafer or a piece of fresh bread is needed. One should make the sign of the cross, then write the full name of the afflicted on the wafer/bread, followed by this formula:

\+ *Erkrejson* + *Katubijan* + *Zawaty* +
\+ *Ostro* + *Odta* + *Kyra* + *Ira* + *Kata* +
\+ *Katuza* + *Bryszcza* + *Bryzeda* +
\+ *Bryndyos* + *Monus* + *Amont* +

Then, the wafer/bread should be given to the afflicted while saying: "*Takowy chleb daję w Imię Pańskie, Amen*" ("This bread I give in the Name of the Lord, Amen"). The wafer should be eaten first thing in the morning over the course of three days.

Zamawianie to Cure a Child from Sleeplessness and Night Terrors

At dusk, a mother takes her child out into the fields. While facing the setting sun (West), she repeats the formula thrice to aid her child with sleeplessness and night terrors.

"Zorzyczki, zorzyczki,
trzy was jest:
jedna porankowa,
jedna południowa,
jedna wieczorna.
Weźcie od mego dziecka płaczenie,
oddajcie mu spanie."

"Zoryas, Zoryas,
three you are:
one of daybreak,
one of midday,
one of twilight.
Take weeping away from my child,
give them back their sleep."

Healing Formula for a Child

"Zarze, zarzyce, trzy siestrzyce.
Poszła Matka Boska po morzu zbirając złote pianki,
Potkał ją święty Jan: "A gdzie idziesz, matuchno?"
"Idę syneczka swego leczyć"."

"Zoryas, Zaryce, three sisters.
Our Lady walked through the sea gathering golden foams,
Saint John saw her: "Where do you go, mother?"
"I go to heal my son"."

Zamawianie to Cure Consumption (Tuberculosis)

"Wychodzi słonecko zza góry,
Wychodźcie, suchoty, zza skóry.
Jako Bóg na niebie,
przywróci do ciebie.
O Maryjo z wysokości,
dajże mięsa na te kości!
Boże, prosimy cię o przemienienie,
lub na śmierć, lub na zdrowie."

"The Sun shines from behind a mountain,
Come out, consumption, from behind the skin.
As the Lord is in the skies,
may he restore onto you.
Oh Mary from above,
give some meat upon these bones!
God, we beg for transformation,
be it into death, or into health."

A Healing Zamawianie to Cure Róża, Calling upon the Sun High inthe Sky

Róża (Rose) is a folk illness characterized by inflammation and reddening of the skin, rash, and sometimes also swelling. It is believed to be contracted from the winds, waters, dryness, or even sent by someone else. This healing formula is to be said while standing before a chimney/fireplace, while holding one's hand up high. Once the formula is recited, one should say *"Hail Mary"* thrice.

"W imię Boże, skądeś się wzięła, różo, czy to z wiatru, czy z śmieci, czy z jakichś wiechci? Ustąp, różo, z bólem, z kołtunem, dobrowolnie; wleź w ziemię głęboko, jak słońce na niebie wysoko."

*"In the name of God, where did you come from, rose? Was it from the wind, from trash, or from some wisps? Yield, rose, with pain, with kołtun**, voluntarily; enter into the earth as deep as the sun is high in the sky."*

Another Healing Zamawianie for Róża

"Oróżo, różo!
Strasznieś bolesno.
Z czegóś się ty obraziła?
Czy z jedzenio?
Czy ze spanio?
Czy z picia i gadanio?
Proszę cię bardzo:
Ustąp za przyczyną Jezusa i Maryi!"

"O rose, rose!
How terribly painful.
What have you come from?
Was it from food?
Or from sleeping?
Or from drinking and talking?
I beg of you:
Give way with the intercession of Jesus and Mary!"

CHAPTER ELEVEN

UROKI AND KLĄTWY: EVIL EYE AND CURSES

The magic of the common folk is never free from baneful work. Nowadays, as we commonly witness in the modern, globalized eclectic practices of witchcraft, many shy away from the malefic aspects of the craft. And while this remains within the bounds of one's personal ethics and choices to practice as one sees fit, to judge and look down upon those who engage in this work is rather short-sighted and ignorant, stemming from a place of systemic privilege and the colonial monotheist understandings of good and evil. Folk magic rises as a tool of the dispossessed, outcast, discriminated, and forgotten, as a tool of retaking one's due, dignity, and rights in the face of oppression and systemic injustice. Where no law or authority is willing to protect one's human rights and grant fair access to the fulfillment of one's basic needs, baneful work may be the only weapon at one's disposal. Our peasant ancestors living under the feudal enslavement of *pańszczyzna* have experienced this firsthand for centuries. And while we may consider ourselves lucky to be relatively free people in Poland over merely the past century, countless folks across the globe continue to struggle in ways all too familiar. All this to say never judge people for the magic they are systemically forced to work and know that your ancestors fully support your baneful work—they understand because they've been there.

The baneful or malicious variety of Polish folk magic includes different types of practices, some of which are explained below, followed by simple ways of removing them, should one fall prey to magical offense. Matters of cleansing, protection, and prevention will be detailed separately in the subsequent sub-chapters.

UROK: MALEFICIA CAST WITH THE EYES

Urok is a type of baneful magic that is cast with one's eyes alone. This is commonly recognized as "the Evil Eye." It was believed that some people or animals were born with the evil eye, especially those who were breastfed for a longer period of time and then abruptly replaced with a newborn sibling—such folks would be unknowingly prone to cast the evil eye all the time. However, the eye could also be unknowingly cast by folks who were jealous of someone, even saying well-meaning compliments could be indicative of jealousy, and thus of potential casting of the evil eye. Naturally, it could also be cast with conscious malicious intent, simply by fixating one's furious gaze upon the target while imagining bad things happening to them or giving fake compliments. Because of the method's simplicity, an urok is considered especially easy to cast, and thus rather common. Most folks would experience a singular urok cast upon them at a time, but it is also possible to be afflicted with a triple, or even ninefold urok if an enemy was really hellbent on them.

When afflicted with urok, the common symptoms include persistent headaches, nausea, stomachache, or general weakness of the body. Similar symptoms could be observed in animals (which were quite commonly targets of urok as well), such as loss of appetite, loss of milk, disturbed balance, and anxiety.

If an urok was left untreated, it was believed to cause permanent health loss or even death.

A common preventative measure against urok includes veiling (wearing a scarf on one's head) and a red thread or ribbon tied around one's wrist or neck.

KLĄTWA: CURSE WORK

Most commonly performed curses historically had to do with stealing one's *pożytek* (surplus of resources, such as milk, butter, crops, etc.), causing one's cows to cease giving milk, making one's animals sick or causing their death, sending illness upon one's homestead, causing failure of crops, and inflicting infertility or even death. Similarly to workings done for any other purposes, curses are also performed in accordance with the rules of sympathy and contagion (as explained in "The Rules of Polish Folk Magic"). This means the tools and ingredients used for the working had to be of baneful or death-related variety. In addition, there always needed to be a direct connection to the target of the curse by use of taglocks (such as one's hair, nails, piece of clothing, footprint, etc.), or, more commonly, by planting the curse within the bounds of the target's place of dwelling.

PROCURING TOOLS AND INGREDIENTS FOR BANEFUL WORK

Some of the most commonly listed tools and ingredients for baneful work include human bones, animal bones, animal feet, animal excrement, hair, fur, moss, baneful herbs, items stolen from church (Paschal candle wax, the Eucharist), old coffin nails, graveyard dirt, and other graveyard "souvenirs."

Alternatively, various kinds of waters were procured for curses and spoken over, thus infusing the fluid with malice. Examples of this include:

- Waters taken from a source of Dead Water (as explained earlier in "Sacred Waters")
- Waters from nine springs combined and spoken over
- Waters gathered before dawn on a significant date, such as Good Friday, Corpus Christi, St. John's Feast Day, etc.

According to lore, items used in baneful work should always be procured at night, with no witnesses. Should someone witness the taking of such an item, it would lose all its power. One example of a perfectly preserved piece of instructions for this practice comes from the Highlanders in the Western Beskids Mountain Range: It is said that to procure a human bone for cursing, one should go to the cemetery naked at midnight of Good Friday. Once obtained, the bone should be wrapped in a piece of fabric, ideally the shirt of a dead person or bedding from a deathbed. As the item is taken, it should be told its function and what it will be used for. Sometimes, formulas such as the *Paternoster* spoken backwards would also be employed to empower the item. When returning with the item, one should never look back.

PLANTING THE CURSE

To afflict one's target with a curse, the procured item would be spoken over and instructed on its wrongdoings. Such an enchanted item would then be planted in the place where it's supposed to work:

- To curse the animals: place inside the farm enclosure or the farm buildings

- To curse the inhabitants of a household: bury under the threshold or stick inside a slit in the walls or roof

If water was used as a carrier of the curse, it was usually poured over the threshold of the house or farm building, as it was believed that whoever stepped over such a threshold would be afflicted. This type of work could end up being less precise because technically, anybody could step over such a threshold. On the other hand, it was more effective because water couldn't be easily noticed and removed.

If an old coffin nail was procured, it would be hammered into the enclosure or building, while speaking a formula: *"Aby ci te krowy uschły, jak ten umarły uschnął"* ("May your cows dry us as this corpse dried up"). Naturally, it could be altered to address whoever was supposed to dry up. Examples of similar formulas have been discussed earlier in "The Rules of Polish Folk Magic."

ODCZYNIANIE: UNDOING A CURSE OR EVIL EYE

In case one is unfortunate enough to catch the evil eye or get cursed, it is necessary first to perform acts of divination to confirm the curse. This was traditionally done by placing hot coals in multiples of three (three or nine) into a pot filled with spring water. If the coals drowned, it confirmed the curse. Nowadays, as practitioners have access to a wider range of divination methods, any of them may be employed in this work.

Once the curse or evil eye is confirmed, acts of *odczynianie* (undoing the curse) are performed. The first thing to do when a curse has been confirmed would be to find the item planted on one's property and dispose of it by burying it at the crossroads or burning it. Similarly to the curse itself, this should also be performed at night, alone, and without witnesses. If one chooses to burn the cursed items, the fire should be started near the source of running water (stream, river), and blessed herbs should be placed inside the flames to purify the curse.

Here is a traditional example of an odczynianie spoken formula:

"Święta Zochfija trzy córeczki miała:
Jedna praczka,
Druga szwaczka,
A trzecia po świecie chodziła, uroki odczyniała.
Odczyń-że panieneczko i temu człowiekowi grzesznemu.

Jeżeliś chłopski urzek, wleź pod szafkę.
Jeżeliś panieński urzek, wleź że pod warkocz.
Jeżeliś kobiecy urzek, wleź że pod chustkę."

"Saint Sophia had three daughters:
The first was a laundress,
The second a seamstress,
And the third one walked around the world, undoing spells.
Have mercy on this sinful man, my lady.
If it came from a man's charm, chase it under the cupboard.
If it came from a maiden charm, chase it under a braid.
If it came from a woman's charm, chase it under a scarf.
To close off the formula, "Hail Mary" is spoken thrice."

Other, more complex forms of odczynianie include: *obmywanie* (washing), *okadzanie* (fumigation), *jajowanie* (egg cleansing) or a combination of several of these methods—all detailed in the following chapter, accompanied by methods of prevention and protection.

CHAPTER TWELVE

OKADZANIE AND CLEANSING

Every traditional culture has its sacred ways of utilizing plant allies for fumigation. In Polish folk practices of cleansing, protection, healing, and blessing, we engage in the practice of okadzanie. For this purpose, bouquets, wreaths, or bunches of herbs blessed on specific occasions are used whenever the need arises.

The practice begins by taking the gathered bunch of dried herbs and lighting them just enough so that they continuously produce smoke without being on fire. Little embers should be visible inside the bunch when one blows on it. Then, the practitioner carries the fumigating bundle around the person or place receiving the treatment, sunwise for beneficial work, healing, or protection, and widdershins for baneful work. When fumigating buildings, it is often documented that one should walk around the property three times (or three times three) to achieve a good result.

Depending on the aim of okadzanie, various spoken charms, rhymes, or prayers are added so that the purpose of the work is clearly stated and delivered. Whilst walking the smoke, practitioners would often include the phrase, "*rozpędzam na cztery wiatry*" ("I chase [this thing] away into the four winds") to banish unwanted forces. Alternatively, phrases like, "*niechaj się rozwieje na cztery strony świata*" ("may it disperse into the four directions of the world") were popular as well. Both clearly call upon the wind's power, relying on its mutable nature and abilities to blow things away and make them dissipate.

HOLY DAYS FOR GATHERING AND BLESSING MATERIA

While an experienced folk practitioner knows how to awaken and bless their plants for purposes of fumigation at any given time, there are several times of year when the common folk would procure blessed herbs for their daily needs, usually (but not exclusively) by getting them blessed with holy water in church. The dates aren't accidental—they align with the cycles of vegetation, relying on the availability of fresh plants to be foraged, for it's always been freshly gathered materia that was blessed for magical and medicinal purposes. The plants were usually gathered either on the eve of the holy day or early in the morning, before dawn.

- ***Niedziela Wierzbowa/Palmowa* (Willow/Palm Sunday):** On this day, willow twigs can be consecrated to be used as an aspergillum (to sprinkle holy water) or to be burned for ash.
- ***Boże Ciało* (Corpus Christi):** Wreaths of herbs are consecrated by the priest during the procession. Alternatively, plants from blessed procession altars are gathered by the folk and later woven into wreaths and bundles for use in okadzanie.
- ***Noc Świętojańska* (St. John Feast Day/Summer Solstice):** Herbs, especially mugwort, gathered on the Eve of St. John's are believed to possess especially potent magical properties. They are collected on the Eve and later worn on the body, dried for okadzanie, or stuck around the household for protection.
- ***Matki Boskiej Zielnej* (Our Lady of Herbs/Assumption Day):** Folks gather bouquets of herbs, which are then consecrated in church with holy water, to be later used in okadzanie.

All the dates and their significance are further elaborated on in the "Polish Folkloric Year" section.

For gathering plants outside of the holy days, it was usually done according to moon phases: waxing moon for foraging aerial parts (or parts visible above the ground like leaves, stems, flowers, and fruits), and waning moon for roots.

SPRING CLEANING AND OKADZANIE

While okadzanie is practiced all year round, it is especially important around springtime, when it is part of a larger process of deep cleaning the house and the entire property. Folks traditionally clean all the windows, scrub the floors, beat the carpets, wash all the clothing and bedding that were used during winter, and fumigate the household and the entire property—sheds, barns, coops, everything. Spring cleaning is important because it helps remove all the stagnant energy that accumulated on the property throughout winter, and it helps welcome fresh energy, good health, fertility, and luck in the coming year. The herbs most often used for magical smoke cleansing were mugwort and rue, believed to banish bad energies and protect from magic and witchcraft.

Here's a traditional Polish folk song that was sung when smoke cleansing with *bylica* (mugwort) and *ruta* (rue) during summer festivities:

"Myśmy przyszły tu z daleka,
opaliły ognie święte!
Nie odbiorą nam już mleka,
czarownice te przeklęte!
Niechaj ruta w ogniu trzeszczy,
czarownica w ogniu wrzeszczy!
Niech bylicy gałąź pęka,
Czarownica w ogniu stęka!"

"We came here from afar,
Kindled sacred fires!
They will not take away our milk anymore,
Cursed witches!
May rue crackle in the fire,
Witches screaming in the fire!
May the branch of mugwort snap,
Witches groaning in the fire!"

PLANTS MOST COMMONLY USED FOR OKADZANIE

The list of plants that have been documented for this use is extremely long, depending on the region, as well as the plants that were realistically available in people's gardens. Sometimes folks would choose plants based on their folk medicinal properties, while other times, based on sympathetic properties derived from their physical properties (thorny, or stinging plants for protection, heart-shaped for love, etc.). Therefore, we shall limit the list to those most notorious for use in practices of fumigation.

- *Bylica* (mugwort)
- *Ruta* (rue)
- *Piołun* (wormwood)
- *Dziurawiec* (St. John's wort)
- *Biedrzeniec* (pimpinella)
- *Mięta* (mint)
- *Czarny bez* (European elder)
- *Leszczyna* (hazel)
- *Sosna* (pine)
- *Pokrzywa* (nettle)
- *Jałowiec* (juniper)

CLEANSING

In addition to okadzanie, our ancestors engaged in various other forms of magic for cleansing, removing, and chasing away unwanted influences from a place or person. Oftentimes, these cleansing practices were combined with or followed by protection magic, which will be expanded on in the next chapter. Unlike in modern eclectic witchcraft, where things are often very clearly separated into neat categories, for our ancestors, these practices blended together. They served several purposes at the same time, making them much more organic and intuitive, in alignment with the old animist perception of the forces that were employed for such work.

Noise Cleansing

Unlike modern practitioners who have access to fancy bells and drums, our ancestors used pots and pans to sound cleanse and chase away evil spirits. This practice was especially popular around springtime to banish all lingering old, sickly energies of winter, and to make space for a healthy new beginning. For this purpose, folks would pick up pots, pans, and utensils and bash them around the property, sometimes accompanied by loud stomping and shouting as well, ensuring that every nook and cranny is covered.

Wymiatanie: Sweeping

Spirit cleansing would always go hand in hand with physical clearing. In rural households, a simple broom made of birch or willow twigs—*drapaka*—was used to sweep the area and cleanse it of dirt, visible and invisible alike. Back in the day, households didn't have foundations and flooring like they do today; instead, they had a threshing floor known as *klepisko,* made of natural smooth clay, similar to how barns and farm buildings still do today. A simple twig broom would be used for sweeping and cleaning such a floor. When rural architecture began to change and wooden houses were built on foundations with wooden flooring, brooms like that started being used only in the vestibule and outside at the front of the house. It was believed that ill-disposed witches and spirits couldn't cross a threshold if a broom stood nearby. I can still remember my grandparents making and using such simple brooms, and at least one always stood in the vestibule, near the threshold. It was also believed that whenever moving to a new house, an old broom should always be left behind. After all, over time, they accumulated a lot of unclean energies, and it would be bad luck to bring all that to a new place.

Obmywanie: Washing

One of the most popular cleansing, as well as healing practices, was baths and washes—*obmywanie.* Washing oneself in water infused with plants for specific purposes was an accessible way of improving one's dire situation. As explained earlier in "The Rules of Polish Folk Magic," maintaining balance in moisture and dryness was crucial for one's well-being. Similarly to okadzanie, both mugwort and rue were used in cleansing baths to wash away unwanted influences. A later, post-Christian influence included hyssop, as well as salt, when it became more accessible to common folk. However, one plant above all was believed to be especially powerful for stripping oneself clean, even of curses. This plant is known as *czarcie żebro* (devil's rib), Cabbage thistle *(Cirsium oleraceum)*. Whenever you feel like someone has cast the evil eye on you, or worse, attempted malicious works, devil's rib will save your skin.

To prepare a cleansing bath with any chosen plant, one needs to prepare an infusion of the herb in advance—a mug or bowl of saturated infusion should do. While it's infusing, one can start filling the bathtub with water. Do not add any bath products. Once the bath is ready, pour the infusion into the bath and step in. Wash thoroughly with the bath water and soak in it for a while. Once out of the bathtub, one should allow the water to dry on the skin without using a towel, if possible. Observe the water in the bathtub, the grimier it is afterwards, the more gunk it has stripped off. Repeat baths for three days or until the water looks "healthy."

Traditionally, such water after a cleansing bath needed to be disposed of in a place where no humans or farm animals walk; otherwise, it could "infect" them back with what was removed. Today, with modern plumbing accessible to most, it is no longer a concern.

Odczynianie: Undoing

As has been discussed in "Uroki and Klątwy," *odczynianie* is a practice of undoing harmful charms and curses. Many of the methods employ a hybrid approach, combining several types of cleansings.

To remove a curse or a charm from someone by the zamawianie of water, take a vessel and fill it with spring water. Take nine burning coals, and as you drop them into the vessel one by one, say a blessing prayer. Traditionally, it was usually the *Zdrowaś Mario* (Hail Mary), *Pacierz* (Our Father), or *Skład Apostolski* (Apostle's Creed prayer), sometimes spoken backwards, depending on who said it. When done with the prayer, and once the coals sink, one takes some of the water in their hand and rubs it onto the cursed person's/animal's forehead. After that, pour the water from this vessel facing West.

Odczynianie can also be combined with obmywanie. For this purpose, one should place three coals, three pieces of bread, and three twigs cut off from a broom into a vessel filled with water. This should be done thrice. With the water prepared in this way, the head of the afflicted should be thoroughly washed, and some of it should be drank as well.

Another method for odczynianie is to use a woman's or child's shirt, turn it wrong side out, spit on it, and use that fragment of fabric to rub on the cursed person's forehead three times, or rub the cursed animal from tail to head three times. No need to say any words or formulas while doing this—it is enough to focus on removing any curses or harmful charms while doing this. In Polish folk magic, spitting is considered "magical first aid" in removing baneful workings.

CHAPTER THIRTEEN

PROTECTION MAGIC

Out of all the types of magic practiced by our ancestors, historically, apotropaic magic must is the most prominent kind. It is practiced by all in ways elaborate and small, increasing one's chances of survival in a world filled with many dangers, yet disproportionately little access to resources, medicine, or privilege. The most common reasons for practicing protection magic have been:

- To protect the household from disasters (storms, fires, floods), thieves, and evil spirits
- To protect oneself from harm, illness, curses, the evil eye, and jealousy
- To protect farm animals from illness, witchcraft, theft of fertility, milk, or eggs
- To protect fields from being blasted by weather or witchcraft alike
- To protect the living from spiritual forces, such as demons, ghosts, and the undead

In today's world, these are the equivalents of protecting one's health, safety, and nourishment—some of the most basic of human needs. While it can be safely assumed that most folks reading this book have many of their basic needs covered, and thus don't need to rely solely on magic to survive, that wasn't necessarily the case for our ancestors, whose lived reality was very different. However, despite the life quality improvements that many of us are able to enjoy today as a result of our ancestors' hard work, we can still learn a lot from their wisdom about the things truly worth protecting, and how to support ourselves the way they did should crisis inevitably reach our doorstep in the form of illness, curse, natural disaster, or spiritual emergency.

THE RED THREAD AND KNOTS

It is believed that the color red symbolizes blood, thus directly relating to the spark of life—the life force and vitality of all living beings. Unlike the colors white and black, which were more often perceived as liminal colors, assigned to ghosts, spirits, and beings of the otherworlds, red stood for beings enfleshed. Therefore, in accordance with sympathetic rules of magic, objects of red were used for the purposes of protecting one's lifeforce and one's living body from forces that may wish to feed on it, destroy it, or otherwise use for their own purposes. By extension, red was utilized in folk medicine to treat illnesses of blood and internal organs.

The color red became especially prominent in Polish and Slavic clothing and accessories, which can still be witnessed in traditional embroidery designs, as well as regional folkloric clothes: shirts and tunics embroidered with protective symbols in red thread, woven belts with symbols in red yarn, red ribbons tied around children's wrists and necks for protection from malicious spirits, or strings of red beads worn by women to ward off the evil eye and curses of jealous folks.

Whenever threads and fabrics are concerned, knot magic should be considered as part of the tradition. The tying of knots plays an important role in harnessing the powers at play and ensuring that they can be both kept and released, depending on what is needed.

Historical examples of belts illustrate how the knot's function was to help hold whatever is inside it together. Wherever a knot is tied around a perimeter or a person with a thread, string, or belt, it preserves or catches whatever is inside it. Wearing a belt for a specific purpose will thus maintain the forces invoked on the wearer. It is important to note that belts were originally tied into a knot around the wearer's waist; only later were they developed to have a buckle instead. When a belt is thrown into the wind with the intent of empowering the wearer with its powers, it will hold that empowerment as long as it is worn. Likewise, when a belt is woven with the intention of protection, it will provide that protection to its wearer.

The red thread proved useful in protection magic outside of clothing as well, especially popular for tying the thread around coffins or even entire buildings or places to ward off demons and curses. Similarly to how red threads and ribbons were used to protect children, they were also used to protect newborn cattle and farm animals from malicious influences and illnesses. Ribbons and strings tied around the wrist or even an entire perimeter work in a very similar manner—they hold whatever is inside them together, just as any length of cord holds things with the power of the knot. Likewise, whenever something like an illness or unwanted influence needs to be caught and released, a knot would be tied around it and then thrown into a river or otherwise disposed of far away from human dwellings.

When it comes to embroidery, it should be done with clear intent for protection—the patterns themselves are often regional and chosen based on the intended recipient of the design. As the pattern is embroidered, spoken charms, prayers, or intentions are repeatedly spoken, thus weaving the formulas into the threads themselves, preserving them in the tight needlework.

Finally, strings of red beads as a woman's accessory are especially popular in the context of warding off the evil eye and jealousy related to matters of attractiveness or marital status. For this reason, red beads were a staple of wedding attire, or other occasions where matrimonial matters were concerned. Outside of love and romance, they could also be perceived as a woman's amulet, worn on the body to reflect all the unwanted attention and preserve the life force and vitality of the wearer.

HOLY OBJECTS, ROSARIES, AND SIGN OF THE CROSS

The dual faith aspects of folk magic are visible when matters of safety and protection are concerned. In the magic of the common folk, anything that is consecrated is believed to either hold apotropaic powers itself or remain protected while being used for its specific purpose. This characteristic is observed and shared across cultures where Catholicism was or still is the main religion, such as Poland, Italy, Latin America, Scotland, and Spain, to name a few. It is still quite popular to have a flask of Holy Water at home, at least one statue or medallion of Mary, or a chosen saint, rosaries and chaplets, reliquaries of soil or water from holy places, prayer cards, blessed herbs, and such. Due to their holy nature, all such items are believed to be especially effective in warding off evil spirits, demons, devils, curses, and other potentially malevolent influences during moments of spiritual crisis.

The rosary, as a symbol of Our Lady, was commonly advised to be worn when traveling or doing work outside. It was believed to protect against evil forces and extreme atmospheric phenomena (often perceived as one and the same). Should danger approach, one could always whip out the rosary and begin praying to improve their chances of remaining unharmed, or perhaps even compel infernal forces to do their bidding, as is advised in old folk legends.

The sign of the cross must have had the easiest time being accepted as non-pagan in the process of Christianization. In reality, folks of these lands have been using the sign of the cross in its various iterations long before they knew what Christianity was. It was frequently used as a protection symbol, marking an impenetrable barrier for any and all evil forces, acting as a stop sign of sorts. A simple protective gesture included crossing one's fingers as a way of negating the evil eye and curses. The cross was gestured with a hand before starting work, before baking and cutting bread, or marked on someone's forehead as a blessing. It marked the beginning of labor in the fields and farms and blessed its outcome. It was carved or painted on tools, toys, pots, furniture, in barns, and houses. And finally, it served as a marker of property, designating where one place ended and another began. To this day, it is seen on marker stones in forests and on hills.

In many Polish families, the sign of the cross remains an important tradition to this day. For example, my father would always mark the sign of the cross on bread with a knife before cutting the first loaf. When asked about the purpose, he simply said: "That's what we've always done, as a sign of respect."

The most commonly documented historical forms of crosses include X-shaped, equal-armed, equal-armed in a circle, swastika, curved, with wider ends, etc.

Historical practices sometimes also describe the inversion of using holy objects for heretical purposes: stealing holy water or the host directly from the church seems to have been especially popular. Such stolen objects could then be used in more heretical acts of not only protection, but also justice, retribution, or attack.

ANIMAL PARTS AND BONES

Animal bones and remains also played an important role in older practices of protection. The animal part is chosen depending on the type of protection needed, based on their perceived character and spirit. For example, a bear, elk, or wolf have been historically chosen for fierce and fearless protection. In accordance with animist perception of the world, the bone or animal part is believed to be ensouled with the qualities of the animal, thus granting its powers to the wearer. Similarly, wearing the hide of an animal, or an animal-shaped mask, helps shed one's human perception and shapeshift the wearer into the animal. Such animal parts would either be worn as a necklace or incorporated into a *nawęza*—a type of amulet that will be described in the next chapter.

Most commonly used bones and animal parts come from wolves, bears, foxes, wisents (bison), elks, boars, deer, cats, snakes, horses, moles, fish, and shells.

STONES AND FOSSILS

Any common stone that stands out in some way—has an unusual shape, color, or texture—is great to use for protection magic. For example, heart-shaped stones are especially lucky.

Baltic amber, in particular, is used to protect against the evil eye and promote good health. Baltic amber can also be burned the same way other resins are used as incense. Amber smoke protects from evil influences, evil spirits, and witches who wish to cause harm. Amber tincture is used medicinally to protect the heart, boost immunity, help with anxiety, and more.

Belemnites and fulgurites, also known as *strzałki* (arrows), *palce* (fingers), *paznokcie* (nails), and *laski* (rods), are well known for their use in protection magic. They were believed to come from thunder; therefore, they can be used both to protect from storms and to employ the power of thunder to guard us and smite our enemies.

TYPES OF ITEMS USED IN ACTIVE PROTECTION MAGIC

Joanna Wawrzeniuk in her *Magia ochronna Słowian we wczesnym średniowieczu na ziemiach polskich* (Protection Magic of the Slavs in early Middle Ages in Poland) offers an exhaustive summary of the most commonly encountered categories of items used by the Slavs for apotropaic purposes (Wawrzeniuk, 2016, p. 107):

- **Sharp:** Thorns, needles, knives, claws, teeth, fangs, horns, blackthorn, wild rose, hawthorn, juniper, thistle
- **Noise:** Bells, rattles, items making squeaking, buzzing, or other annoying noises.
- **Shiny/reflective:** Shiny stones, metals, glass, mirror
- **Stinging:** Nettles and other stinging plants
- **Intoxicating:** Poisonous plants
- **Bitter:** Wormwood and other bitter plants
- **Repulsive:** Feces, animal dung, urine, and other disgusting substances

All the items listed possess clear deterrent qualities, causing active harm, annoyance, or unpleasant consequences to the recipient upon contact. This illustrates how our ancestors had a clear preference for active protection as a first "line of response," repelling or wounding the attacker before they could cause trouble, rather than allowing the attack to occur and having to rely on passive protection alone.

CHAPTER FOURTEEN

NAWĘZA: TRADITIONAL POLISH AMULETS, TALISMANS, AND CHARM BAGS

Nawęza or *nawąz* is an object that protects from enchantments and witchcraft. The consensus is that amulets are considered protective, while talismans are believed to bring luck. *Nawęzy* (plural), however, most likely served both functions, sometimes even simultaneously. They are the perfect example of passive magic, which means that once properly created, they would continue to do their job without additional actions needed from the wearer. According to tradition, nawęza should be tied around the neck with the length of the cord reaching the dimple just below the breasts, and it should be worn until it falls off by itself. This meant that the piece had completed its job and should be replaced with a new one. Let us look at historical examples of the amuletic and talismanic nawęzy, as well as modern examples of these magical objects used by folk witches today.

ANIMAL FANGS, CLAWS, BONES, AND TEETH

In the early medieval period until the fifteenth century, animal claws, fangs, and teeth (including human teeth) were especially popular as protective nawęzy, but sometimes also talismans. Folks would drill a little hole in the tooth or fang, string it, and wear it around their neck. These were believed to not only protect the wearer but also bestow the powers of the animal to whom they belonged upon the wearer. The most popular were wolf fangs, bear claws, wisent horns, and moose hooves—all belonging to animals believed to be fierce, strong, and dangerous. Fox, deer, boar, beaver, and dog teeth nawęzy were common as well. Amulets made of bones, as well as fish vertebrae and sturgeon gills were also popular finds. An example of a bone charm worn for protection from the evil eye was traditionally made from a chicken wing bone.

WEAPON AMULETS: AXES AND HAMMERS

It could be surprising to some that hammers resembling the well-known Scandinavian "Thor's hammers" design were quite commonly found in Poland as well. Many of those, made of amber, were found in Gdańsk and other northern settlements by the Baltic Sea. Some of these hammers have been discovered in local amber workshops from as early as the tenth century. Interestingly, the designs of some of these hammers were so unique that it prompted a hypothesis that, despite the apparent Scandinavian association, they could've also played a role in the Slavic cult of Living Fire.

Other than hammers, miniature axes made of copper or bronze were also discovered, some in burial mounds and some in medieval settlements. These bear a more easily recognizable connection with the Slavic deity Perun.

CULT POUCHES AND KAPTORGA

Cult pouches could be best described as a Polish equivalent of "mojo bags" worn around the neck. They were traditionally made of wool or silk, stuffed with items specific to the purpose of the talisman. One such historical example of a cult pouch found by archaeologists in northern Poland included a pouch made of wool, containing a beaver's chopper tooth, a fragment of an amber cross, a piece of moss, and a bundle of red thread—items commonly used for protection.

Evolved directly from cult pouches, *kaptorga* is a type of pouch-shaped jewelry made of precious metals, decorated with plant ornaments on the outside, and designed to carry objects inside it, similarly to a locket. They were a type of cult pouch for wealthy elites. *Kaptorgi* (plural) were made in Poland as early as the eleventh century. They were used for carrying items meant for specific types of protection or healing of particular ailments.

CROSSES

Across Poland, several types of cross-shaped *nawęzy* have been found. The majority would be based on the equal-armed cross shape, fairly common as a solar symbol in pre-Christian times. The Latin cross (with its longer lower leg), however, most likely comes from the Christianization period, when the religion was still new and most people couldn't understand the difference between the crosses. It is an interesting example of religious and magical thinking intertwined and used for a specifically magical purpose. They were often discovered in cult pouches alongside other miniature pagan symbols, usually carved in amber.

FOLK CATHOLIC AMULETS

Around the fifteenth century, folks eventually started replacing the older talismans and amulets with Catholic devotional jewelry, which appeared more socially acceptable at the time. *Agnus Dei* medallions (called *Agnuski)* seemed to be especially popular for protection from illnesses and sins. These medallions were made of beeswax, with the image of the Lamb of God on one side. and the image of a saint on the reverse. The kaptorga necklaces also underwent a process of syncretization—from cult pouches carrying plant materia, to reliquaries, carrying relics of folk saints or other holy items. Likewise, rosaries, chaplets, medallions, and prayer cards of saints became frequently used as amulets and talismans, which remains common practice today.

CHARAKTERY

Charaktery (characters, writing) is a type of amulet documented around the fifteenth century, which consisted of formulas written on parchment or etched into metal. These were most often based on formulas found in the Bible or heretical formulas circulating in grimoires across Europe. Fragments of gospels or psalms were inscribed for specific ailments or magical purposes. Pieces of *Epistola manu Dei scriptae* (letters written by the hand of God)—an apocryphal anonymous text dating back to the sixth century—were also extremely popular as formulas used for charaktery. Even the names of saints were enough of a formula for simple charms of this kind. For example, to protect cattle from illness, folks would inscribe the name of St. Luke (whose attribute is the ox) and place it in their cattle's mouth.

STONES, SHELLS, AND OTHER MATERIA

Other popular nawęza amulets were traditionally made of *Strzałka piorunowa* (Thunder arrow, a Belemnite), holey stones, cowrie shells, miscellaneous bones and teeth, and magical plants, such as lovage or *alraune* (white bryony root).

NAWĘZA IN CONTEMPORARY FOLK MAGIC

Folk witches still use nawęzy talismans in their practice today. The types commonly witnessed among fellow folk witches most resemble the folk Catholic amulets, the older cult pouches, or a combination of both—little hand-sewn baggies made of linen or wool and decorated with embroidered symbols corresponding to the purpose. The contents of the bag would differ depending on the practitioner and the purpose. They are usually stuffed with herbs of chosen correspondences, parchments with symbols, prayers, or charaktery inscribed on them, sometimes also devotional cards or medallions, or animal parts like teeth or bones.

The creation process of a cult pouch nawęza today consists of:

- Sewing the baggie
- Embroidering it with relevant symbols
- Filling it with corresponding plant and animal matter, as well as other chosen devotional items
- All the above steps are done with intent and prayed over, usually with zamawiania (spoken charms) and prayers directed to specific spirits or gods with whom the witch works.

A talisman created in such a way is ready to be worn, either by the witch or their client. Nowadays, the tradition is not lost and seems to be regaining its popularity in Poland.

CHAPTER FIFTEEN

EGG MAGIC AND JAJOWANIE

Eggs are one of the most important tools and ingredients in Slavic folk magic. Their uses range from being the primary offerings to spirits and ancestors, to being used as sacred gifts and divinatory tools, and for healing and cleansing practices.

In Slavic mythology, one of the creation myths tells a tale of how the world emerged from the Cosmic Egg. Thus, an egg can be perceived as a pure manifestation of life force. It is not yet born, and yet it exists, holding potential for life. Eggs are a symbol of rebirth, renewal, triumph of good over evil, good beginnings, and, of course, life itself. Before we explore how to utilize eggs for the practice of *jajowanie,* an introduction to the springtime traditions related to eggs is in order.

MAGIC OF EGGS: PISANKI, MALOWANKI, AND KROSZONKI

The tradition of *pisanki* predates Christianization, with its roots stemming from practices related to the spring equinox and *Dziady Wiosenne* (spring rituals honoring the dead). In practice, there are various kinds of egg ornamentation, depending on the region and technique. For example, in Silesia where I grew up, we would traditionally make *kroszonki,* which is a type of egg dyed with natural dyes (such as onion peels or red cabbage), and then the ornaments are skillfully scraped on the surface with a tiny knife or another sharp object. In comparison, pisanki are painted on with wax to create multi-layered designs, whereas *malowanki* are dyed, with no additional ornaments.

No matter the type of ornamentation used, all Easter eggs still share the same properties.

In the past, decorating eggs was an activity reserved for women only. Traditionally, women would gather on Maundy Thursday or Holy Friday to decorate the eggs together. No man was allowed to help or even look at how it was done. Should a man stray into the room where eggs were being decorated, he would be chased away and all the eggs, as well as tools had to be cleansed with salt, accompanied by a spoken formula, *"Sól tobie w oczach, kamień w zębach!"* ("Salt in your eyes, and stone in your teeth!"). Similar cleansing practices were employed if a menstruating woman touched the eggs.

The most traditional color for dyeing the eggs was red. As we know, in Slavic tradition, red is the color of protection, as well as blood and life force, which naturally enhances the properties of the egg.

Post-Christianization, the eggs were customarily consecrated at church on Holy Saturday in a traditional *święconka* basket (see: "Polish Folkloric Year: Spring").

In households where folk practices remained alive, the first completed eggs were usually gifted to family members or hidden around the garden to be found by the children. Sometimes, they would also be gifted to animals to grant them good health.

Other than the living, eggs were also gifted as offerings to the ancestors and nature spirits. During *Dziady Wiosenne* (Spring Forefathers), it was customary to roll eggs on graves and leave them as offerings for the dead. Generally speaking, eggs are among the most popular food offerings for spirits in Slavic culture, along with bread.

In a Slavic household, nothing goes to waste. Both the water used for boiling eggs and the eggshells are used in folk magic as they are believed to possess powerful properties. Ground eggshells were commonly buried in the field to multiply the harvest and protect the crops from natural disasters, as well as witchcraft. Some folks would also bury eggshells in the garden and around the property for similar purposes. Single girls would add a pinch of eggshells into their beloved's food to make them fall in love. They would also wash their faces in egg water as a rejuvenating beauty treatment.

Easter eggs were also used in love magic and courting. Both girls and boys would gift the prettiest decorated eggs to each other; it was seen as a token of love, representative of fertility and readiness to commit to a relationship. Naturally, because boys couldn't decorate their own eggs, they would usually receive them from their mothers or sisters to gift them to their chosen girl. While it seems like an innocent and cute custom on the surface, it could get dark pretty fast. If a girl or her parents didn't approve of a boy, they could refuse to receive the gift of an egg. This was perceived as rejection and letting the boy know that he has no chance of becoming a future husband for the girl.

There are also plenty of fortune-telling traditions using the egg. One such universal method utilizes raw eggs. After cracking open the egg, one would separate the egg white from the yolk and ask a question—this could be a question about anything, such as love, job, health, happiness, etc. Then, one would pour the egg white into a transparent glass or jar filled with cold water and set it aside for 24 hours. The next day, one would divine from the shapes that the egg white created in the glass. Similar, albeit more elaborate egg scrying methods were employed in conjunction with the cleansing practice of egg rolling, which shall be expanded upon below.

JAJOWANIE/EGG ROLLING

Jajowanie (read: yayovanie) is one of the signature Slavic folk magic practices. We know that similar practices exist in other cultures across the globe—I've personally heard of practitioners similarly using eggs in Mexican folk magic, for example. This practice appears to be very old, and it is nearly impossible to trace its origin in the Slavic culture. At its core, it is a method of cleansing a person from illnesses, curses, bad luck, the evil eye, internal struggles, addictions, and so much more. Some people say the egg can also help with things like insomnia, menstrual pains, weight loss, removing wrinkles, supporting the kidneys and bladder, regulating metabolism, and such. While some of these seem like a rather long stretch, I believe that jajowanie is generally great for internal cleansing—a powerful spiritual detox that helps get rid of malicious influences (both external and internal), which can go a long way. Sometimes, a small change can be the first step in creating a ripple effect that will help tackle much bigger problems.

Depending on the issue, one session may be sufficient, while multiple sessions may be necessary. Jajowanie is performed using a single egg per session. The egg draws out all the unwanted influences, illnesses, and such, and neutralizes them within itself. The egg can be used for divination afterwards to learn more about the nature of the ailment, but it is not necessary.

Traditionally, it is said, the egg should be freshly taken out of the chicken coop so that it is still buzzing with life force energy. If one doesn't have chickens, eggs acquired from someone locally work just as well. Some say that store-bought eggs will not do, but that is up to the practitioner to assess and decide. Once the egg is acquired, the practitioner would then roll the egg around the person's body in specific ways, sometimes accompanied by reciting prayers, until the person is cleansed or until the egg becomes full, which signals the end of the session. It is also possible to perform jajowanie on oneself. I will attempt to describe both ways of approaching it, so that you can both help someone, as well as do it for yourself if needed. As you continue to practice jajowanie, you will develop your own ways of rolling the egg, as well as interpreting the signs from a cracked egg afterwards.

Supplies

- One fresh egg
- A glass or jar of water that is only used for this purpose alone

Setup

Both you and the person should wear loose, comfortable clothes and remove all jewelry that could get in the way. The person should sit on a simple stool with hands gently resting on their thighs or knees. They should close their eyes and try their best to relax and be receptive to the work being done on them. It is wise to warn them that they may experience strange sensations in the body, such as feeling hot or heavy, nausea, pain, tingling, or other sensations, indicating where in the body the illness or curse is located. Such sensations are a natural reaction, but they don't have to occur for jajowanie to work. Some folks are more receptive than others, so a fair warning goes a long way. If the person feels safe, it is advised to withstand this brief moment of discomfort until the working is complete.

There are two basic types of egg rolling.

- Touching the patient's body by rolling the egg directly on the skin
- Holding the egg just above the skin and rolling it "contact free" in circular motions

No matter the chosen kind of rolling, you should first establish and feel a connection between the person being cleansed and the egg. This is often done by gently placing the egg in the lap or hands of the person, allowing them to hold it and simply feel into it, blurring the boundaries between the person and the egg. Some folks even believed that holding an egg in this way, and allowing it to absorb an illness or curse was enough. In return, the egg would pour its life force into the recipient. This can feel like a pleasant buzzing or warmth between your hand and the egg, kind of feeling like you and the egg are extensions of each other. Everyone feels these things differently, so be receptive to your bodily sensations. Once you feel the connection, the rolling can begin.

It is generally agreed upon that you should hold the egg with all your fingers, with the broader side of the egg directed towards the inside of your palm and the narrow tip of the egg out towards the person being cleansed. Depending on sources, some say you should always hold the egg in your right hand and roll it clockwise, while other sources say the practitioner should establish a way that feels most powerful for them. You begin at the top of the head and start rolling the egg in spiral-like motions, while remaining aware of a connection between you and the egg.

Rolling the egg directly on the skin is easier to use when you are already familiar with jajowanie and are confident in your experience with controlling the egg under the palm of your hand. It doesn't take much to have the egg slip from under your hand and break; therefore, it takes a bit more practice to master. It is usually best to begin by placing the egg on the top of the person's (or your own) head, placing the palm of your hand on top. Then, you begin to slowly roll the egg in spiral-like motions, while remaining aware of a connection between you and the egg. You allow the egg to roll as it feels right, remembering not to press too hard (or else it might break).

Another type of direct contact is rubbing the egg on your body as if the egg were an eraser. It is easiest to perform this while completely naked, which is why this method would be best used on yourself. While rubbing ourselves with the egg, we try not to think about anything in particular—the more we relax and keep our minds empty, the better the results. We try not to rub too vigorously or aggressively, but maintain a calm and steady pace until the entire body has been equally rubbed.

You would usually begin from the top of the head, rolling in spiral or circular patterns. Begin with the front of the body, from head to toes, and then on the back, from toes to head. As you begin to roll on the head, pay special attention to the eyes, ears, nose, and mouth—all the openings through which we experience the outside world. From the face, you proceed to the front of the body. Pay special attention to the major organs and all the joints. Once you get to the back, begin with the heels and move up. As you roll up, pay attention to the joints, to the base of the spine, all the vertebrae up to the base of the skull.

Alternatively, some folks prefer to focus on each body part separately, rolling around one body part before moving to another, instead of top-down on the front, followed by bottom-up on the back. In this way of rolling, you still begin with the head, then move on to the neck, and from there, you can roll around the shoulders and arms, front and back of the torso, front and back of the hips, then around each leg, and so on.

I believe that everyone should establish a way and order of rolling that feels right and is genuinely guided by the body instead of strictly following a book. In this way, you get to reach a subtle trance state as you roll, and follow what you're seeing and feeling in the person's body— thus, being able to provide a better, more thorough cleansing.

During egg rolling, it is generally best to focus on connecting with the person's body on a deep level. Some people call it "energy work;" however, that is more in line with modern eclectic paradigms, rather than folk magic. As you roll the egg, you should be feeling how the egg is collecting pieces of unwanted gunk from their body. You may see them as debris, shadowy strands, mucus, etc. Always trust your inner sight. As you grow experienced with this method, you will notice that you can intuitively feel which body parts feel inflamed, dark, or heavy—that is where it needs the most thorough work. Once you feel a body part being thoroughly cleansed, you move on to the next. You should be focusing on the task at hand and seeing how everything is collected within the egg and neutralized inside it. The eggshell acts as an impenetrable barrier for all the gunk. Once the process is complete or the egg is full and it feels like it won't hold any more, you will know—that is when you stop.

Removing curses with egg rolling

According to some egg rolling practitioners, to remove a curse by jajowanie, you should make thirty-three clockwise circular movements on the patient's head while whispering chosen prayers or spells. You begin with small circles above the forehead and then continue to make larger and larger circles above the entire head. Once all thirty-three circles above the head are finished, you drag the egg from the base of the spine up to the base of the skull and then begin to cleanse the entire back with circular motions.

Prayers used during the procedure

This component is often present, especially when jajowanie is performed by folk witches who practice in the ways of dual faith. East Slavs would recite Orthodox prayers, while West Slavs would recite Catholic prayers. In Poland—in the context of Catholic dual faith—the prayer used is either the Hail Mary *(Zdrowaś Mario)* or the Lord's Prayer, also known as Paternoster *(Ojcze Nasz)*. There are also several folkloric versions of Paternoster adapted and explicitly used in folk magic across the globe, such as the White, Black, and Green Paternosters. The prayer should be said in whichever language feels most powerful to you. Below, I share an example of what this can look like in Polish. Skip ahead for non-Catholic alternatives.

Polish Paternoster / Pacierz

"Ojcze nasz, któryś jest w niebie,
święć się imię Twoje;
przyjdź królestwo Twoje;
bądź wola Twoja, jako w niebie tak i na ziemi.
Chleba naszego powszedniego daj nam dzisiaj
i odpuść nam nasze winy, jako i my odpuszczamy naszym winowajcom.
I nie wódź nas na pokuszenie,
ale nas zbaw ode złego.
Bo Twoje jest królestwo i potęga, i chwała teraz i zawsze i na wieki wieków.
[Odejdźże wszelkie zło z (imię i nazwisko osoby) i spal się w ogniu bożym.]
W imię Ojca i Syna i Ducha Świętego.
Amen."

English Paternoster

"Our Father, who art in heaven,
hallowed be thy name;
thy kingdom come;
thy will be done on earth as it is in heaven.
Give us this day our daily bread.
And forgive us our trespasses, as we forgive those who trespass against us.
And lead us not into temptation;
but deliver us from evil.
For thine is the kingdom, the power and the glory, for ever and ever.
[All evil flee from (name and surname of the person) and burn in god's fire.]
In the name of the Father, and of the Son, and of the Holy Spirit.
Amen."

Catholic prayers aren't part of everyone's practice or faith. Naturally, one should only use prayers, spells, or enchantments that have meaning and power to the practitioner. You can address the spirits and deities that you work with for aid in this work. Alternatively, which is also traditionally accurate, you can directly address the illness, curse, or whatever else you're removing with the egg. Folk witches of old were animists, and thus they addressed the illnesses or other forces as spirits with their own agency. It was customary to say zamawiania, directly addressing the forces, sometimes by a forceful command, other times by bribing or kindly asking them to leave and never bother this person again. This can be easily done by speaking from the heart and improvising. All you need to do is genuinely connect to this force that you're looking to remove and speak to it directly, just as it intuitively comes through you. Generally, the prayer or spell should be whispered. The recipient does not need to hear or understand the words.

Divination with the egg

Once jajowanie is complete, one can use the egg for divination to learn more about the nature of the ailment or curse. It is generally agreed upon that the egg shows you what was, not what will be. For this, you will need a transparent glass or jar filled two-thirds of the way with clean water (some suggest using only rainwater or spring water, but follow your gut). Crack the egg on the side of the glass and pour everything into the water. You can then use this for scrying. As with all forms of scrying, there are no meanings that are set in stone, but it may be helpful to look for any abnormalities or patterns. The yolk can be perceived as representative of the inside of the person's body, while the whites represent outside influences and environmental factors. If the yolk has any anomalies, that could point to internal issues. The whites may form various strands or patterns that could hint at what's happening around the person—if most strands are attached in a specific place, for example, all are above the yolk, that could indicate outside influences trying to get into this person's mind; likewise, strands from below can point to issues with stability, family, or health. In general, the more "normal" and undisturbed the egg looks, the better; the more strange, abnormal, discolored, muddy, etc., the more issues there are/were.

Once the process is complete, discard the egg. If you did the divination, remember to get rid of both the egg in the glass and the shells. Traditionally, the egg should be blessed and thanked for its service and disposed of away from your property. You can take it to the crossroads and throw it behind you, or bury it under a dead tree or bush. Less traditionally, but still works well, you can flush the egg in your toilet, as long as you declare that you're flushing it away from your property and that it'll get cleansed and neutralized in the sewage treatment plant. Remember to thank the egg for its service. As for the glass or jar you used for divination, wash it thoroughly with water and salt. Remember never to use this vessel for anything else. Best keep it for next time.

CHAPTER SIXTEEN

LOVE MAGIC

Love magic has always been one of the most popular kinds of workings. After all, young people back in the day couldn't always choose their partners the way we are free to do so today. Marriages were often arranged by the parents to ensure mutual benefit and prosperity for the family. To try to better their chances of getting a good partner, young ladies and lads alike engaged in love magic all year round, but especially around St. John's Eve or the Summer Solstice, known as *Noc Świętojańska* or *Sobótka*, when celebrations of water and fire—sex, love, and fertility—took place. This shortest night of the year is a culmination of fertility in nature and agriculture, when everything is at its peak, together with the sun. To secure a partner or lover, folks would dedicate the time between the Spring Equinox and the Summer Solstice to exercise an array of love magic practices.

HERBS FOR LOVE MAGIC

Some say that herbs harvested in May are extra potent for love magic and potions. Plants gathered on the full moon and on a Friday were most powerful. Such plants were later added to the drink or food of the chosen beloved, worn on the body, or secretly planted in their garden to make them fall in love.

Some of the most popular herbs and plants used in love magic include:

- **Edelweiss (*Leontopodium alpinum*):** When worn around one's neck, the plant brings about the love of all people.
- **Common vervain (*Verbena officinalis*):** Among various other uses, the plant is believed to bring about lust and debauchery.
- **Bog Star (*Parnassia palustris*):** Popular for its qualities of changing

the hearts of those who were reluctant to fall in love, opening them up to love.

- **Lovage (*Levisticum officinale*):** One of the most popular love magic herbs. When worn on the body, it would evoke sympathy in others. Bathing in lovage would make someone easy to fall in love with. Children bathed in lovage are said to be granted happy love in the future. When added to food and eaten by the beloved, it makes them fall in love. Lovage should be harvested at midnight during the full moon, while reciting the following spell:

"Lubieniec, ja cię rwę pięciu palcami, szóstą dłonią,
niech się za przyjaźnią moją ludzie gonią."

"Lubieniec, I pluck you with five fingers, with my sixth hand,
let people chase after my friendship."

- **Martagon lily (*Lilium martagon*):** Known for its qualities of arousing love.
- **Common beech (*Fagus sylvatica*):** For igniting love, one should look for a beech tree that grows close to a fir tree, so that when the wind blows, they rub against each other. One should scrape a small amount of bark from the place where the trees touch, burn it, and add the ash to a beloved's drink to make them fall in love.
- **Rosemary (*Rosmarinus officinalis*):** It was believed that rosemary granted stability of love and partnership; therefore, it was often used in wedding wreaths and bouquets to grant lasting love to the newlyweds. In love magic, if a girl managed to stick a sprig of rosemary in her beloved's shirt, he would surely love her back.
- **Periwinkle (*Vinca minor*):** Similarly to rosemary, periwinkle is especially useful for maintaining and reigniting love in marriage.
- **Ivy *(Hedera helix):*** The juice of the plant should be rubbed into one's hands; touching one's beloved with such hands would make them fall in love.
- **Common hazel (*Corylus avellana*):** It is believed that hazel releases a magical flower at midnight on Christmas Eve. Should a girl procure such a flower, she will be loved by many and will be able to choose her perfect husband. Children bathed in hazel, similarly to lovage,

are granted happy love in the future. If a dried-up hazel grows green again, it foretells the return of one's lost true love.

- **Horseradish (*Armoracia rusticana*):** Recommended for males anxious about their performance. It was believed that consuming horseradish would strengthen their potency, which may be reflected in the plant's popularity in dishes eaten around Easter.
- **Rue (*Ruta graveolens*):** The juice of the plant, when squeezed into wounds (especially snake bite), helps attract someone's caring love. Rue was also commonly used by parents of girls as a repellent of horny boys, when planted in the front garden, it restrained the lust of potential suitors.
- **Silver birch (*Betula verrucosa*):** When secretly planted in a beloved girl's garden, it would make her fall in love.
- **Rowan (*Sorbus aucuparia*):** Girls use rowan roots in love spells to attract mutual affection, as well as wear strings of red rowan berries to attract a partner. Newlyweds hang a blessed rowan above their beds to help keep sinful thoughts at bay and protect the marriage. A suspicious husband wanting to test if his wife had been faithful should place a bunch of rowan berries still wet with the morning dew on his wife's forehead. If she continued sleeping, she had been faithful.
- **Wild pansy (*Viola tricolor*):** Believed to bestow attraction and irresistible charm. Some say that the Polish name of the plant *(bratek,* "brother") comes from two brothers who fell in love with each other and couldn't resist it; thus, they were punished by God and turned into wild pansy. Ladies would rub the juices of the plant into their eyebrows to attract their beloved and make them reciprocate the feeling. A spoken charm could accompany this:

"Niech me spojrzenie nabierze takowej jasności,
Byś ty [imię] za mną usychał z miłości."

"May my gaze become so bright,
To make you [name] pine for my love."

DEW AND BEAUTY BATHS

Dew has been known for its magical properties, which include restoring youthfulness, removing wrinkles and freckles, and granting extraordinary beauty. On St. John's Eve, before dawn, ladies would sneak out to wash themselves in dew and thus become beautiful and impossible to resist.

On the night of St. John's Eve, women would prepare special ritual baths for themselves with some of the love herbs mentioned earlier. Similar to dew, such baths were believed to grant extraordinary beauty, making one irresistible. This bath could also be performed on another date, if the herbs were harvested around St. John's Eve.

BLOOD AND SECRETION MAGIC

Some of the traditional Polish and Slavic love spells fall under the category of blood magic, sometimes also involving other bodily fluids. Although this is an authentic folk tradition, nowadays we are more aware of the safety hazards that come with these types of practices. Reader discretion is advised.

Old sources, such as *Katalog Magii Rudolfa* (Rudolf's Catalogue of Magic) from the thirteenth century (Karwot, 1955, pp. 23-27), detail practices of love magic with the use of blood and secretions. This could be regular or menstrual blood of the witch or other bodily fluids (such as urine or discharge).

A popular practice for ensuring that the husband continues to love the wife was to add her menstrual blood to food, which would then be fed to the man. An alternative would be to bake cookies with the woman's hair (from all body parts) and blood added to them. Nettles soaked in urine were also used; however, details of the practice are rather blurry. It is unknown whether they were added to food or made use of otherwise.

To make one's chosen beloved reciprocate the feeling, one should prick a finger of the left hand and put a few drops of blood into a jug of beer, then add a bit of saliva. As one adds these fluids into the drink, a spoken formula should be recited:

"Jako ja nie mogę przez swojej krwie,
tak ty krzczony, mianowany [imię],
nie możesz żyć beze mnie."

"Just as I cannot live without my blood,
so you christened and called [name],
cannot live without me."

ANIMAL PARTS

Some practices involved the use of animals or animal parts to attract love or force someone to fall in love. Unfortunately, oftentimes the animal was only useful for its blood, heart, or bones. While it is historically relevant to shed light on such practices, harming animals is entirely unnecessary in our modern reality. Animal parts can be accessed via more ethical means, in ways that honor them.

One such example of a love spell called for the use of three small fish. One should be placed inside the mouth, another under the breasts, and the third inside one's vagina. Once the fish die in this way, they are then turned into a powder and added to the husband's food or drink to ensure he continues to love his wife.

Another calls for a chicken or dove to be killed in a hole in the ground, then extract the heart or blood of the animal and turn it into powder, to be used in food or drink as well.

Finally, a rather drastic example of love magic involves "rakes" made of bat ribs that were used for enchanting people. To create such a tool, one had to capture a bat and kill it at midnight. Afterwards, the bat was to be placed inside an anthill. After a few days, the bat's skeleton was stripped clean by the ants and was ready to be used. If pricked with such a bat rib rake, the victim would be enchanted to fall in love or otherwise be receptive to the wishes of the perpetrator. Another version of this working is performed on the night of St. John's Eve, where a group of women would take a bat and bury it in an anthill in the forest. As the bat was being stripped clean to the bones, they would dance around the anthill and chant:

"Kacoperz, kacoperz, z kacoperzów rodu,
Służył ci u Jana białnego za młodu,
Zdejmujewa z niego siaty,
Ostaną się ino gnaty - Leluja!"

"Bat, bat, from the bat bloodline,
He served you with John the White in his youth,
We remove the nets from him,
Only the bones will remain - Leluja!"

The bones would then be split between the women and inserted by them under the pillows of their chosen boys to fall in love with them.

FERN BEAUTY SPELL

Girls performed this spell to achieve irresistible beauty, which helped them attract the best lovers. They would use a specific type of fern called adder's-tongue fern *(Ophioglossum,* known as *nasięźrzał* or bovine tongue) and rub its leaves into their skin to become beautiful. As they were harvesting the plant at night or before dawn, they would recite a zamawianie:

"Nasięźrzale, Nasięźrzale,
Rwę cię śmiale,
Pięcią palcy, szóstą, dłonią,
Niech się chłopcy za mną gonią
Po stodole, po oborze,
Dopomagaj, Panie Boże."

"Adder's-tongue fern, adder's-tongue fern,
I harvest you boldly,
With five fingers, sixth, my hand,
May boys chase after me
In barns and cowsheds,
With God's help."

After harvesting the plant, they would rub its leaves into their skin to enhance beauty, or otherwise add it to love-related baths, concoctions, and spells.

While the above examples of love spells are far from exhaustive, they illustrate some of the most well-known Polish folk magic practices related to love, fertility, and attraction. As may be apparent from some of the enchantments, most of these folk practices come from post-Christianization times; however, their roots are much older than that.

Other than love spells *per se,* love divination and fortune-telling were also extremely popular, especially in late autumn during *Andrzejki* (St. Andrew's Eve), which shall be explored in the autumnal section of the "Polish Folkloric Year."

PART FOUR

SPIRITS AND ALLIES

CHAPTER SEVENTEEN

HOUSEHOLD SPIRITS AND FAMILY SPIRITS

Under the broad umbrella of Indo-European mythologies and folklores, which includes the Slavs, we recognize two main types of spirits categorized based on their relationship to humans as well as places of dwelling:

1. Spirits of the wild, unknown and/or unknowable, often perceived as hostile to an average human.
2. Spirits of civilized places and social structures that are tamed and familiar, such as households, farms, and other places of human dwelling, as well as families and social contexts. These spirits were also generally perceived as *demony opiekuńcze* (protective demons) of a family, community, or place.

It is the latter type that was intimately familiar with and involved in the daily lives of our ancestors, and welcomed as part of the family and community.

Unlike the souls of those who died of unnatural causes, who then transform into dangerous and vicious demons, mares, and evil water spirits, our average household or family spirit is said to originate from the soul of an ancestor who died a natural death. However, it's important to note that not all household spirits are of human origin; therefore, we cannot ascribe these traditions to the cult of the dead alone.

Household spirits are usually considered helpful and somewhat friendly, or at least not extremely disruptive. Those who dwell near the hearth or in the attic help take care of the household, perform various chores while we're asleep, or even protect the family from harm—both of mundane and otherworldly origin. These spirits also reside within farming enclosures, helping to care for cattle, as well as guarding our property and food supplies, such as grain.

Cultivating a good relationship with the household spirits was extremely important to our ancestors. Regular offerings of food and drink would be placed in fixed spots such as the attic, in corners of the house, near or on the main hearth stove, or laid directly into the Living Fire in the stove.

DOMOWIK

The household spirit most commonly known across all Slavs is called *domowik* or *domowy*. The name comes from the word *dom*, meaning "house." This spirit is usually treated like a family member and is believed to be a good ancestor of the family, often looking similar to the head of the family, except older, other times resembling a dead grandfather or other dead relative, and usually dressed in their clothes. On rare occasions, especially at night, domowik can be seen in his otherworldly form, which is very different from the above description. He appears dark, hairy, and horned.

Alternative names for the domowik include: *damavik* (Belarus), *domovyk* (Ukraine), *domovoy, domovoy ded, dobrochot, posteń* (Russia). In Poland, other than domowik, he was often also addressed as *sąsiad* (neighbor), *gospodarz* (householder), *dziadek* (grandfather), or *ojczulek* (father, affectionately). Sometimes, the male domowik would also have a wife, *domacha* or *domowicha*, who dwells under the floor and especially enjoys spinning and weaving.

It is believed that every household has its own domowik whose primary job is to share the responsibility of taking care of the household with the family, being an appointed spiritual protector of the Ród (bloodline), caring for the well-being of the family, and delivering important news from the spirit world concerning potential incoming dangers, as well as blessings. For this reason, the domowik can be seen as more than other household spirits; he is also the protective spirit of the family.

Domowik was thought to originate from the first person who died a natural death in the household. Others say that the first person who crosses the threshold of the house after it's been built will become the household spirit after they die. For this reason, people would often let a cat or other animal go inside first, so it could become the familiar spirit resident. Yet, others hint at the possibility that domowik could be a collective of spirits—both ancestral and land spirits—who dwell in the building. They could be thought of as the soul of the house. However, I will explore the soul of the house separately to demonstrate the difference between domowik and other household spirits.

In the past, common folk would live in one household for many generations, and so the original owner of the house would be a blood relative from previous generations. This made relating to the domowik much easier, and the role as protector of the Ród much more pronounced, due to direct familiarity and long-standing tradition. Nowadays, as we tend to move away from our families and rent apartments, the matter of domowik works slightly differently.

When moving to a new house, folk would traditionally invite their domowik to come with them. One such way of taking the spirit with the family was to leave a shoe for them near the hearth stove overnight so that the domowik could hop inside and be carried to the new place.

When building a new house or digging up a new well, specific offerings were expected to be made for the domowik and other land spirits during the construction phase. Some archaeological finds revealed sacrificial offerings of black roosters, eggs, or animal heads placed in the corners of the house, under the floor beams, or under the main door threshold. Other finds revealed clay pots filled with grain, groats, meat, and drinks buried under the dyke of the settlement, hinting at a larger scale belief in powerful local spirits of entire collectives—extended families, or even entire villages or tribes—illustrating how these traditions were very similar on both the micro and macro scale.

SOUL OF THE HOUSE

Dusza domu, the soul of the house, is a collective of spirits inhabiting the household. They are generally divided into anthropomorphic and zoomorphic types of spirits, meaning that some take on a somewhat humanoid form, while others resemble animals or hybrids of various creatures. No matter their shape or apparition, they can be generally characterized as a community of spirit roommates who share the dwelling with the humans and animals on equal rights. They contribute to the well-being of the homestead and the family in ways that are conditioned by how they are being treated, if their needs are met, and if offerings are left on a regular basis.

The anthropomorphic spirits are imagined as rather tiny, with big heads and feet, living in nooks and crannies of the household, most notably behind or near the stove, under the threshold, in the pantry, or in dishes. While domowik belongs among these spirits, he is not the only one. Various types of tiny humanoid beings dwell in different areas of the house, feeding on offerings and leftovers, helping to multiply abundance, giving and taking good luck, ensuring that the humans act appropriately, cleaning and repairing things, tending to animals, and sending dreams and visions to humans when information has to be passed on. Some of their names include: *bożątka, domowe dziadki, banniki, krośnięta, kłobuki, płonki,* and many more.

The zoomorphic beasties are also rather small and inconspicuous, often capable of flying, changing shape, or disappearing. They generally help multiply the household's abundance but can also cause mischief or even disaster if not properly respected. Some of them look like snakes or other reptiles, birds, or a variety of imps and devils. Some live around the corners of the household, attic, and cellar, while others may dwell under the outside threshold, under the stairs, or elsewhere close to the house. Some of their names include: *diabły domowe, węże domowe, gwizdy, kikimory, skrzaty, zmoki,* and many more.

Both categories of spirits also include those who are protectors of the property as a whole, not just the house itself. Some take care of farm buildings, others guard the fences, while others look after tools, animals, or plants growing in the garden. From a broader perspective, every homestead is a complex ecosystem of spirits and beings enfleshed who coexist and depend on each other for well-being and survival. When all are taken care of and respected, the homestead flourishes and is blessed with abundance. When neglect or disrespect creeps into the homestead, spirits may rebel and punish the human caretakers to make them realize and make up for their mistakes.

FAMILY SPIRITS AND ANCESTORS

Household spirits share a significant overlap with the ancestors and the cult of the dead, which is still very prominent among the Slavic people. Some of the anthropomorphic household spirits, such as the domowik, in fact, *are* the ancestors, and their job is to bestow blessings and wisdom upon the living generations of their Ród.

The cult of the dead in Polish culture is ever present and interwoven into our daily lives, as well as into agrarian traditions and seasonal celebrations. To this day, it is customary to visit and dress the graves of our loved ones several times a year, to invite the souls of our ancestors to our homes and the dining table on all major seasonal and family celebrations. Many of these customs will be introduced and explained in "Agrarian Traditions and Polish Folkloric Year" chapters.

As for the everyday ancestral cult present in our homes, it is usually integrated with the cult of household spirits. Traditionally, every household used to have a *święty kąt* (sacred corner)—a shrine in the corner of the house (often close to the stove), where the ancestors and spirits relevant to the family would be addressed, prayed to, and given offerings and gifts. Today, many of us continue to cultivate this tradition by having a shared shrine in the living area.

HOW TO ESTABLISH A RELATIONSHIP WITH HOUSEHOLD SPIRITS

In today's world, when many of us rent property, buy a home second-hand, or we relocate much more often than our ancestors would, one might wonder if it's still possible to invite a domowik in and how to establish a relationship with him. For our ancestors, this process would have been much easier because people lived on the same land or in the same house for many generations, so the household spirits were "inherited" with the home.

It is, however, possible to invite a domowik and other household spirits into one's home, simply by starting to leave regular offerings of milk for them overnight. While it might take some time for the spirits to become attracted and start visiting your home regularly, it's worth the time and patience. Many people choose to build shrines for the ancestors and household spirits, usually in the kitchen or the main living area, as modern houses rarely have the traditional hearths, fireplaces, or tiled stoves that our grandmothers had (the traditional importance of such stoves is explained in the "Living Fire" chapter). However you choose to honor the domowik and other household spirits is up to your preference—what matters more is the dedication and regularity in feeding them. With time and patience, as your relationship develops, one might even get lucky enough to encounter the spirit at night and see their true form.

HOW TO CULTIVATE A RELATIONSHIP WITH HOUSEHOLD SPIRITS

For our relationship with these spirits to flourish, we are expected to give regular offerings—it is up to you to decide the frequency with your household spirits. The most well-known and documented offerings consist of milk, honey, oatmeal, or the first slice of bread. All offerings are supposed to be left overnight near the hearth of the home. If we get lazy or otherwise fail to give offerings with regularity, we can expect a number of consequences to follow: illness, visitations from malicious spirits, failure of crops, arguments, and even the spirits abandoning our household. After all, nobody wants to live with neglectful roommates, not even spirits.

When properly respected, thanked, and fed with regularity, the spirits will take care of our well-being and protect our household from harm, disaster, and all malicious spirits—the more regular and generous the offerings, the more powerful the soul of the house collective becomes.

WORKING WITH HOUSEHOLD SPIRITS IN A MODERN HOME

From my personal experience, working with household spirits can be very rewarding. It's nice to be surrounded by friendly spirits, to look out for each other, and to be warned of potential danger approaching. Today, things may not always look the same as they did in the lore of old due to the demands of modern life, but whenever in doubt, filling in the blanks with simple animist practices works wonders where local spirits are concerned.

Several years ago, we went through the process of building our forever home on a previously uninhabited plot of land. Up to that point, we had rented apartments; therefore, no domowik could move in with us from any previous homes. As the house was being built, we laid offerings at the foundations and at certain corners of the plot to befriend the local land spirits, apologize for the disturbance, and in preparation for our coexistence. Once the house was built and we moved in, we could initially feel the absence of spirits—the space felt rather sterile. Over several months, ancestors and spirits of the land were repeatedly invited and given regular offerings at a living room shrine until the soul of the house was awakened—inhabited not only by humans and animals, but also by the invited spirits.

Daily offerings of drink and food are laid in a simple, inconspicuous shrine in the living area, dedicated to the ancestors and the household spirits, together. We offer various drinks and foods interchangeably, but the staples are fresh water, coffee, the first slice of a loaf of bread, seasonal flowers, rocks, or acorns. On occasion, special dishes (such as *kutia)* are offered along with a shot of natural, herbal alcohol. Additional gifts are given on death and birth anniversaries of our beloved ancestors. As the daily offerings are given, a simple formula is spoken:

"Kochani przodkowie, domowiku, duchy domu, duchy miejsca,
Oto świeża (kawa/woda/kromka chleba) dla Was.
Nasyćcie się nią i chrońcie nasz dom od wszelkiego złego.
Dziękuję."

"Beloved ancestors, domowik, household spirits, land spirits,
I offer this (coffee/water/slice of bread) to you.
May you be nourished by it and protect our home from all evil.
Thank you."

CHAPTER EIGHTEEN

DIABEŁ: FOLKLORIC DEVILS

The devil is most commonly referred to as *diabeł*, but his older pre-Christian titles include *czart* and *bies*, meaning monstrous or terrible. In Polish demonology lexicons, one can find pages upon pages of documented local names and nicknames for the folkloric devils—a testament to how many there are, as well as to the fact that folks were always rather careful not to name the devils directly if they could help it, to avoid drawing their attention or attracting their presence in vain. Common folk would rather refer to them as *tyn zły* (the evil one), *łon* (he), or *tyn ogoniasty* (the tailed one) than call their name. It is important to stress that folkloric devils are not synonymous with the Devil or Satan of Christian theology. Rather, they are a group of spirits who existed long before Christianization. Although the folkloric perception of devils was undoubtedly influenced by this new faith over time, equating them all with an imported figure was (and remains) a tool of cultural erasure that we shall not entertain.

The devil of old could be seen as one being and many beings, simultaneously. In his folkloric figure, both pre- and post-Christian elements continuously merge and intertwine, resulting in the coexistence of numerous types of devils, as well as the enmeshment of old land spirits and chthonic deities with said devils. In pre-Christian times, devils such as bies or czart were regarded as ancient beings residing in the depths of the wilderness, dark forces beyond human comprehension, and terrifying and powerful guardians of the very laws of nature. They were either openly hostile or largely unconcerned with human affairs, except to make common folk hellbent on destroying unnatural man-made hierarchies or overthrowing lords and oppressors. This aspect of old devils, when combined with a persistent low interest in Christian theology among the common folk remained well preserved within the folkloric perception of the devil as wielder of folk justice and prosecutor of men in power, accusing and punishing those who dare abuse their authority, act out of greed, or commit cruelty against the powerless. It was even believed to be against devilish ethics and standards to cause harm to the common folk, and especially those living in poverty. According to folklore, should a devil steal a poor man's only meal or otherwise wrong them, the spirit would be punished by other devils and denied access to hell until he makes up for it. To gain his reputation back, he'd have to repay the wronged person by offering his labor, as well as punishing any man who treated them poorly.

As dual faith beliefs developed and evolved over the centuries, one ontological truth remained as relevant as ever, carried over from the pre-Christian world's creation myths straight into folk Catholicism—"*Panu Bogu świeczkę, a diabłu ogarek*" ("A candle for God, and a wick for the devil")—meaning that a wise folk will never place all their bets on one spirit, but rather alternate with cunning to achieve the best results. Notably, the Slavs were largely unbothered by the Christian dualistic perception of good and evil well into post-Christianization times. This means that the devil and other chthonic beings weren't perceived through the typical Christian lens as representations of evil until centuries later. The importance of cultivating good relations with all powers—both heavenly and chthonic—remained at the forefront of folk magic practices throughout the centuries. This was, naturally, good news for all the devils and land spirits whose role beyond the hedge and in the rural household never truly lost its prominence. The familiar, local devils were thus perceived as more caring and reliable than the foreign God. After all, the Christian God was the one perceived as a force in support of the oppressor, because the authority and power wielded by the aristocracy or the clergy was often abused in the name of no other than the Christian God. The devil, therefore, remained a protective figure of those less privileged, dispossessed, or neglected.

TYPES OF FOLKLORIC DEVILS

Folkloric devils are likely the most widespread category of spirits present in Polish folklore. Every area of life and every place you can think of has its own patron devil. Folks will meet them at the crossroads, in deep forests and old ruins, crowded taverns, and even churches. Folks will encounter devils of illness, love, abundance, travel, magic, crime, and more. Every town and village have its own local devils—spirits responsible for making people fall for temptations, offering empowerment, access to magical abilities, knowledge, or wealth in exchange for one's soul.

In terms of appearances, folkloric devils are adept at shapeshifting and would rarely show their true form in front of regular mortals. Usually, they are either invisible or camouflaged to resemble an animal or human, which helps them slip by unnoticed or even be accepted into the community as needed. One physical characteristic that is often attributed to a devil is that they limp on one leg, and that leg is often hooved. This limping seems to be related to beliefs that syncretize the devil with fallen angels (according to folk belief, the devil broke his leg when he fell from the heavens). Another characteristic could be thick hair or a hat that conceals their horns. Additionally, they may have no nostrils or have claws instead of regular human nails. They may also be recognized by their strong scent of sulfur or tar, leaving behind dark marks wherever they go.

Devils of Human Origin

As has been hinted at earlier on (see: "Visions of Spirits, Hypnagogia and Life Beyond Death"), there are devils of human and non-human origin. The human devils largely originate from men who signed a pact with the devil while alive, thus signing away their souls. While not all of them would become devils themselves posthumously, some of the most notorious would. If they were of noble standing while alive, they could continue to maintain their status in their devil era, hence why so many of the Polish devils hold recognized noble names and crests. Such devils would be referred to as *diabły szlacheckie* (noble devils) or *diabły kontuszowe* (named after kontusz, a traditional piece of clothing worn by noblemen).

Wild Devils

Many devils, however, are of non-human origin. Those that dwell in nature are broadly referred to as *diabeł dziki* (wild devil), which betrays their direct relation to land spirits and guardians of place. The most common natural places of dwelling include forests and groves, crossroads, caves and mountains, inside old trees (especially willows and elders), dikes, swamps, and marshes. Some wild devils are personifications of natural phenomena, mainly the winds or whirlwinds. Others could be seen disguised as animals. The most common animal forms of devils include rooster, black dog, cat, owl, black horse, wolf, goat, fox, bat, hare, toad, ram, and bull. Sometimes, they would appear as a hybrid of human and animal. Wild devils are unable to take the form of a dove or a lamb.

Household Devils

Other devils of non-human origin, such as *diabeł domowy* (household devil) or *diabeł chowaniec* (familiar devil), are the type of devils that were somewhat "tamed" and used to the presence of humans. They dwell in man-made structures, often working alongside humans in exchange for payment. Their favorite places of dwelling include ruins, abandoned buildings, old mills, forges, taverns, attics, and basements.

Devils as Witches' Familiars

Our folkloric devils sought love and partnership among mortal women, usually witches. Curiously, most devils weren't interested in open relationships; they would rather marry the chosen woman and stay in a long-term relationship with her. This overlaps with traditional witch lore across Europe, especially the numerous stories of spirit spouses. For example, witches would regularly have sex with their chosen devil familiar, and this intercourse was an important part of where they acquired their magical powers. This could be recognized as one of the most common witch-familiar relationships, where the devil (or other spirit) is a lifelong companion, lover, helper, and teacher of the witch.

Let's look at some of the folkloric devils known for working with witches:

- ***Inkluz:*** Also known as *diabeł szczęścia* (devil of luck), it is a peculiar type of folkloric devil who brings money, specializing in returning all the money spent back to its owner. To employ such a familiar for a job, one must go to the crossroads at midnight and whistle to summon the inkluz. If one would prefer to employ inkluz long-term, one must carry the egg from a black hen and black rooster in one's armpit for nine days and nine nights. If successful, such an egg would then bear a tiny inkluz devil ready to bestow abundance onto its owner.
- ***Odmieniec* (changeling):** While the same name was used interchangeably for children swapped by demons, this particular devil is a shapeshifter, capable of taking up many forms. When in the shape of a werewolf, he was commonly employed as a means of transport for witches or sent by witches to harm or kill humans or cattle. He wields northern winds to reverse the fates of men, turning all that's

good into ill, and vice versa. In witch lore, he could be perceived as the equivalent of a witch's fetch (the beast/animal form).

- ***Chowaniec* (familiar):** In folklore, it is described as a lesser devil of unknown rank and background, hinting at the fact that it is a role that any devil could take up, rather than a name of one particular devil. He is a companion and helper of the witch, running errands for her, helping around the homestead, protecting the animals and other inhabitants from illness and harm, empowering the witch's magic, and ensuring overall prosperity in exchange for food, payment, and safety. Chowaniec usually dwells around the stove or under the threshold and feeds on groats, milk, and alcohol—similarly to household spirits. He looks like a tiny humanoid with a long beard, but he can also shapeshift to appear as an animal, especially a rooster.
- ***Farmazon:*** Known as *sobowtór* (doppelganger), he is a being of mysterious origin. Some say he is a devil born of the soul of a freemason who sold his soul to the devil. Capable of taking up any form, he works for witches and sorcerers by taking up their physical form and doing their work or running errands for them. He can take care of elaborate tasks, tending to the practitioner's business, granting them money, and fulfilling complex tasks. Similarly to odmieniec, in witch lore, he is perceived as one of the forms a witch can take up in their subtle body, or spirit double (the non-physical vehicle of the witch's soul).
- ***Latawiec:*** Also known as *diabeł ulatujący* (flying devil) or *czart nocny* (night devil), it is believed to originate from the ghost of an unbaptized child or miscarried fetus. After seven years of causing harm to humans, the spirit transforms into a devil. It is also associated with falling stars and meteorites. The spirit comes to the witch at night disguised as a fair young man, offering sex in exchange for mutual aid. Latawiec is known to bring money, grains, and other gifts when treated well. Aside from his disguise as a young man, he may appear as a flying fire, a falling star, a flying mole with membranous wings, or a rooster.
- ***Farel:*** A bird-shaped devil, he was banished from hell for his cunning, but he is beloved by witches for granting great effectiveness to magical potions and flying ointments. He can reveal treasure hidden in the earth. He is often summoned by sorcerers for aid in mirror scrying and conjurations.
- ***Kacperek:*** Also known as *barani łeb* (blockhead), he is a witless and primitive devil, capable of doing simple jobs. He has long claws, a hairy head,

and giant horns, which make him so ugly that he was often used for scaring children. Generally, he is rather harmless and easy to work with.

An interesting "species" of devils employed by witches in their work are the twisted heretical versions of Catholic saints and angels, functioning almost like their evil shadow twins. For example, Marchel is a devilish counterpart of St. Melchior, or Czarny Jurk (Black George) is the evil twin of St. George. These devils were recognized as having the opposite functions to the saints, where the saint would protect against something, such a devil would be the cause of this evil in the first place. Witches would work with such devils by sending them upon people or cattle to cause harm in their name.

On the other hand, there is a folk saying, *"Gdzie diabeł nie może, tam babę pośle"* ("Where the devil cannot go, he will send a woman"), which seems to solidify further this interesting dynamic of mutual fondness between women (witches and non-witches alike) and the devilish kind. According to folklore, women are the most "susceptible" to devilish influences, which actually means that women were traditionally perceived as the most gifted seers and spirit workers, and most effective in asserting control over devils and taking advantage of their infernal powers. Much of this is supported by the belief that devils generally looked for long-term relationships with human women who (unlike men) are believed to be capable of having a sort of equal, mutual working relationship with any chosen devil.

Meanwhile, men—especially ones of noble blood—are more likely to sign contracts with the devil in exchange for their souls. This suggests that transactional relations were perceived as a more accessible way for men to bargain with the devil. Without much wiggle room for fair negotiations or partnering with the devils, these men would usually end up becoming their servants or eventually be transformed into devils themselves posthumously.

FAMOUS FOLKLORIC DEVILS

At last, here are some of the most infamous devils of Polish (and sometimes more broadly Slavic) folklore. They belong to various types of devils and have different functions, but what they all have in common is the notoriety and fame preserved in well-known myths, legends, and fairy tales.

- ***Boruta:*** Classified as one of the noble devils, Boruta was originally a nobleman living in the fourteenth century. Though he's been dwelling in Łęczyca Castle for as long as it stands, some say that he is much older than his noble heritage, and that he's been existing under a different guise long before taking on the name Boruta. Others claim that the nobleman was transformed into a devil upon his death as punishment for daring to appropriate a treasure given to him for safekeeping by the king. Boruta appears under many guises, as an owl, black horse, wolf, giant fish, giant bird, or even a monk. In his favorite original form, he appears as a nobleman with a long black mustache and dark eyes, wearing a rich traditional outfit. While he is known for being intimidating due to his tremendous strength and cunning, he is known in legends for helping the poor by giving away food and grain. He may be petitioned for matters related to finances, politics, and social standing.

- ***Rokita:*** Classified among the wild devils, he is named after a type of willow—*wierzba rokita (Salix rosmarinifolia)*—inside which he is known to dwell. Because the bush commonly grows in marshes and swamps, Rokita is known as a swamp devil. He is known for controlling the fog, which he calls his "milk." Capable of sending fog upon people to confuse them, drive them mad, or get them lost in the swamp, as well as flooding his enemies with mud and swamp water. It is said that witches visit him on Thursdays to partake in his foggy milk and cheese, which makes their cows produce a lot of milk. When called with the saying, *"Rokita, dam ci duszę ciało, daj mi mleko, bo mi się zachciało"* ("Rokita, I'll give you my soul and body, give me milk, for I crave it"), he appears under the guise of a cat and purrs. Some lore says Rokita is very tall, monstrously strong, and fond of slinging curse words. He may be petitioned for matters related to concealment, confusing enemies, finding hidden treasures, seeing past illusions, and finding one's path.
- ***Czart:*** He is another wild devil of the pre-Christian era. The name czart most likely comes from *czary,* or sorcery, hinting at his close association with practitioners of magic and witchcraft. This is further solidified by his association with winds, which were perceived as the primary carriers of spoken enchantments and spells. Described as a "typical" devil—half-man, half-goat—he is capable of shapeshifting into intimidating animals, birds of prey, bears, stags, dragons, angels, or even Christ himself. His favorite form is said to be that of a goat. He is believed to have especially hated the new faith and was often

responsible for throwing large boulders and rocks at newly built churches. These rocks, called *czarci głaz* (czart's rock), can be found all over Poland, each one having its own local legend attached to it and displaying the devil's claw marks or hoof prints to show for it. He may be petitioned for matters related to practices of magic, aid, and teachings of witchcraft, sorcery, and heretical practices against the church.

- ***Bies:*** One of the pre-Christian devils of the wild, he is the personification of untamed forces of nature. He lives in ancient forests and inaccessible swamps where he guards treasures hidden deep in the Earth. Described as a hybrid beast of strange shapes and capable of shapeshifting, he is known for causing absolute terror and madness in those who encounter him in the wild. He can possess people and act through their bodies. A possessed person would be referred to as *zbiesiony* (adjective: *"biesed"),* which hints at a particular state of frenzy or ecstasy. Witches would call his name for aid in traveling to the sabbat. For this purpose a chant was used (see: "Zamawianie and Spoken Formulas"). Here are some examples of Polish sayings about bies:

    - *Bies nie śpi:* Bies doesn't sleep; evil constantly preys upon us.
    - *Pójść do biesa:* Go to bies; go to hell.
    - *Zły jak bies:* Angry like bies; very angry, evil.

  He may be petitioned for matters related to trance and altered states, spirit flight, the witches' sabbat, navigating the wilderness, and shedding one's humanity.

- ***Iskrzycki:*** Classified as a household devil, the name Iskrzycki comes from *iskra* (spark), hinting at his relation to the cult of Living Fire. He is one of the most intelligent devils out there, a businessman and entrepreneur, willing to aid humans in achieving great success. He's believed to be the best companion for homesteaders and farmers, especially, cunning and knowledgeable in matters of management, often serving his human as a personal accountant, granting unbelievable wealth. Due to being extremely unappealing visually, he never shows himself to his "clients" and always gives his advice from behind the stove. He usually stays faithful to his chosen humans until their death. He may be petitioned for matters related to business, entrepreneurship, homesteading and farming, land-based work, finances, and success.

There are countless hordes of other folkloric devils unique to the region of Poland—many of them tied to specific regions and places, often accompanied by local legends and devilish rocks to show for it. Some of the local legends and stories also speak of more widespread European devils and demons, such as Lucifer, Beelzebub, Belial, and many others associated with the Goetia, whose lore usually overlaps across Europe. One such example local to where I live is the legend of *Lucyper* (Lucifer) and how his hordes of lesser devils accidentally created the Mount Ślęża.

THE LEGEND OF MOUNT ŚLĘŻA AND THE BURIED PORTAL TO HELL

In the same spot where the Ślęża Mountain stands today, once stood an open portal to hell. One day, the devils emerged from hell to the surface of the Earth and climbed the nearby Radunia Mountain to marvel at the world from above. On the neighboring hill called Gozdnica, they noticed a host of angels. Upon this sight, the devils became possessed with hellish anger. In an instant, a fierce fight broke out between the angels and the devils. They grabbed stones and boulders and threw them at each other. The battle lasted a long time. As the sun began to set, it was getting darker, and the stones were still flying from side to side, but hardly ever reached the opponents.

When the fight finally ended, it turned out that a great mountain, made of boulders and stones, had grown between the angelic hosts and the devilish legions, closing the entrance to hell. This angered Lucyper. Enraged, he kicked the slope of Radunia mountain so hard with his devil's hoof that the ground collapsed, creating the Tąpadła Pass. Finally, the devil unleashed a terrible storm above the newly created Ślęża, angrily throwing lightning at it in hopes that the entrance to hell would open back up—to no avail. In the end, Lucyper was defeated as the mountain would not budge. To this day, when storms rage above Ślęża, people say it's the devils trying to find the portal back to hell.

HOW TO CONTACT THE FOLKLORIC DEVILS

Folkloric approaches to communing with local devils vary. We know that common folk used to go to the crossroads, devil's rocks, or cemetery gates at midnight and whistle or call the devil by name to conjure him from the dark. It didn't take much elaborate work to have them come forth. Alternative methods include going to trees of the devil, such as willow or elder—ideally around liminal times of dusk or midnight— speaking to the tree, and asking its inhabiting devil for aid. While it wasn't hard to make the devil appear, it may have been slightly more challenging to ensure he didn't snatch or injure the conjurer. To avoid getting hurt or followed home, folks were advised to never look back on their way home, no matter what they heard.

A very peculiar example of historically documented ways of communing with a local devil, which may be easily adapted for use in one's practice, entails preparing a bucket of soapsuds, along with a comb, a meal of oats, and a piece of meat. These items should be set next to an outdoors lavatory at night, and the devil should be addressed as follows:

"Przyjdź, diable, wykąp się i uczesz. Koniowi twojemu daj owsa, jastrzębiowi mięso, a mnie pokaż męża swego."

"Come, devil, wash yourself and comb your hair. Give oats to your horse, meat to the hawk, and show me my future husband."

As for more sophisticated methods employed by sorcerers of nobility, such as the notorious Polish sorcerer Twardowski (known for outsmarting hordes of devils), conjuring the devil was done through mirror scrying or summoning the spirit into one's place of dwelling while standing inside a circle marked with chalk. When the devil appears, the sorcerer must be prepared to sign a pact in exchange for the spirit's labor.

Should one wish to re-create the Renaissance scrying mirror of Twardowski for conjuring spirits and the devil, the original Renaissance mirror (still displayed in a church in Węgrów) was created from an alloy of silver, gold, zinc, and tin, and framed in black wood. The frame is inscribed with a phrase in Latin: *"Luserat hoc speculo magicas Twardovius artes, lusus at iste Dei versus in obseqvium est,"* meaning "With this mirror Twardowski played, performing magic arts, now it is dedicated to the service of God." To modify the inscription to maintain the mirror's originally intended use, the word "Dei" may be replaced with "diaboli" or "spirituum."

Alternatively, a very popular heretical method employed in folk magic across Europe, including Poland, entailed speaking the *Paternoster* (Lord's Prayer) backwards.

Pacierz (Lord's Prayer) Backwards in Polish

"Nema
ogełz edo wabz san ela
eineszukop an san źdów ein i
mocjawoniw myszan ymaczszupdo ym i okaj,
yniw eszan man ścupdo i
jaisidź man jad ogenideszwop ogeszan abelch
imeź an i kat eibein w okaj, ajowt alow źdąb
ejowt owtselurk źdjyrzp
ejowt eimi eś cieiwś
eibein w tsej śyrutk szan eczjo."

The above formula is adjusted to be reversed phonetically rather than just in writing. This would be closer to a realistic reconstruction of how it was potentially spoken.

WAYS OF PROTECTING ONESELF FROM FOLKLORIC DEVILS

Before we move on to discuss another prominent folkloric figure, one should be aware of traditional ways of protecting oneself from the devilish kind.

Highlanders believed that if they found themselves overwhelmed by sin or temptation, it was a clear sign that a devil was present with them. To reject his influence, one should take a piece of blessed chalk and draw a circle around oneself—as long as one stays inside the circle, it grants total protection. Alternatively, a blessed whip can be used to scourge devils, should they appear in visible form. Similarly, to deal with the devils of the wind, throwing a knife at the wind will wound them, thus chasing them away.

To trap and kill a devil, one should lure him into a vessel filled with blessed bladdernuts *(Staphylea)*—a plant ally whose nuts were traditionally used for making rosaries with strong apotropaic properties.

CHAPTER NINETEEN

MARYJA: FOLKLORIC MARYS

In a somewhat heretical, dual-faith fashion, we shall mirror all the devils with figures of folkloric Marys. The cult of Our Lady has been quite prominent in Poland for as long as we can remember. Mother Mary became the primary spiritual source of solace, support, maternal protection, and intercession between the common folk and the larger divine powers. We can witness it in common prayers, how the larger powers are rarely addressed directly—often, prayers would be addressed to Mary (or a chosen saint) as an intermediary who can help make our prayers heard by the distant, larger powers. As psychopomp and a compassionate messenger, Mary understood and deeply felt the pains that come with feminine grief, the challenges of motherhood, and the trials of womanhood. Countless folkloric stories and legends of Mary's everyday struggles reflected the reality of an average Polish woman, thus portraying her as a heavenly advocate of mothers and children, as well as protectress of vegetation and wildlife, blessing and guarding the fields, saving and guiding souls, aiding in labor, soothing grief and despair, teaching humanity respect for all life, and sometimes even going against the rules set out by god. Indeed, this was reflected in the common involvement of Mary in folk prayers, magical charms, and novenas, as well as the popularity of the rosary and pilgrimages to holy places of Our Lady as a way of obtaining miraculous healing and support when all else failed. To this day, Mary remains crowned as Queen of Poland, and her shrines remain a common sight both at crossroads and in people's homes.

It is quite well documented that post-Christianization, Mary assumed the role of an "umbrella figure" for the more feminine land spirits and deities, standing in contrast to the folkloric devils who were syncretized with more ambiguous or masculine spirits and deities. Similarly to the devils, there are countless folkloric Marys present in Polish folk tradition. They could be divided into two primary kinds: Marys related to local land features and Marys connected to seasonal agricultural celebrations. The land-based ones tend to be associated with sacred springs, wayside shrines, Mary's rocks (mirroring the devil's rocks), sacred trees, caves, and sanctuaries built in places of her apparitions, contributing to the continuity of old land spirit veneration practices concealed in this new syncretic form. Meanwhile, the seasonal Marys are related to the days of the most important agrarian traditions and cross-quarter days, echoing older celebrations honoring seasonal shifts and marking dates of important agrarian work.

LAND-BASED MARYS

Every region and culture has its ways of marking spots where the *genius loci* (spirits of place) have been present and revered. In Poland, areas associated with genius loci activity were commonly situated at the crossroads, or recognized in rock formations, sacred springs, hills, and trees. After Christianization, such places were syncretized with folkloric Marys, figures of saints, or local devils. Therefore, while the original names of the spirits may have been lost to time, the sacred places themselves remained important and tended to by local communities, primarily expressed in the folkloric cult of Mary.

Kapliczki: Wayside Shrines

Wayside or crossroads shrines dedicated to Marys or saints are a common sight across Poland, especially in rural areas and on wild trails, but they are also regularly incorporated into urban environments. Some resemble small wooden birdhouses attached to trees in the wild, usually holding a figurine of Mary, along with rosaries, prayer cards, stones, and offerings from the folk. Such a tree hosting a shrine of Mary is considered holy—reminiscent of the pre-Christian wooden cult pillars dedicated to deities or ancestors— and forbidden from being cut down. Other shrines may be deliberately built structures of stone, featuring a larger statue of Mary inside the shrine, decorated with multicolored ribbons and flowers. When paying attention, one can notice how local wayside shrines continue to be frequented by members of the local community, with fresh votive candles regularly lit at their base, and new offerings of flowers or rosaries being hung at Mary's hands. The shrine Marys often have a name unique to the place where the shrine stands, such as one of my personal favorites: *Matka Boska Izerska* (Our Lady of Izery Mountains), who stands on the wayside of a mountain trail, and whose prayer touches upon themes of blessing and protecting the place, its nature, animals, and pilgrims.

Kamienie Maryjne: Mary's Rocks

Sacred rocks are often geologically classed as *"glacial erratics"*—massive stones dragged with the long-forgotten Ice Age glaciers, resting far from their native place, thus appearing alien and seemingly out of place when compared with the landscape around them. For such a rock to have been accepted as holy, it needed to be naturally marked with imprints interpreted as feet, knees, hands, shoes, spurs, and other marks proving the presence of a spirit. Local communities revere the rocks as sacred spaces, offering them gifts and continuing to tend to them to this day. As can be expected, every such sacred rock's existence is surrounded by local legends of Mary and her journeys and deeds. Some of them gained fame due to miraculous sightings of Mary or folks being cured by them. Thus, chapels and sanctuaries were built nearby to accommodate the increasing number of pilgrims. In contrast to the Mary rocks, very similar rocks across Poland are classed as Devil's rocks—these are often naturally marked with what appears to be claws or other unusual "unholy" signs—equally surrounded by legends and folk stories of devilish deeds. While the Devil's rocks are feared rather than revered by the common folk, some were approached by witches and sorcerers alike. Out of the 168 documented rocks tied to folk spirituality, approximately 130 have survived in Poland to this day, with the majority associated with Mary, and others with folkloric devils or saints.

Cudowne Źródełka: Miraculous Springs

Sacred water sources are believed to spring forth in places of Mary or saints' apparitions. The water of such springs is believed to possess healing qualities and sometimes other miraculous properties. Often, such springs are places of the old pre-Christian cult of local water spirits, and the water in them, regarded as *Żywa Woda* (Living Water). Many of the folkloric stories surrounding miraculous springs share a similar motive: how the local community was saved from a plague (or other dangers) by the miraculous apparition of Mary or a saint—sometimes they would appear to folks in dreams or visions, other times in person—and how, in the place of the apparition, a spring had been (re)discovered in a dark moment when the community needed it most to survive. It is said that there may be over 120 such sacred springs recognized across Poland.

Święte Góry: Sacred Hills

Sacred hills were originally sites of pagan cults, dedicated to local deities and spirits, some of which have been thoroughly documented to have possessed remains of cult walls, offertory mounds, and simple ritual items and dishes. As the cult of Mary gained prominence in medieval times and old places of land worship were transformed into places of Marian cult, the number of Marian sanctuaries grew exponentially, reaching a peak around the seventeenth and eighteenth centuries, with over a thousand established locations of Marian cult at that time. While not all of these were sacred hills, the most revered ones were indeed built on hills known for older worship, thus retaining their original status as holy mountains, places of mass pilgrimage, and hubs of miracles and apparitions of Mary. The most prominent ones standing to this day include the Black Madonna of Częstochowa and Our Lady of Kalwaria (or Our Crying Lady).

Święte Drzewa: Sacred Trees

Folk Marys were notorious for apparitions in forests and trees, echoing the old cult of trees and sacred groves, so prominent in Slavic pre-Christian traditions. An example of this is the sanctuary in *Święta Lipka* (Sacred Linden), dating back to the fourteenth century and remaining one of the most important places of Marian cult to this day. There, Mary apparitions took place in a linden tree until a chapel and then a larger sanctuary were built on the spot, with countless pilgrims visiting the place for healing and blessings over the centuries. The Mary-related cult of trees is still alive to this day, with the latest apparition occurring in 2023 in Parczew, where the face of Mary was said to appear in the bark of an old red oak. While most people consider it a hoax, the apparition attracted pilgrims and folks praying *en masse* to the tree nonetheless, echoing the ancestral instinct of the folk towards revering the land.

Rośliny Maryjne: Plants of Mary

Other than the genius loci aspects of Mary, we also recognize plants dedicated to her, many of which, incidentally, bloom in May (the month of Mary) and are used in folk practices. Some of these plants include:

- **Rose:** Related to Mary as Rosa Mystica
- **Daisy:** Believed to have been created from Mary's tears
- **Mullein:** Mary's braids
- **St. John's wort:** Mary's blood
- **Greater celandine:** Hand of Mary
- **Marsh gentian:** Mary's dresses or Mary's fingers
- **Common toadflax:** Mary's shoes
- **Milk thistle:** Mary's thistle
- **Carlina thistle:** Mary's thistle
- **Wild teasel:** Mary's brush
- **Shepherd's purse:** Mary's purse
- **Yellow loosestrife:** Mary's pears
- **Southernwood:** Mary's tree

There are nearly a hundred plants that we know of that are related to Mary, either through their properties, through their folkloric names, or specific folk legends telling stories of Mary's life and how she created these plants. Interestingly, many of the plants dedicated to Mary are also known from folklore for their connection with other spirits and deities; for example, most thistles are also related to the Devil, mullein is the herb of goddess Dziewanna, and so on. The syncretism is apparent—the plants that have been known for their healing or magical properties, and often associated with specific nature spirits or deities became syncretized with Mary, allowing folk to continue benefiting from their medicine without being accused of heresy.

SEASONAL MARYS

Unlike the land-based Marys who represent the genius loci of old, seasonal Marys stand for old patron goddesses of the agrarian cycles, seasonal shifts, atmospheric phenomena, as well as various creatures and plants. They appear to wield larger forces of transformation, begin and end cycles, and tend to the Earth and local communities.

Matka Boska Gromniczna (Our Lady of Gromnica, February 2)

Our Lady of *Gromnica* (Thunder Candle) is a folkloric Mary celebrated at the cross-quarter day marking the very middle of wintertime. Her other folkloric names include *Matka Boska Wilcza* (Our Lady of Wolves) or *Matka*

Boska Niedźwiedzia (Our Lady of Bears). According to folk stories, Our Lady oversees winter grains and guards human dwellings by illuminating them with the light of the blessed thunder candle at this darkest time of midwinter, instilling hope and reminding folks to take things slow. As Our Lady of Wolves, she's portrayed with a fiery sword, surrounded by wolves. Legends say that, during this time of year, Our Lady can be seen walking through the forests and tending to wild animals who may struggle with the snow and frost, especially protecting wolves from being hunted down by humans by hiding them inside her cloak—very reminiscent of Dziewanna, the goddess of wilderness and non-cultivated lands.

The thunder candle made of beeswax, sometimes poured onto a mullein stem (incidentally, also called dziewanna), bestows protection upon the household and all its inhabitants, possesses healing qualities, and symbolizes light, hope, and renewal of life. In folk beliefs, she accompanies people in passing away, "leading the dead through the gate"— echoing the psychopomp duties of Marzanna. This is why people nearing their death are often given Gromnica candles to hold in their hands, to lead their souls beyond.

Matka Boska Roztworna (Our Lady of Openings, March 25)

According to Catholic faith, the Annunciation is the day that celebrates Our Lady discovering new life growing within her. However, in Polish folkloric tradition, it has been syncretized with traditions surrounding the coming of spring and the equinox. The name *Matka Boska Roztworna* (Our Lady of Openings) comes from the belief that, around this time, Our Lady would wake up the Earth and open her up in preparation for receiving new seeds in spring. Alternatively known as *Matka Boska Strumienna* (Our Lady of Streams)—coming from the belief that Our Lady helps unfreeze streams and release the lifegiving waters to sustain new life—as well as *Matka Boska Zagrzewna* (Our Lady of Warmth)—because she orders the sun to shine brighter, thus warming up the soil in preparation for the new vegetative cycle. On this day, Our Lady is venerated as the patroness and creatrix of all new life, waking all creation up from winter slumber and entering into the joyful spring, echoing the symbolism familiar from older, pre-Christian fertility cults. Her familiar animal is the stork, a bird revered by the West Slavs as a herald of spring, fertility, and abundance.

Matka Boska Jagodna (Our Lady of Berries, July 2)

Several versions of folk legends surround Our Lady of Berries, but the base motifs remain consistent. According to lore, on July 2, Mother Mary roams the forests and gathers berries to feed the souls of deceased children. Some legends say that Mary, who is pregnant with Jesus at this time, gathers the fruits to nourish herself so that her baby grows strong. Because of this, one should refrain from picking berries until this day to give way for Mary to gather as much as she needs for herself and the children's souls first.

On this day, mothers who miscarried or who suffered the loss of a child are especially looked after by Mary, as they pray to her for solace and healing from the depths of their grief. It is believed that Mary knows of and understands their sorrow and despair, and that is why she continues to feed and look after the souls of deceased children in their mothers' stead.

Matka Boska Zielna (Our Lady of Herbs, August 15)

On August 15, also known as Assumption Day (in Catholicism) or The Dormition of the Mother of God (in Eastern Orthodox), Mother Mary falls asleep and is taken into the heavens. In folkloric tradition, Our Lady of Herbs is associated with the magical and healing properties of plants, believed to be at their peak at this time of year. In the morning, we harvest bouquets of herbs, which are then blessed and kept in bundles or bouquets for later use in magical and healing practices. As the plants are harvested, the spirit inhabiting them is believed to be gathered with them for safekeeping and protection during the dark half of the year. Some believe it to be the spirit of an agrarian goddess such as Marzanna, others believe it is the spirit of the plants, or Mother Mary.

Matka Boska Siewna (Our Lady of Sowing, September 8)

Our Lady of Sowing is a patroness of the winter grains that are sown around this time. In folk wisdom, both grains and Mary are the primary symbols of fertility, life, and sustenance—physical and spiritual alike. After all, grain is the primary ingredient for bread, containing the holy spirit of the land, which later merged with the symbolism of the Eucharist. Our Lady of Sowing watches over this process from the very conception—the sowing of the seeds, through the growth of the plants, to its final stages in the baking and partaking in bread as a life-sustaining substance. As the grains are sown, Our Lady is also born. After all, September 8 is also Our Lady's birthday.

CULT OF MARY

The folkloric cult of Our Lady is alive and well to this day. Present-day devotees of Mary attend regular pilgrimages to Marian sanctuaries located at sacred sites, such as the famous *Jasna Góra* (Luminous Mountain Sanctuary) in Częstochowa. On Marian feast days, as well as in May (Marian month), local communities gather at local wayside shrines to decorate them with fresh flowers, pray, and sing together.

Catholic Marian devotees usually also have a humble shrine set up in the household, consisting of icons, prayer cards, a statue of Mary, and a selection of relics, such as Mary-shaped bottles with holy water, reliquaries with soil from the holy land, and rosaries from various places of pilgrimage. Votive candles, similar to Gromnica, are traditionally dedicated to Mary and lit during prayer of novenas, feast days and celebrations. Blessed bouquets, such as the one acquired on Our Lady of Herbs (August 15) are customarily kept on a Marian shrine, as well. Such shrines are reminiscent of the *święty kąt* (sacred corner) of old—a place in the household where offerings were given to the family spirits and the ancestors. Some modern folk practitioners who work with Mary often include the Marian shrine in their shrine for ancestors and household spirits, honoring the fact that most of their recent ancestors were Marian devotees themselves.

THE ROSARY

In the folk Catholic cult of Mary, the rosary is the most popular form of prayer, especially among women. For petitioning Mary, the rosary is used either as an everyday prayer routine, or in novenas, which are prolonged prayer routines in sets of nine (days, weeks, months, etc.), usually leading up to an important feast day corresponding to the petition. Another form is known as *koronki* (chaplets), which either utilize the rosary itself or prayer beads like the rosary, created for specific types of prayers dedicated to saints (for example, St. Michael) or aspects of Mary (like Our Lady of Seven Sorrows). If you're a practitioner of folk magic, you're probably aware of the use of Psalms in witchcraft—reciting specific psalms for specific outcomes. One could perceive the rosary similarly, except the timing, structure, and prayers used are chosen by the practitioner based on petition/need, instead of already prescribed for specific purposes like the Psalms. Many of the novenas or prayers are surrounded by a deep lore of miracles and aid in the most hopeless of situations, making it an accessible last-resort tool for folk who otherwise can't count on anybody else, like many of our ancestors, especially those from the lower class and deep rural environments.

The rosary as an item is also surrounded by folklore, generally believed to possess protective qualities and to repel all evil. Some believe that you should always carry a rosary with you, just in case something happens and you need protection. For example, in Polish highlander folk magic, it was believed that the rosary could aid one in protection from strong winds. The highlanders believed that strong winds and mountain gales arise when a witch or sorcerer dies. Alternatively, such winds may arise because of devils dancing. Gusts of such winds bring misfortune and illness. Therefore, to protect oneself from the effects of the winds, one should carry a rosary in one's pocket when leaving the house. Additionally, for good measure, one should spit thrice while whispering Hail Mary or saying the name of *białe ziele* (white herb), which is a folk name for garlic.

Since purchasing a rosary wasn't accessible for most village folk back in the day, there were plants that the rosary would traditionally be made from at home. One such plant is *Kłokoczka południowa* (European bladdernut, *Staphylea pinnata L.).* Its tear-shaped, brown and shiny seeds make the perfect rosary beads. The tree, or rather, bush's folk name is *drzewo różańcowe* (rosary tree), and it is currently among endangered species in Poland. The plant is surrounded by deep folklore and almost an aura of veneration. It is hard to say whether it is because of its connection to the rosary, or the other way around. According to folk beliefs, those who make beads out of their seeds and carry them will be protected from thunder and all witchcraft. It was also believed that the devil is afraid of this wood and flees from it, and that any evil forces are horrified by this bush. This would explain why the wood of this bush was also used to make little crosses that were hung at home for protection. Other than bladdernut, rosaries could also be made from rowan berries, rose hips, and various nuts.

To this day, folk Catholics still acquire rosaries from places of pilgrimage. Oftentimes, certain holy places carry unique rosaries, with reliquaries, with images of their specific miraculous figures, with a grain of soil from a holy place, or a drop of water from a holy spring. Even though it doesn't seem like much, such customs echo older traditions related to venerating local land spirits and making pilgrimages to places of cult, miracles, and worship.

Prayer to Our Lady of Thunder Candle

"Matko Najświętsza,
Pani Gromniczna!
Przed Twym obliczem,
przy świetle gromnicy,
Ciebie wzywamy.
Pod Twoją obronę się uciekamy!
Czuwaj nad nami,
broń nas od złego,
niech Twoja łaska
zawsze nam przyświeca.
Bądź nam Matką i Opiekunką
w życiu i w śmierci godzinie.
Amen."

"Holy Mother,
Our Lady of Thunder Candle!
Before your countenance,
by the light of Gromnica,
We call upon you.
We flee to your protection!
Watch over us,
protect us from evil,
may thy grace
always shine upon us.
Be our Mother and Protector
in life and in the hour of our death.
Amen".

Devotional Song *Witaj Jutrzenko* (Hail, Morning Star)

"Witaj, Jutrzenko rano powstająca,
śliczna jak miesiąc, jak słońce świecąca!
Ty świecisz mile światu w Częstochowie,
gdzie czołem biją świata monarchowie.
Tobie koronę z gwiazd dwunastu dano,
świata wszystkiego Panią Cię nazwano;
na Jasnej Górze jaśniejesz nad słońce,
tu lud upada do nóg swej Patronce.
Pocieszycielko ludzi utrapionych,
do Ciebie, Panno, w nędzach niezliczonych
lud się ucieka, prosi Cię serdecznie,
by z Twej przyczyny życie wiódł bezpiecznie.
Tam Twoje Serce, kędy skarb przebywa,
gdzie stół królewski obraz Twój nakrywa;
niech odrobiny z niego nam spadają,
Twoi synowie głodu niech nie znają.
Otwórz swój skarbiec, rozdziel nam swe dary,
któreś dawała synom tu bez miary;
niechaj doznają dziatki Twojej mocy,
strzeż nas, o Pani, we dnie jak i w nocy."

"Hail, Morning Star rising in the morning,
beautiful as the moon, shining like the sun!
You shine pleasantly to the world in Częstochowa,
where the monarchs of the world bow their heads.
A crown of twelve stars was given to you,
you were called the Lady of the whole world;
on Luminous Mountain you shine above the sun,
here the people fall at the feet of their Patroness.
Consoler of the afflicted,
to you, Virgin, in countless miseries
the people flee, beseech you heartily,

that through your intercession they may lead a safe life.
There your heart, where the treasure dwells,
where your image covers the royal table;
let crumbs fall from it for us,
let your sons not know hunger.
Open your treasury, distribute to us your gifts,
which you gave to your sons without measure;
let the children experience your power,
guard us, O Lady, day and night."

Pod Twoją Obronę/Beneath Thy Protection

"Pod Twoją obronę uciekamy się,
święta Boża Rodzicielko,
naszymi prośbami racz nie gardzić
w potrzebach naszych,
ale od wszelakich złych przygód
racz nas zawsze wybawiać,
Panno chwalebna i błogosławiona.
[O Pani nasza,
Orędowniczko nasza,
Pośredniczko nasza,
Pocieszycielko nasza.]"

"We fly to thy protection,
Holy Mother of God;
Do not despise our petitions
in our necessities,
but deliver us always
from all dangers,
O Glorious and Blessed Virgin.
[O Our Lady,
Our Advocate,
Our Mediatrix,
Our Comfort.]"

Our Lady of Herbs Modern Novena Prayer (fragment)

"Zielna Matko Boża,
Opiekunko żniw, Duszo zboża,
Ty, która kładziesz do snu duchy roślin
I śnisz wraz z nimi w fałdach ziemi,
Pani dzierżąca sierp i widły,
Matko pracująca w pocie czoła,
Ty, która znasz znój i cierpienie,
Objawiasz się w liściu i korzeniu
Ku pokrzepieniu, ku uleczeniu,
Zielarko, Lekarko dusz, Mądra Babo,
Nosząca nasiona wichrem przez łąki,
Błogosławiąca nas ranną rosą i mgłą,
Ziemna Mateczko przekochana!
Usłysz moje serce zwrócone ku Tobie,
Ofiarujące modlitwę niczym bukiet polnych kwiatów.
Sierpem swym wytnij tam gdzie boli,
Polną apteką uleczaj rany.
Widłami przegoń wrogie moce
I ziemią sypnij im w zęby i oczy.
Pochwyć z wiatru szept mej modlitwy
I zanieś ku spełnieniu."

"Our Lady of Herbs,
Guardian of harvest, Soul of grain
You who lulls plant spirits to sleep
And dreams beside them in folds of the earth.
Wielder of sickle and pitchfork,
Mother who labors with sweat on Her brow
And knows the weight of toil and sorrow,
You reveal Yourself in leaf and root
To soothe, to mend, to make whole
Herbalist, Midwife of souls, Wise Old Mother,
Scattering seeds on the wind across meadows,
Blessing us with morning dew and mist,

Earthen Mother, so deeply loved!
Hear my heart's plea as I turn to You,
Offering my prayer like a bundle of herbs.
With your sickle, cut out where it hurts,
Heal wounds with medicine of the land.
With your pitchfork, drive out wicked powers
And fling soil into their teeth and eyes.
Catch the whisper of my prayer on the wind,
And carry it into becoming."

PART FIVE

AGRARIAN TRADITIONS AND POLISH FOLKLORIC YEAR

CHAPTER TWENTY
FOLKLORE OF DAILY CYCLES

TIMES OF DAY AS REPRESENTATIONS OF A GREATER CYCLE

Most of my pre-industrial ancestors came from Polish peasants—farmers and field workers who spent large chunks of their days engaging in physical labor on the land around them. The folklore and folk traditions that we know today mostly survive thanks to the peasants, whose lives were largely dependent on taboos and rules of sustaining right relations with the land, the seasons, and the unpredictable forces of nature. All natural cycles played a crucial role in how they organized their work and family life, how and when they celebrated, and how they planned for the future. The world was believed to be organized in triads—the three worlds (upper *Jawia,* middle *Prawia,* and lower *Nawia)*, the three stages of life (birth, life, and death), the three ages of the moon (young, full, and old), and so on.

Our ancestors did not perceive time as linear, but rather as cyclical, moving in repeating spirals. The most intimately experienced and relatively longest cycles directly observed by our ancestors were the cycles of their own lives, and the lives of the members of their *Ród* (family bloodline): birth, life, and death. On a natural macro scale, they found these cycles reflected in the four seasons and the celestial tides that corresponded with them on an annual basis: spring as birth, summer as life, autumn as death, and winter as a period of regeneration and gestation leading up to rebirth. Smaller-scale cycles were observed monthly with the lunar phases: The new moon was perceived as youth, the full moon as an adult, the waning moon as an elder, and the dark moon as a period spent in the otherworlds, leading up to rebirth (similarly to winter). In fact, the moon was believed to be so closely related to humans that it is very likely due to the observances of the lunar cycles that the Slavs developed a belief in rebirth after death. The young moon was most often addressed and prayed to for health and good luck, while the old moon was generally avoided, believed to be old and sick, capable of bringing illnesses and misfortune upon humans. By extension, times of day—morning, day, evening, and night—were also perceived as even smaller scale representations of the same natural cycles of birth, life, death, and rebirth, reflected in the movement of the sun across the sky. Once we grasp this, it becomes easier to understand the origins of certain folk practices and the mindset that accompanied them.

PORANEK: GREETING THE DAY

Similar to most cultures rooted in animism, the Slavs were taught to commune and communicate with the world around them, which also included daily greetings of natural phenomena, places, features of the land, as well as celestial bodies, and even times of day. You may have heard of practices such as "salutation of the sun," "adoration of the sun," "greeting the moon," and "drawing down the moon," present both in traditional cultures, as well as adapted into Western occult traditions. Such traditions can be traced back to the animistic roots, when the human species still paid attention to cultivating positive relationships with other than human persons and natural phenomena around them.

Our ancestors believed that you should do most of the work starting in the early morning hours until midday. Then, during midday, it was forbidden to work. Afternoons were again safe to work, until the sun began to set once more, leading to evenings, yet again taboo in terms of work. Ideally, everyone had to be back home at dusk.

As is evident, times of day corresponded heavily with the larger cycles mentioned earlier. Time was precious, and none of it was wasted. But "waste" wasn't perceived the same way we see it today, where unnatural amounts of "productivity" are required of us all year round, irrespective of the natural cycles that still influence our functioning just as much as they did our ancestors, whether we choose to see it or not. Our forebears understood that there are periods of intense work, intertwined with periods of rest and withdrawal, when other beings emerged from their dwellings and completed their tasks, without humans getting in their way. Everything had to be done in accordance with the natural order of things.

In terms of morning traditions and rituals, we know that our forebears would usually wake up early in the morning with the rooster. They took their time to pray to and greet *Jutrzenka* (dawn), welcome the morning sun, or wash their faces in morning dew—all to ensure a good day of work ahead. They would then work until noon. While working, they had to remember that they must never turn their back toward the sun while reaping the grain, as it was considered disrespectful to turn away from the force that guides our lives. Work in the field was always conducted with the sun, from East to West. Working with the Sun ensured that the work was properly done, as the journey of the sun in the sky dictates the order of everything in life, thus making East the direction where everything begins and West where everything ends.

POŁUDNIE: MIDDAY TABOOS

According to tradition, all field work had to be conducted during the day, with the exclusion of midday. At noon, with the sun in its zenith, field workers would take a mandatory break to rest and eat their lunch. It was believed that dangerous demons, such as *południce* and *płanetnicy* (demons responsible for atmospheric phenomena), appear in open fields at noon, and so working during this time was dangerous and could result in death.

On a practical, mundane level, working in the fields at midday could result in a heat stroke, rendering one unable to work, and thus making labor much more difficult for the entire community. The taboos relating to dangerous demons hunting people down at midday are a direct reflection of this. While it might not seem like a big deal from the perspective of a modern person, pre-industrial life was much more community-focused, and the well-being of one could severely impact the well-being of all. There was no space for selfishness. Therefore, while the midday demons roamed free in the fields, folks had no choice but to utilize this time for a lunch break. They would sit in the shade of trees or barns to consume their daily rations, usually consisting of a piece of bread and some seasonal plants or fruit, accompanied by legumes, butter, or cottage cheese on occasion. Those who were wealthier could afford a slightly more wholesome meal, perhaps even a piece of dried meat.

Each meal was blessed and thanked for as food was considered a blessing and privilege. Every piece of bread would be marked with the sign of a cross before cutting, and no crumbs could be wasted. Some folk beliefs go so far as to believe that, if you drop a crumb into honey, it will transform into an ant. This deep reverence for bread remained especially prominent in Polish folkloric culture, as grains had been the main product from farming these lands for centuries. Some would say that bread itself was an object of cult and reverence, similar to that of the sun, with countless stories, prayers, spells, taboos, and beliefs surrounding it. Some versions of the Slavic folkloric ontological myths describe how God shaped humans from bread dough, thus equating bread with the primary matter of creation.

This implies—at least in the folkloric perception of the world, which operates on sympathetic connections—that bread possesses magical powers, which can be used to heal, harm, and otherwise impact the living who were created from it. The countless healing spells, prayers, taboos, and magical formulas that utilize bread remain a testament to its prominent use for magical purposes.

The midday sun was perceived as a representation of the highest good, the sacred guide in the skies, the great parent who sustains life. To this day, the sun is still commonly called upon as a witness of oaths and promises. Folk would swear upon the sun: "*Jak mi słońce na niebie!*" or [X is as true] "as the Sun is in the sky!"

While the sun was generally perceived as a benevolent, life-sustaining, and affirming force, the merciless aspects of fiery heat, droughts, heat strokes, and conflagration were taken equally, if not more seriously. The sun's lethal powers were, however, believed to be primarily directed against those who showed disrespect or failed to display appreciation, which is directly represented in the most common taboos surrounding our relationship with the sun. Other than the practice of showing respect by always working the fields facing the sun (working from East to West), we know of other such taboos regarding the midday sun, existing outside of the agrarian context. It was considered taboo to:

- Throw away trash in the direction of the sun, as it was believed that it could accidentally get into God's eyes.
- Point a finger at the sun for similar reasons as above.
- Urinate or spit facing the sun, as this was considered a great offense.
- Leave dead animals beneath the scorching sun, especially adder snakes, which were embodiments of household spirits and regarded as holy themselves.
- Say profanities and use filthy language in the presence of the sun.

WIECZÓR: EVENING FRIGHTS

Evening is a time of liminality—an in-between state of transition from light to darkness and *vice versa.* According to folklore, humans are only truly safe during the sunlit hours of the day. As soon as the sun begins to set, strange and untamed forces begin to emerge from their places of dwelling. Some are drawn to the darkness itself, others feeding off the moonlight (such as werewolves and *utopce*). A plethora of demons, vampires, mares, devils, ghosts of the dead, and night-dwelling spirits begin their regular nightly activities. Many of the most terrifying *upiory* (phantoms, ghouls) were believed to be spirits of humans who died unusual or premature deaths, such as miscarried fetuses, children who died from fatal accidents, young lads and girls who died from a broken heart, drowned women, and especially victims of suicide. They were often considered to be more dangerous than other types of spirits—those that come from the land—because their unfair deaths could've made it impossible for their souls to move on, trapping them in their undead bodies and making them vengeful, hungry for human flesh and blood, clingy, or otherwise threatening.

Those who are caught outdoors after dark and unlucky enough to encounter a spirit like that, end up being the ones spoken of in local legends as those who disappeared and were never seen again—be they devoured by a hungry ghoul or led to their death in the swamps by will-o'-the-wisps.

It was also absolutely forbidden to trade or borrow certain things after dark. Folks who were reckless enough to borrow money, bread, milk, cheese, and fire embers in the evening or at night would doom themselves and their homestead to misfortune and the diminishing of resources from their property. Evenings and nights were certainly not the best time to prove that one is a good neighbor.

However, not all individuals were subject to the usual rules of traditional societies. Those living on the fringes of their communities or brave enough to break taboos in times of need knew how to take advantage of the evening hours for purposes of committing sorcerous deeds, making pacts, and sometimes engaging in crime.

While the regular, godly folk would spend their evenings locked up indoors, sharing supper with the family and saying prayers for protection from malicious and wild forces, witches, criminals, and those desperate for aid from the spirits would engage in their cunning routines. They would venture to the edge of the forest, crossroads, graveyards, openings of caves, sacred wells, or roots of old elder trees to make pacts, speak *zamawiania*, lay offerings, bury spells, or otherwise petition the forces of these liminal places for all kinds of deeds. More experienced witches would also be gathering graveyard dirt or crossroads dirt for use in spells of bane and healing. This all took place at the liminal time of the evenings due to the firm belief that all the spirits and supernatural powers were growing in strength at this time. Thus it was both easier for humans to perceive them and speak with them, as well as easier for the spirits to enact their will.

Similar taboos to those observed around evening time, albeit intensified, were also observed during sun and moon eclipses. Folks believed that eclipses were anomalies caused by their depravity and wrongdoings, sent upon them as punishment and a sign to right their wrongs. Folks expected that an eclipse heralded the coming of illness, death, destruction of property, and other misfortunes. They believed that the eclipse of the sun happened because the star was swallowed whole by a dragon or other evil forces, depending on the region. During an eclipse, folks would lock their cattle and other animals in barns, cover up wells and water sources, and hide indoors. The only way to save the sun and make the demons spit it back out was by continuous zealous prayer.

Should a modern witch wish to take advantage of the evening time for their unspoken deeds in accordance with the Polish tradition, it is wise to keep in mind that in the dark, one is subject to the mercy and favor of spirits more than ever. A wise folk practitioner always moves stealthily in the dark and pays attention to the moon phase, which is the ruler of all magic performed after sunset.

FOLK CORRESPONDENCES OF DAYS OF THE WEEK

In Western countries where Latin had an impact on the language, names of the days of the week are usually related to planetary correspondences, such as Monday coming from the moon, Saturday from Saturn, etc. In Polish and generally Slavic culture, days of the week are mostly named after their order, which may not be very poetic but rather simple and practical.

- **Sunday/*Niedziela:*** The name comes from *"nie działać"* ("not acting" or "not working") because Sunday was customarily the day of resting and attending church.
- **Monday/*Poniedziałek:*** The name comes from *"po niedzieli"* ("after Sunday").
- **Tuesday/*Wtorek:*** The name comes from *"wtóry"* ("second") because it's the second day after Sunday.
- **Wednesday/*Środa:*** The name comes from *"środek"* ("middle") because it's the middle day of the week.

- **Thursday/*Czwartek:*** The name comes from "*czwarty*" ("fourth") due to Thursday being the fourth day of the week.
- **Friday/*Piątek:*** The name comes from "*piąty*" ("fifth") due to it being the fifth day.
- **Saturday/*Sobota:*** The name comes from "*szabat*" ("sabbath"), which has roots in Judaism and that, in the Bible, God finished creating the world in six days and on the seventh day he rested. In Jewish tradition, this seventh day was Saturday. However, in Polish tradition, it is Sunday.

While in some cultures Sunday is considered the first day of the week, in Polish folk perception, it is Monday that is most often perceived as the first day, and Sunday the last day. This was dictated by common folk's daily lives: peasants who worked from Monday until Saturday and were allowed to rest on Sunday. Just as they rested on Sunday, so they would perceive Sunday as the day on which God also rested. This is a great example of how religion and its dogma are always verified by the lived experience of the folk, and in the end, it is the agrarian cycles that dictate the folk perception of the world, and shape the practices of folk Catholicism.

Similarly to how folk lived by the seasonal cycles and seasonal lore, they would also have beliefs surrounding days of the week, which dictated when it was best to do certain works, when it was best to travel or get married, and when to avoid certain actions. This can prove extremely helpful in timing one's magic workings today, too.

Poniedziałek (Monday)

Monday was generally considered not to be a good day for starting any new work due to it being too close to Sunday, a holy day. It was the best day for proposing marriage, bringing good luck and prosperity for the couple. However, it was not a good day to get married.

Wtorek (Tuesday)

Tuesday was generally considered to be a universally good day. It was the best day to start new work, be productive, and get things done.

Środa (Wednesday)

Because Wednesday is the day dedicated to Our Lady, it was traditionally regarded as a favorable day for undertaking important endeavors. It was the best day for moving house if you're a people person as it will bring good luck and a lot of guests into your home. Proposing marriage on Wednesday meant there would be no arguments in the relationship. It is the best day for starting a new business, especially if it's a shop. Wednesday is also the best day for sowing flax. Kids born on Wednesday were believed to be good and hardworking.

Czwartek (Thursday)

Similarly to Tuesday, Thursday was considered to be a good day for all sorts of work. It is the best day for travel. In sources, Thursday was most often identified as the day when witches would fly to the Bald Mountain to feast and do witchcraft. Thus, it is a good day for doing magic, spirit flight, and contacting spirits.

Piątek (Friday)

Friday is the day of fasting and solemnity, in remembrance of the death of Christ. On this day, folks would not eat meat. A Polish folk saying goes: *"W piątek zły początek"* ("Friday is a bad beginning"), as it was generally considered to be an unlucky day. However, Friday is possibly the best day for contacting the dead. It is also considered a good day for witches and devils (especially Good Friday), as it was believed that when Jesus was lying dead in his grave, witches, devils, and all other spirits and demons could roam free.

Sobota (Saturday)

Saturday is a good day to begin and end various works because it is dedicated to Our Lady. It was believed that on Saturday, the sun must always come out from behind the clouds even during the worst weather, because on Saturdays, Our Lady was drying her son's diapers. It is the best day to get married. Same as Wednesday, Saturday is an equally good day for starting a new business, especially if it's a shop. It is also the best day for sowing flax. Kids born on Saturday were also believed to be good and hardworking. It is a good day for moving house,especially for those who'd like to avoid lots of guests. Moving on Saturday brings overall good fortune to the family.

Niedziela (Sunday)

Sunday is a holy day and a day of rest. A Polish folk saying goes: *"Myślał kogut o niedzieli, a w sobotę łeb mu ścieli"* ("The rooster was thinking of Sunday, but they cut off his head on Saturday"), warning against planning too far into the future. Kids born on Sunday were believed to be lazy and superficial (an absolute tragedy for farmer families).

Based on the above folk beliefs and superstitions, folks can apply specific rules and correspondences to their work routines or witchcraft practice. For example, I would consider Thursday to be the best day for practices of spirit flight, trance work, divination, dream work, and other such practices that involve altered states. Friday, being an "unlucky day" to most folk but lucky for "evil witches and devils," could be utilized as the perfect timing for any type of heretical workings and baneful magic, as well as contacting the dead and necromancy. Tuesday and Thursday seem to be generally good days to get work done as they are fairly neutral and productive, with few taboos. Wednesday and Saturday are the perfect days for work related to Our Lady as she outstretches blessings to folks who start new endeavors or make significant steps on this day. I would consider Wednesday and Saturday to be good days for workings of protection, blessing, prosperity, etc. Monday, in my opinion, is a great day for planning ahead but not necessarily for getting things done. And lastly, Sunday should be the day of rest and replenishment.

The above descriptions and correspondences may not have much in common with the more widely utilized Western planetary correspondences; however, they may serve as an additional source of inspiration and knowledge for when workings of a more ancestral nature are considered.

CHAPTER TWENTY-ONE

POLISH FOLKLORIC CALENDAR

Those who are interested in learning about ancestral cultural practices and folk magics often begin their search by exploring a chosen culture's "Wheel of the Year" and seasonal celebrations. Most contemporary practitioners out there are aware of the existence of the Celtic "Wheel of the Year," which seems to have become the mainstream go-to for land-based celebration of the seasons across the globe, with the eight seasonal sabbats that can be engaged with to honor the old traditions. Less often discussed, however, is how the "Wheel of the Year" is a contemporary eclectic construct, partially based on folklore and scarce records of pre-Christian traditions and partially drawn from synthetic reconstructionism of "what could have been" in "ye olde times"—all rooted in the seasons as experienced in the climate of the British Isles, as well as the astronomical solstices and equinoxes. Despite its shaky background, the usefulness of the concept itself is undeniable, and, at this point, it is so widely recognized that pagan practitioners and groups from other cultures have attempted re-creations of similar reconstructionist systems on their native grounds. The Slavs are no exception in this regard; in *Rodnovery* (Slavic native faith), it is customary to organize the seasonal rites around a neo-pagan Slavic equivalent of the "Wheel of the Year."

While the seasonal Wheel system can be a good start for understanding the seasonality of the agrarian traditions and incorporating said traditions of our ancestors into one's practice, it is but a humble fraction of the entirety of what constitutes the Polish Folkloric Year—a system that remains a living tradition to this day, as well as the foundation upon which the modern Wheel has been reconstructed. Therefore, what I would like to present to you is the whole spectrum of what's out there. We shall explore the Polish Folkloric Calendar season by season, and, wherever it is appropriate, it will be noted which celebrations are simultaneously recognized as the neo-pagan ones as well. Although it is impossible to include every single folkloric celebration specific to every region of Poland (indeed, there are plenty of lesser-known local celebrations or their variants), the ones that are most broadly recognized across the country will be detailed. In this way, I hope that you will be equipped with as much of a "full-picture" perspective as possible, including both the older and the newer understandings of Slavic land-based spirituality—and thus will be appropriately geared to make more informed decisions when it comes to celebrating our ancestral traditions yourself.

Keep in mind that the Polish Folkloric Year is rooted in old pre-Christian traditions honoring the agrarian cycles and seasons, as well as the syncretic folk Catholic celebrations of specific feast days dedicated to saints, spirits, and such, which are still widely celebrated in Poland to this day. For readers who may struggle with religious wounds or aversion toward anything remotely Christian, I advise you to approach these celebrations with an open mind. It is crucial to understand that, as our ancestors were slowly Christianized over several centuries, the only organic option for preserving the old traditions and continuing to honor the land and the local spirits was to integrate the surface-level syncretisms with the Catholic faith—to reimagine the land spirits as figures of saints, to build wayside shrines dedicated to folkloric Marys in places of ongoing communion and worship, to consecrate items and herbs for magic and healing in church, and so on. It was not necessarily a quick process, but one that occurred gradually over hundreds of years, as preachers attempted to integrate more and more of the Christian faith into pre-existing beliefs in a way that would make sense for the common folk, and not the other way around.

The syncretisms present in folk magics and traditions are, ultimately, survival mechanisms that helped preserve our traditions and ancestral wisdom and continue to keep them alive to this day. Over the centuries, these beliefs and perceptions became inseparably linked. Today, there is no authentic folk spirituality devoid of these religious syncretisms. Trying to strip them away and sanitize these practices severs the old ties that link us to the very origins of our ancestors' traditions, and the land itself. However, how these syncretisms are applied in one's individual practice is up to the individual. Some may choose to follow a more "godly" path of folk Catholic magic. Others may find themselves thriving in more heretical, taboo, and inverted expressions that only present as "acceptable" on the surface, while deep down they couldn't be further away from monotheisms. Folk magic adapts to all conditions, wherein lies its very survival.

For readers more accustomed to the modern expressions of the craft and thus less familiar with animism and folk magic and their deep rootedness in folkloric and cultural traditions of a people, it may appear confusing as to why a magical practitioner would heed dates of Catholic feast days if they're not religious, or the agrarian cycles of working the land if they're not a farmer. If you are this reader, I ask you to keep in mind that in folk magic, the folkloric year is an expression of the cycles of the Earth, the sun, and the moon as the primary forces to whom a folk practitioner may turn to for guidance and timing one's workings and magical operations. All the materia we work with is heavily dependent on these cycles, and so is the activity of various land spirits and other allies we engage with for aid. Where an average Catholic sees an opportunity for strengthening their faith or perhaps praying to a saint for aid, a folk witch sees correspondences of the saint with specific spirits, materia, and intentions that can be worked in heretical ways, far exceeding what appears to be there on the surface.

CHAPTER TWENTY-TWO

SPRING

The folkloric year begins in spring, which has always been recognized as the true "new year" in Slavic traditions. Due to the agrarian roots of our celebrations, the emphasis is laid upon the seasonal transformations of the land, rather than the astronomical cycles of the sun.

MARZEC: MARCH

March is an unpredictable month. While the days are getting noticeably longer compared to the winter months, the weather doesn't always reflect that. This is why one of the most well-known sayings about March is, "*W marcu jak w garcu*" ("In March it's like in a pot"), meaning that we get a little bit of everything, as if the gods were cooking us a weather soup—we get rain, sun, frost, wind, snow, hail, often drastically changing within a single day.

The name *marzec* is related to the god Mars, but also—closer to home—to the goddess Marzanna, who happens to be a central figure of this month's spring equinox celebrations. There is, however, an older name for marzec, which was in use in Old Polish before the current name took over. *Brzezień*, which is directly related to *brzoza*, the birch tree. In March, birch trees begin to come to life after the winter season, and thus people would usually start collecting birch syrup around this time.

At the beginning of March, we slow down, as if in anticipation of the upcoming bursting forth of life at the spring equinox. This is beautifully signified by the traditions surrounding *Wielki Post* (Lent), which is a movable period of 46 days leading up to Easter.

March Calendarium:

- **46 days before Easter:** *Środa Popielcowa,* Ash Wednesday (movable, usually between February 4 and March 10)
- **46 days before Easter:** *Wielki Post,* Lent (movable, starts usually between February 4 and March 10 and lasts until Easter)
- **March 12:** *Św Grzegorza,* St. Gregory Feast Day
- **March 19:** *Św Józefa,* St. Joseph Feast Day
- **March 19-21:** *Równonoc Wiosenna,* Spring Equinox (movable)
- **March 25:** *Matki Boskiej Roztwornej/Strumiennej,* Our Lady of Openings/of Streams

You will notice above that some of the dates are movable. This means that the exact dates will vary from year to year and are calculated based on lunar cycles, as well as the solstices and equinoxes. As an example, Easter is celebrated on the first Sunday after the first spring full moon, which is the first full moon after the spring equinox. Celebrations such as Ash Wednesday, Lent, Palm Sunday, and Pentecost are then calculated based on the date of Easter.

Środa Popielcowa/Ash Wednesday and Rites of Womanhood

Ash Wednesday used to be referred to as *"Wstępna Środa"* (Preliminary Wednesday) as it marked the entry into Lent—a time of solemnity, penance, and modesty.

The ash that was used to mark people's foreheads traditionally came from burned Easter palms from the previous year. It is especially interesting to consider that these palms were originally made of willow twigs—a tree connected to the dead and grieving, as well as deep healing, in Polish folk medicine and magic. It is reminiscent of the much older practice of sprinkling oneself with ash as a way of marking a period of grief or mourning.

The custom of marking people's foreheads with ash was originally reserved for individuals in the community who were publicly recognized as having deserved penance. It was a way of giving local criminals the opportunity to change their ways and seek betterment. Over time, the custom shifted to include everyone, making space for acts of symbolic penance for personal sins. Priests would usually sprinkle the heads of fathers (head of the family) and give them some ash to take home so that they may mark the rest of their family in the comfort of their home.

Ash Wednesday was also a special day for women, filled with traditional rituals related to womanhood. For example, women would gather in local taverns to perform a traditional dance to enchant a good crop of flax and hemp in the coming season. This folk magic dance involved setting up a stump or a bench in the middle of the room and women jumping through it while chanting spells and songs about the fertility of said plants. In the meantime, men would also perform similar acts for a good crop of oats.

Women would also perform "chasing away the fat" from their kitchens for Lent. This meant getting rid of or thoroughly cleaning all pots and bowls that were previously filled with fatty foods during the *Zapusty* (carnival) period. They would also set up clay pots by the stove filled with leaven for *żur* (sour rye soup).

Finally, Ash Wednesday was a time when older married women would welcome newlywed women into their circle, marking their attainment of the *gospodyni* (matron) role. During such rites of passage, older women would dress up as men and visit all the newlywed women, asking them out for a run to the tavern. After drinks, all gathered women would begin singing traditional songs and orations wishing the new wives all the best, mainly focusing on prosperity, good health, and beautiful children.

Wielki Post/Lent

Wielki Post means "The Great Fast." Our ancestors treated this time very seriously and willingly denied themselves certain things, like alcohol, tobacco, hearty foods (especially meat), music and dance, and even social gatherings of any kind. It was a time of introspection, quiet contemplation of the meaning of life, as well as inner purification in preparation for spring and the resurrection of life all around. One could look at it as an old-school precursor of contemporary "meditation retreats" or the "Depth Year" that's become popular in the past few years. The idea was to truly look inward and examine one's life without the distractions of pleasures. As an old saying goes, "*Polak woli rękę stracić niż złamać post*" ("A Pole would rather lose their hand than break their fast"), which leaves no doubts about how serious it was.

When it comes to food, common folk would completely deny themselves meat, animal fats, sweets, honey, and all dairy products. They would mostly live off of *żur postny* (a type of lent rye soup), potatoes, cabbage (pickled, raw, and cooked), cooked rutabaga, dried fruit, herring, and bread.

Wielki Post lasts for 40–46 days, and precisely in the middle of this solemn period, folks would celebrate *Półpoście* ("Half Fast"). All the peace, seriousness, and silence were put on pause for a day. Young boys would run through the streets with various wooden knockers, clappers, and flappers and make as much noise as physically possible. While it may seem annoying, this custom was welcomed with relief by the young and old alike. After all, it meant that they were already halfway through Lent and happy celebrations were fast approaching.

Świętego Grzegorza/St. Gregory Feast Day (March 12)

St. Gregory is a patron saint of teachers and students. March 12 used to mark the beginning of the school year in rural parish schools. St. Gregory's feast day also marked the date when folks would start releasing their cattle to graze in the open field after a long period of keeping them in the outbuildings overwinter. This is reflected in folk sayings that helped preserve the memory of customary acts, as well as observable weather changes and signs foretelling and determining the agrarian work.

Agrarian sayings for St. Gregory Feast Day:

- *"Na świętego Grzegorza idą rzeki do morza."*
  "On St. Gregory's rivers go to the sea."
- *"Na świętego Grzegorza nie stoi już świnia u gospodarza."*
  "On St. Gregory's, the pig doesn't stand in the sty anymore."
- *"Po świętym Grzegorzu nie paś bydła na zbożu."*
  "After St. Gregory's, stop feeding grain to your cattle."

Świętego Józefa/St. Joseph Feast Day (March 19)

St. Joseph is a patron saint of carpenters, lumberjacks, and families. On this feast day, people would focus on repairing the stork nests in anticipation of their migration back to these lands. Cultivating human-stork relationships is an old tradition, stemming from times when allyship with the natural world was of utmost importance, sacred even. In Polish folklore, all migratory birds represent the souls of our ancestors clad in zoomorphic forms, as well as omens from the spirits. Storks, in particular, are at the forefront of these relationships, even having been invited to spend overwinter in people's houses.

Having storks make a nest on the roof of one's home was considered to be a blessing, which is why folks would repair existing nests, or even go as far as building new nests for storks to use when they return from the "warm lands" for spring. It is taboo to destroy their nests or hurt the birds in any way. Killing a stork was as serious an offense as homicide. A stork is a friend whose presence brings fertility, abundance, luck, and blessings to the home. Both humans and farm animals were well acquainted with "their" storks and treated them well, as if the stork was an incarnation of some deity. But the truth is that people would revere them for who they were—allies and friends.

Agrarian sayings for St. Joseph's Feast Day:

- *"Jak na święty Józef bociek przyleci, to na skrzydłach resztki śniegu przynosi."*
  "If the stork returns on St. Joseph's Day, he will bring leftovers of snow on his wings."
- *"Święty Józef trawę sieje, Najświętsza Panna z niego się śmieje."*
  "St. Joseph sows the grass, Our Lady laughs at him."
- *"Jak na świętego Józefa chmurki, to sadź ziemniaki, gdzie górki; a jak pogoda, to sadź, gdzie woda."*
  "If St. Joseph's Day is cloudy, sow your potatoes on the hills; if it's sunny, sow them near the water."

Równonoc Wiosenna/Spring Equinox

The spring equinox culminates between March 19 and 21, marking the astronomical beginning of spring. In older folk traditions, people didn't have the means to recognize equinoxes as precisely as we do today, which means that the start of spring was often celebrated on set feast days (like March 25), based on moon phases, or based on Lent, the fourth Sunday of Lent, also known as *Laetare, Czarna Niedziela* (Black Sunday) or *Biała Niedziela* (White Sunday). Nowadays, some of the spring welcoming traditions and celebrations occur on the actual equinox, recognized in Polish pagan tradition as Jare Gody.

Jare Gody means "Spring Festivities". It heralds the resurrection of nature, times of joy, light, and new vitality. The sun finally wins over darkness, bringing us much-needed warmth, light, and fresh air after a long, dark winter.

In common folk tradition, we celebrate *pierwszy dzień wiosny* (the first day of spring) with a series of rituals and magical acts focused on banishing winter and calling in spring. The most important tradition that remains broadly recognized and celebrated is the ritual of burning and drowning of the effigy of Marzanna.

To this day, especially in rural Poland, communities create human-sized Marzanna effigies made of straw, dressed up to imitate the goddess. The effigy is created on a long stick, dressed in human clothes (preferably of natural fabrics), and adorned with colorful ribbons, flower wreaths, and such. After the effigy is created, it is then paraded through the village in a colorful and loud procession culminating in stripping the effigy, setting it on fire and, finally, drowning it in a river. This ritual is older than most folk can remember (stemming from pre-Christian traditions) and believed to symbolize the banishing of winter, and with it, all the illness, death, and bad luck accumulated over the dark half of the year. Alternatives to this ritual include tearing the effigy made of straw on the fields, thus scattering the old seeds from last year's season and marking the beginning of a new agrarian cycle.

Matki Boskiej Roztwornej/Matki Boskiej Strumiennej (March 25)

March 25 marks the celebration of the Annunciation *(Zwiastowanie Pańskie)* in Catholicism. However, in Polish folk tradition, it is better known as *Matki Boskiej Roztwornej* (Our Lady of Openings), *Matki Boskiej Strumiennej* (Our Lady of Streams), or sometimes also *Matki Boskiej Zagrzewnej* (Our Lady of Warmth), regarded as the older date of the first day of spring festivities.

The many names or epithets of Our Lady recognized at this time of year reflect her stewardship over the agrarian cycles of vegetation, related to preparing the earth to receive new seeds, unfreezing rivers and other water reservoirs across the land to moisten it, as well as encouraging the sun to grow in power, thus blessing all plant matter with the best conditions for healthy, abundant growth.

In folk tradition, Annunciation is not only the day when Our Lady finds out that there's new life growing within her, but She also becomes a patroness and creatrix of all new life. She wakes all creation from winter slumber and enters into the joyful spring, which bears symbolism familiar from the pre-Christian rites of spring equinox. The most anticipated omen of new life to occur on this day was the storks returning from the "warm lands" of Wyraj, which explains why just a few days prior (on St. Joseph's feast day), everyone would be repairing their nests. This may also help explain why storks became the "birds who bring children" in folk belief, combining themes of fertility with the blessing-bearing powers of storks.

To convince the returning storks to nest on one's property, people would bake special offering cakes shaped like a stork's foot. Other shapes of cakes would also be baked, mainly in the shapes of various agricultural tools like plows and harrows. Such cakes would then be placed in the storks' nests or inside the thatch of the roof as offerings, to attract prosperity and ensure the success of early spring field works. Alternatively, when people saw storks flying above their homes, they would come outside carrying the stork foot cakes high up and calling, *"bocian! bocian!"* ("stork! stork!"), thus inviting the storks to nest on their property.

KWIECIEŃ: APRIL

April is still a somewhat unpredictable month weather-wise. This is reflected in folk sayings about this month, such as, *"Kwiecień-plecień poprzeplata trochę zimy, trochę lata"* ("April-weaver weaves in a little winter and a little summer"), which is a very accurate description of typical Polish April weather. Some days it's hot and sunny, so one can venture outside without a jacket, and then the next day it could be sub-zero temperatures and snowing.

The name *kwiecień* comes from *kwiaty* (flowers), which signifies that the first flowers begin to bloom this month. However, in the past, April also had two older names, *łżykwiat* (lying flower) or *zwodzikwiat* (deceiving flower), warning that the first blooms shouldn't fool us, because winter weather is still lurking around the corner.

Depending on the moon phases, April is often the month where all of the folk celebrations of Easter and welcoming spring culminate, followed by the tradition of *Dziady Wiosenne* (Spring Forefathers). Most of April's holy days are movable, which means that the exact dates change from year to year. Easter is calculated based on the lunar cycles. Namely, it always falls on the Sunday after the full moon that occurs on or after the spring equinox. If the full moon falls on a Sunday, then Easter is the next Sunday.

April Calendarium

- **April 1:** *Prima Aprilis*
- **Sunday before Easter:** *Niedziela Wierzbowa,* Palm Sunday (movable)
- **Between Palm Sunday and Easter:** *Wielki Tydzień,* Holy Week (movable)
- **First Sunday after the first spring full moon:** *Wielkanoc,* Easter (movable)
- **Monday after Easter:** *Śmigus Dyngus,* Wet Monday (movable)
- **First Thursday after Easter:** *Dziady Wiosenne,* Spring Forefathers (movable)
- **April 23/24:** *Świętego Jerzego* (St. George Feast Day)

Prima Aprilis (April 1)

The custom of pranking people on April 1 arrived in Poland around the sixteenth century and initially was only picked up by the upper class. Over time, however, superstitions concerning this date arose among the common folk. It was (and often still is) believed that one shouldn't do anything serious on this day. No serious business should be conducted, no marriages, no lending money, etc. There are even historical examples of serious political deals having their date changed to March 31, just so that Prima Aprilis doesn't appear on official documents, thus making a mockery of them.

Nowadays, folks still avoid doing anything important on this day and don't accept anything they're told at face value because chances are they're being pranked. It's generally advised not to take anything seriously and enjoy the silly fun of this day.

Niedziela Wierzbowa/Willow Sunday

In Polish folk tradition, Palm Sunday has a few names: *Niedziela Wierzbowa* (Willow Sunday), *Niedziela Kwiatowa* (Flower Sunday), and *Niedziela Palmowa* (Palm Sunday). While the custom of carrying palm leaves is directly connected with the Christian story of Jesus being welcomed into Jerusalem, similar customs predating Christianity have been practiced by our ancestors long before Easter was known in our culture. Around this time of year, folk would carry entire trees known as *wiechy* in a colorful procession around the village. The young tree was usually cut down by a group of boys the night before the celebration, which was a kind of test of skill and strength. Once cut down, the tree had to be dressed with specific plants with magical properties. It was all part of a traditional ritual enacted to bestow blessings of prosperity and ward off evil from the area.

Over time, these big trees were gradually replaced by smaller "palms," usually a handful of willow sprigs with *bazie kotki* (catkins). Willow trees, because of their magical ability to grow easily anywhere, even from a broken twig, have always been a symbol of vitality, life force, and rebirth. Other than willow, sprigs of boxwood and periwinkles, were also traditionally added to the "palm."

Naturally, many regions of Poland have their traditional versions of palms, which differ from the one described above. For example, in Kurpie, they'd be made of tall pine sticks, wrapped in green sprigs and decorated with willow catkins, as well as flowers and ribbons made of colorful crepe paper. Each color and type of decoration had its traditional meanings:

- **Green:** Hope
- **Violet:** Anticipation
- **Red:** Love
- **Yellow:** Rebirth
- **Loose flowing ribbons:** Connection between heaven and Earth

Interestingly, while the common folk were preoccupied with consecrating their palms in church, it was believed that the folkloric devil was also present at the Willow Sunday mass. This meant that the treasures he kept buried in the fields were left unguarded. Those brave enough to risk their lives, would skip church and instead venture out there to look for hidden treasure. Such riches could be identified by a flaming will-o'-the-wisp hovering above the treasure. In order to retrieve it, one should approach the place and throw a piece of clothing or accessories at it, such as a ring, scarf, hat, belt, shoes, coat—thus extinguishing the flame, which would allow for digging. The piece of wardrobe used would determine how deep one had to dig for the treasure. Throwing a coat meant digging up to the neck, throwing a shoe meant digging up to the knees, and so on. The deeper the dig, the higher the chances of the devil catching and punishing the thief.

Easter palms, once consecrated, were believed to possess magical properties. People would whip themselves and their farm animals with consecrated palms to regain health and vitality. They were also used as aspergillum, dipped in holy water to sprinkle around the house and farm buildings for blessing, cleansing, and protection. Traditionally, one would walk around the household three times with the palm, dipping it in water and sprinkling, while also whipping each corner of the house with it. They were also hung from the ceiling or stood in the corner of the living room, placed in the wardrobe, or in the attic to protect the household from evil and illness. If placed in the window, they protected the household from lightning, similarly to the Gromnica candle. Accordingly, some folks used the consecrated willow twigs for fumigation, which was believed to protect from storms and lightning, as well as chase away illnesses and evil spirits. In this way, willow palms bear similarity to other blessed bundles of plants, such as the wreaths consecrated at Corpus Christi or the bouquets of herbs blessed in August.

Because of their rejuvenating, healing, and protective properties, blessed willow palms would also be taken to the fields and either buried or stuck upright in the soil to bless the field and protect the crops from natural disaster.

Catkins from the palms were also believed to possess magical healing properties. Most commonly, one to three catkins were swallowed as a cure for throat infections and fever. For those who had difficulty swallowing the catkins directly, they could be made into a tea-like infusion or steeped in fresh spring water to drink, or added into a rejuvenating, healing bath.

Palms were kept in the house all year, until the next spring. Then, they were burned for *Popielec* (Ash Wednesday), and the willow ash was then used for sprinkling family members' and animals' heads.

Wielki Tydzień/Holy Week

Holy Week is rich in lore and traditions, especially the intensified apotropaic magic practices that were (and often still are) cultivated during this period. One such old practice involves chasing away evil spirits and demons by banging on pots, sometimes filled with mud, ash, and dung (see: "Okadzanie and Cleansing"). Each day of the Holy Week, starting with Wednesday, has its own focus and unique customs.

Holy Wednesday

Wednesday was originally the day of cleaning and cleansing the home for Easter. Today, *Matki Polki* (Polish mothers) still make an entire ordeal out of spring cleaning the house. Everything needs to be deep-cleaned—no excuses. While the date itself may not be strictly adhered to anymore due to the demands on modern life, the tradition itself, of course, is still cultivated.

Back in the day, folks would deep-clean their cottages and ensure that all corners of the home are cleansed of any remains of stagnant overwinter energy. This meant that the home had to be swept thoroughly, all sheets, cloths and linens had to be aired outdoors, and so on. This would often be accompanied by fumigating the house and property with a blessed bundle of herbs. Today, people focus on decluttering the home from any unwanted or broken stuff, washing their windows, hanging fresh curtains, dusting and washing all shelves that may have collected dust for too long, power-cleaning the rugs, getting rid of broken furniture etc. Such cleaning and decluttering traditions were sometimes taken to the next level. In Opolskie Silesia, where I grew up, there are records of folks gathering all old and broken furniture from across the village and organising a communal bonfire to burn them. Although I have personally never witnessed such a tradition being cultivated in my village.

Once the cleaning and cleansing activities are complete, and the house is immaculate, it would then be dressed with spring themed decorations, such as *spring pająki* (traditional decorations made of straw, dressed with eggs, feathers, and flowers) which were hung from the ceiling. Other common decorations include decorated eggs, hares and early spring flowers.

Outside of the spring cleaning traditions cultivated on Holy Wednesday, some regions of Poland would also observe *Judaszki,* a practice recreating the hanging of Judas for his betrayal. Incidentally, Judaszki is very similar to the burning and drowning of Marzanna that occurs around the spring equinox. The practice consists of creating a straw effigy of Judas, mockingly parading him through the village, and finally hanging him on a tree for his crimes. Later on in the day, he would be cut off from the tree, carried outside of the perimeter of the village, to finally be torn into pieces, burned and drowned. No matter the figure personified in the effigy, such traditions echo older beliefs and customs of sacrifices given to the land and water spirits, meant to summon first spring rains and awaken the fertility of the fields.

Maundy Thursday

Thursday, sometimes also known as *czysty czwartek* (clean Thursday), was a day of washing oneself in rivers or streams. It wasn't just an ordinary bath. There were quite a few rules and taboos surrounding the washing. For example, it was ideal to wash in a stream or river that flowed from West to East. It was forbidden to speak during the washing process. Sometimes, folks would also whip themselves with willow or birch twigs during the process. After the ritual wash was complete, the body wouldn't be dried with a towel, but rather allowed to soak up all the water until the skin is dry. Such practices are consistently observed with other types of healing or cleansing washes and baths, too.

It was believed that Maundy Thursday washes and baths in Living Water (see: "Sacred Waters") were magical and could heal any illness, as well as grant beauty. They also removed all hexes and curses.

Thursday also marked a period when all labor in the field was strictly forbidden until Easter. During this time, the soil was considered sacred, as it was believed to hold the body of Christ. Thus, folks weren't allowed to dig in the soil, nor pluck anything out of it.

Maundy Thursday was also an important day dedicated to the souls of the dead, as well as household spirits. It was believed that on this day, the veil between the worlds thinned, and the souls of our ancestors visited our households. It was strictly forbidden to use the stove as the house spirits and the dead were said to enjoy hiding in there. It was likewise taboo to sew, spin, and weave to avoid tangling and thus trapping the souls in between the threads.

Similar taboos were observed around *Dziady Wiosenne* (Spring Forefathers) and other times of the year, when the ancestors were invited into the household, such as All Souls Day or Christmas Eve.

Good Friday

Friday was believed to be an especially dangerous day when all evil forces had an easier way of getting to people, when witches reigned and could easily cast a curse or steal one's abundance from the home. According to old belief, the evil eye could be easily cast on someone by accident, even by praising or complimenting someone. To protect themselves, people would cross their fingers as a repellent gesture. In order to avoid being suspected of casting the eye, folks would commonly add *"bez uroku"* ("without a charm") whenever they said a compliment, looked at someone a little too intently, or walked in on someone eating a meal—this was seen as proof of good intentions and wishing no harm upon anyone.

While Jesus remained in his grave during this day, devils and witches had no one to fear, fully taking advantage of the temporarily expanded freedom. For this reason, additional protective measures were employed to ensure safety around the household. For example, folks would cover all mirrors around the home, which would seal them off as potential portals for malicious spirits and witches, as well as the dead. Other traditions included marking three crosses with chalk on the front door, or circling one's property thrice with apotropaic items, such as salt, holy water, or blessed herbs (see: "Protection Magic").

Friday was also the day of cooking as well as decorating eggs—*pisanki, kroszonki,* and *malowanki.*

Holy Saturday

Holy Saturday is the day of consecrating fire and water, as well as baskets of traditional foods known as *święconka.* In the past, water would be consecrated in the morning, foods around noon, and fire in the evening. Today, baskets are consecrated in the morning, while fire and water are consecrated in the evening.

The contents of the święconka basket evolved over the centuries and depended on what people could afford or had access to. It is speculated that initially the baskets contained mostly meats. Over time, dairy products, salt and pepper, as well as decorated eggs (see "Egg Magic and Jajowanie") were incorporated into the mix. Nowadays, święconka traditionally contains eggs, bread, sausage, salt and pepper, horseradish, babka cake, sugar lamb figurine, *rzeżucha* (cress, Lepidium sativum), and other foods. This may vary slightly depending on the region, and contemporary sweets like chocolate bunnies and eggs are now commonly added across regions.

Interestingly, the consecration was not performed initially by a priest in church (like we see today). Instead, the head of the family (usually the grandfather or father) performed the consecration using holy water at home. Later, entire villages would gather in a public space to have their baskets consecrated by a priest, and this tradition survives to this day.

A traditional święconka basket needs to be covered with a white lace cloth and adorned with sprigs of boxwood, periwinkle, catkins, and spring flowers available locally. The cloth is only removed for the moment of consecration itself, then replaced to protect the contents. Upon returning home from the consecration, folk would often walk around the house three times with the basket to bless the home and ensure prosperity, as well as bury one of the eggs under the threshold of the front door as an offering for the household spirits.

The consecration of fire and water this time of year played an important role in the folkloric reverence for fire and water (see: "Living Fire" and "Sacred Waters" chapters) and certainly predates Christianization. Because springtime was considered the beginning of the New Year in our ancestors' agrarian societies, it was firmly believed that, with the beginning of a new cycle, a new sacred flame needed to be kindled and then taken home to rekindle the hearth. As for water, it was believed to be under the domain of chthonic entities all throughout the dark half of the year. Therefore, with the coming of the light half of the year, water needed to be consecrated so that it no longer posed spiritual threats to humans.

Before consecration, all hearth fires needed to be extinguished in anticipation of the new flame. Back in the day, big bonfires would be lit at the front of the church, and the flame would be consecrated there. Afterwards, folk would take some embers back home to rekindle the hearth flame, as well as some ash to sprinkle on their fields for blessings of good harvest.

As for consecrated water, folks would drink a small amount of it right after the consecration for good luck and strength. The rest would be taken home and sparingly sprinkled around the house for protection from curses and hexes. Whatever remained would be kept for later and used in various household rites throughout the year.

Around midnight on Holy Saturday, all living waters (rivers, streams, and springs) were believed to manifest magical powers. At night, people would go to these sources of water for healing, good health, luck, love, beauty, and other blessings. This was different from the washing that occurred on Holy Thursday. This time, the waters have already been consecrated and thus are much more powerful. These nighttime water rituals were usually done in complete silence and with secrecy, although everybody knew that everybody did them.

Wielkanoc/Easter

The celebrations of Easter or the Holy Sunday begin straight after midnight or very early in the morning, with the three-hour-long resurrection mass. It was believed that one could easily recognize local witches during the procession. While witches were known for their abilities of effortlessly concealing their heretical dispositions from the local community by pretending to be a good Catholic—participating in mass, and even partaking in communion (to discreetly steal the Eucharist wafer)—the resurrection mass presented an opportunity to unmask them. A clear sign of a practicing witch was that she would actively avoid circling the church thrice with the procession during resurrection mass.

After church, all the interesting customs and traditions come into play. Right after mass, folks would sometimes organize cart races. Those who were the first to arrive from church in the village were to be blessed with the greatest harvests in the year ahead.

In the morning, entire families would have a festive Easter breakfast together. It always began with sharing the consecrated eggs from the święconka basket while exchanging best wishes—very similar to the sharing of wafers during *Wigilia* (Christmas Eve). After the eggs, eating could finally begin. Everybody had been waiting for this very moment since the beginning of Lent. Traditional Easter breakfast foods differ depending on region. My family always had *biały barszcz* (white borscht) with bits of święconka foods added into the soup (egg, sausage, bread, horseradish, salt, and pepper). After soup, there would be a selection of *śledź* (herring) dishes, *galareta* (aspic) dishes, *sałatka ziemniaczaka* (potato salad), and egg dishes. Lastly, there would be dessert such as babka or mazurek cake, marzipan, and coffee. Some family members from older generations would wash it all down with a shot of vodka.

Similarly to the previous days of the Holy Week, Easter Sunday also had several taboos and prohibitions in place. Folks were absolutely not allowed to work, kindle a new flame, or lie down in bed during the day. The latter could result in one's grain lying flat later in the season.

Śmigus Dyngus/Wet Monday

Śmigus Dyngus is a day of flirtatious mischief and fun. Nowadays, it is still traditional to pour water onto one's family members (preferably while they're still fast asleep) first thing in the morning. The one who wakes up first obviously wins the race. Growing up, it was known that if you went outside on this day, you would end up drenched in water straight from a bucket or even thrown into the local stream. If you chose to avoid trouble and stay inside, you'd still have visitors. Boys and men would visit from door to door in the neighborhood to sprinkle you with water in exchange for a little chocolate egg, fruit, or a shot of vodka. This tradition is much older and initially rooted in the beliefs surrounding Living Water. It was customary to drench each other with water to awaken fertility. Another part of the celebrations would be to (gently) whip oneself, or each other, with willow twigs to chase away illness and weakness, and awaken new vitality within. Traditionally, males would be drenching and whipping females.

In some regions, Śmigus Dyngus was accompanied by additional fun occurrences. For example, in the Małopolskie region, a man dressed up as Siuda Baba roams the streets. *Siuda Baba* is a hag, dressed in disheveled clothes, dirty with soot. She has a special soot ointment (reminiscent of witches' flying ointment) that she smears on every passerby's face, accompanied by merry wishes, while expecting a payment of food in return. Other regions have *Śmiergusty, Dziady śmigustne, kurek,* and other traditional folkloric figures.

Other than sprinkling and drenching fellow people, fields also received their fair share of water magic on this day. Wet Monday was the day of blessing the fields. Early in the morning, farmers would go to the fields and sprinkle them with holy water. They would then pray for an abundant harvest, prosperity, and ease of labor. It was then customary to make a small bonfire in the field and make scrambled eggs with leftovers of święconka. This would often turn into social gatherings of farmers from neighboring fields exchanging food and drinks around their bonfires.

Dziady Wiosenne/Spring Forefathers

Dziady Wiosenne is a pre-Christian tradition of ancestor veneration. The Autumnal Forefathers, which occur at the beginning of November, is a similar tradition. In fact, our Slavic ancestors held similar rituals for the dead several times per year, with spring and autumn celebrations being the most important ones.

Although it is speculated that these rituals may have occurred initially around the second dark moon after the spring equinox, Spring Forefathers has long been organized on the first Thursday after Easter, and two days after *Rękawka*—a similar celebration regional to Kraków, taking place on the first Tuesday after Easter.

Rękawka is a Spring Forefathers celebration occurring in a particular place: the mound of Krak, the legendary Polish prince and founder of Kraków. During Rękawka, folks hike up the mound to hold a wake feast for the dead, with traditional offerings of eggs, apples, and bread. It has been customary to roll the eggs and other foods from the top of the mound down. This has evolved into a custom of giving away the aforementioned foods to the poor and homeless *(dziady)* so that they may feast with the community, despite having brought no offerings of their own. In Polish folklore, dziady is a word used to describe both the ancestors (forefathers) and old, poor, or homeless people. It was believed that the souls of the ancestors could enter the body of such a person and visit us in this form; therefore, one should always feed the poor and treat them with utmost respect if they knock at the door.

Spring Forefathers outside of Kraków would be celebrated differently, as evidenced from the following example found in Zygmunt Gloger's *Rok Polski w życiu, tradycji i pieśni* (Polish year in everyday life, tradition and song, 1900, p. 214). First thing in the morning, women would dress in white cloth, pack up leftovers of święconka and other Easter foods, and go to the cemetery saying, *"Idę teraz na Dziady!"* ("I'm going to the Forefathers now!"). Processions of women dressed in white would walk to the cemetery in complete silence.

In the past, there were no tombstones, which meant that a few years after the burial, most graves were hard to recognize. This was usually remedied by women, too. They would leave various items, like ribbons, aprons, beads, etc., on their family graves to be able to tell them apart.

Once the women arrived at the cemetery, they would locate their family mounds and clean them. Since tramps, shepherds, and outsiders would often take the items that were meant to help tell the graves apart, women would first have to remember which grave was their family's and place new aprons, beads, and ribbons on it.

Then, they would cover the grave with white cloth and place their offerings of leftover święconka, cake, egg, cheese, meat, and vodka on the cloth. Once the offerings were placed on the mounds, women would sit or squat in front of them and begin their mournful laments and conversations with the dead. This would take a while and almost form a choir of all the women in the cemetery crying and lamenting together, each to their own dead.

After a while, one of the women would stand up, pour a glass of vodka, and say, *"Piję ja do ciebie, (imię) serdeczna, żebyś wiedziała, że ci nic nie żałuję, i światło Boże niech ci świeci"* ("I drink in your name, dear (name), so that you know I hold nothing back from you and pity you not, may God's light shine upon you"). Then, she would pour the vodka onto the mound, beginning a feast. Everyone would get up and start drinking, sharing food, talking about the dead, telling tales about their lives, and sharing memories and feelings. While eating and drinking, it was customary to offer pieces of food and glasses of drink directly to the mounds and graves, thereby feasting together with the dead. Over time, conversations about the dead would shift toward joyful chatter about spring, praising the sun and the longer, warmer days, so that in the end the initial mournful mood lifts completely and is transformed into a joyful community feast.

Eventually, the women would gather up leftover foods, offering cloths and such, and return home. Afterwards, all the tramps and other folk would go to the graves and steal the ribbons, aprons, and beads yet again, while feeding on any leftover foods.

Świętego Jerzego/St. George Feast Day (April 24)

St. George is syncretized with the celestial Thunder God Perun and regarded as the slayer of serpents and dragons (chthonic forcers), as well as the patron of warriors. Common folk would petition St. George for the protection of their cattle. In some regions, St. George's Feast Day was customarily the first day of the year when cattle were taken out into the fields. This was accompanied by prayers to St. George: "*Święty Jerzy, ojcze, zdajemy na twoje ręce bydełko i prosimy, obroń je od zwierza lutego, od człowieka złego*" ("St. George, father, we place our cattle under your protection and we humbly ask so that you protect them from wild animals and evil people").

During storms, folk would imagine that St. George himself is throwing lightning at the devil. These lightnings, when they fell to the ground, were believed to transform into *strzałka piorunowa* (lightning arrow). In actuality, these are fossils of belemnites. Finding one is an omen of good luck. They were traditionally used as amulets, especially useful for protection (see: "Protection Magic"), but also for magical healing practices, for example, healing cattle.

MAJ: MAY

While March and April were both still unpredictable weather-wise, May finally brings us the genuine warmth that we crave and fills the air with scents of blooming trees, bushes, and other plants, This is reflected in a folk saying, *"W maju jak w gaju"* ("In May it's like in a grove"), meaning that everything is green, blooming, and full of life.

The name of the month Maj comes from the Roman *Maius*, similarly to English May. An Old Polish name for this month was *trawień*, which comes from *trawa* (grass).

Before Christianization, this time of year was likely filled with a culmination of rites and traditions honoring land spirits and plant spirits, which could be deduced from how "saint-heavy" this month's folk calendarium is. As documented by researchers such as Claude Lecouteux in *Demons and Spirits of the Land: Ancestral Lore and Practices* (Lecouteux, 1995, p. 68-80), places of former nature spirit worship were appropriated and transformed into places dedicated to figures of Saints or Mother Mary, syncretized with the spirits. Contemporarily, we observe modern neo-pagan reimagining of such traditions. For example, Rusalia, which is believed to be a week-long celebration occurring at the beginning of May, is solely dedicated to Rusałki, the spirits of rivers, lakes, and groves.

May Calendarium

- **May:** *Miesiąc Maryjny/Majówka*, Mary's Month
- **May 4:** *Świętego Floriana*, St. Florian Feast Day
- **May 8:** *Świętego Stanisława*, St. Stanislaus Feast Day
- **May 15:** *Zimna Zośka*, St. Sophie Feast Day
- **May 21:** *Świętego Jana Nepomucena*, John Nepomucene Feast Day
- **50 Days after Easter:** *Stado/Zielone Świątki*, Herd/Pentecost (movable)

Mesiąc Maryjny/Mary's Month

May is dedicated to Our Lady in Polish folk Catholicism. While this tradition has been practiced in certain places since much earlier, the beginning of the thirteenth century is when it truly became popular nationwide and remains so today.

Every evening, people gather in churches or by nearby wayside shrines to pray *Litaniae Lauretanae* and *Sub tuum praesidium* in devotion to Our Lady.

Mary is documented to have become a syncretized psychopomp-type "umbrella" spirit for the *genius loci*. This is beautifully attested by the overwhelming presence of wayside shrines dedicated to her many folkloric images—a staple feature of the rural Polish landscape, marking places formerly known for being inhabited by land spirits. Such places, located at crossroads, by old trees, and by sacred springs, remain places where witches and folk practitioners come to perform specific workings, and ordinary people come to pray for favors and miracles, always leaving offerings behind.

Unlike the folkloric Marys listed in an earlier chapter, the May Mary never received a unique folkloric name like the rest, which may have something to do with the prayer Litaniae Lauretana prayed during this month-long devotion. The prayer lists 54 titles or sacred epithets of Mary that she is honored by—from "Mother of mercy," through "Seat of wisdom" and "Spiritual vessel," to "Queen of the most holy Rosary."

Świętego Floriana/St. Florian Feast Day (May 4)

St. Florian is a patron saint of firemen, metallurgists, chimney sweeps, potters, and bakers—most professions that have to do with fire.

The cult of this saint wasn't initially very popular among the Polish folk. This changed in 1538, when a large-scale fire occurred in Kraków. An entire district largely succumbed to the fire and suffered tremendous losses, except for the St. Florian church, which miraculously remained untouched by the flames. Legend has it that witnesses saw an apparition above the church's roof, pouring water over it. Witnesses identified the figure as St. Florian. Since then, the saint has become the patron who protects against fires. His icons and medallions were often placed inside city walls, buildings, and churches for protection.

While St. Florian may be helpful against fires, his water-wielding powers have been known for aiding farmers and merchants. Here are a few folk sayings about the saint:

- *"Na świętego Floriana deszczyk rzęsisty, będzie plon obfity i dobry, i czysty."*

"On St. Florian's pouring rain, there will be harvest abundant, good and pure."

- *"Deszcz w świętego Floriana, skrzynia złotem napchana."*
  "Rain on St. Florian's day, chest will be filled with gold."
- *"Święty Florek daje podwieczorek."*
  "St. Florian gives supper."

Świętego Stanisława/St. Stanislaus Feast Day (May 8)

St. Stanislaus was a bishop in Kraków, living in the eleventh century under King Bolesław Szczodry's (Boleslaw the Generous) rule. He was known for being rather ascetic and openly criticizing the king and his court's luxurious, wasteful lifestyle. He was also known for his ability to resurrect a corpse so it could testify in court. This eventually got him murdered and dismembered. Legend has it that his body parts grew back together, except for his pinky finger, which fell into a nearby pond, thus bestowing its waters with miraculous healing properties.

Because of his astounding abilities, St. Stanislaus is petitioned for aid in especially tough cases and whenever a major breakthrough is needed. A keen witch may notice the saint's necromantic abilities of animating corpses and growing his dismembered body back postmortem. While this may not be of direct use to common folk for cult purposes, it sure can come in handy for witches interested in harnessing necromantic skills.

As with other folk saints, St. Stanislaus's feast day is also significant in agrarian traditions, especially for sowing flax. A selection of folk sayings sheds light on the customs and beliefs:

- *"Jak się zasieje len w świętego Stanisława, to tak urośnie jak ława."*
  "If you sow flax on St. Stanislaus day, it will grow thick like a bench."
- *"Święty Stanisław len sieje, Zofia konopie, a Urban jęczmień i owies każe kończyć, chłopie."*
  "St. Stanislaus sows flax, Sophie sows hemp, and Urban orders barley and oats to finish, peasant."
- *"Po świętym Stanisławie sadzą fasolę prawie."*
  "After St. Slanislaus we almost plant beans."

Zimna Zośka/St. Sophie Feast Day (May 15)

St. Sophie's feast day is known as *Zimna Zośka,* or Cold Sophie. The day is of crucial importance to those who grow their own plants and crops. The Three Cold Saints—also known as Cold Gardeners, Pankracy, Serwacy, and Bonifacy (May 12–14,) culminating with Saint Sophie (May 15)—are regarded in Polish farming and gardening folklore as the last four days of spring, when harsh frost can still be expected to come overnight after warm days, thus ruining all the work and killing the plants or damaging crops. According to almanacs, fragile and frost-sensitive leafy plants, as well as many vegetables, are advised to be planted in the ground after May 15.

As with other folk saints, there's always a wealth of traditional sayings to back up the predictions and observations:

- *"Pankracy, Serwacy, Bonifacy—źli na ogrody chłopacy."*
  "Pancras, Servatius, Boniface—boys angry at the gardens."
- *"Pankracy, Serwacy, Bonifacy, i Zośka to zimni święci."*
  "Pancras, Servatius, Boniface, and Sophie are the Cold Saints."
- *"Święta Zofija kłosy rozwija."*
  "St. Sophie sprouts ears of grain."

Świętego Jana Nepomucena/St. John Nepomucene Feast Day (May 21)

St. John Nepomucene is one of those saints whose syncretism with nature spirits is obvious. In his case, similarly to St. Florian, it is water spirits. His story is rather grim. He was the Czech queen's confessor and refused to tell the king her sins, for which he was tied and thrown from a bridge into the Vltava River. Since his canonization in the eighteenth century, his cult grew in association with water-related matters. For example, John Nepomucene could be petitioned to help find the missing corpse of a drowned person.

Statues of this saint, called *Nepomuki,* were often placed near lakes to protect their local community from floods, droughts, heavy rains, and other water-related weather phenomena. Some of these statues were believed to possess a mind of their own and would be found "swimming" over long distances, to transport themselves into chosen places. To this day, there are a few thousand Nepomuk statues still standing around Poland.

St. John Nepomucene is also considered to be a patron saint of bridges, considering his death resulted in being thrown from a bridge. Back in the day, bridges, due to their liminal nature as connectors of two lands, were believed to be inhabited (or even haunted) by dangerous water spirits. Folks would erect statues of St. John Nepomucene for protection from said spirits.

Statues of this saint were believed to possess great protective powers. However, if treated with disrespect, the saint was known for punishing the wrongdoer.

An agrarian folk saying related to St. John Nepomucene is directly related to the outcomes after "Cold Sophie:"

- *"Na Jana Nepomucena wiadoma już zboża cena."*
  "On St. John Nepomucene, we already know the price of grain."

Stado - Zielone Świątki/Herd - Pentecost (Movable)

Pentecost, which occurs 50 days after Easter, is known as *Zielone Świątki* (Green Festivities). Research suggests that Zielone Świątki replaced an older pre-Christian festival known as *Stado* (Herd), a pagan celebration that occurred around the same time of year. Despite the folk Catholic character of the celebrations today, they remain deeply rooted in land-based customs related to fertility and vitality. In present times, Stado festivities are thoroughly reconstructed and celebrated each year by the Polish Rodnovers. The celebrations are deeply rooted in the old herding customs of shepherds, including choosing a King and Queen of the *stado* (herd) based on their herding skills. The chosen couple is then dressed in flowers and greenery, and a shared feast accompanied by a bonfire dance, as well as various games and friendly competitions ensues.

Many of the customs practiced at this time of year focus around the kind of folk magic aimed at multiplying harvests and prosperity, as well as granting safety from water spirits who would begin to grow malicious by the end of spring. It was believed that the land had to be purified of their influence, to make way for the shifting of seasons. With the growing of the sun and the fast approaching summer time, the water spirits' influence had to recede and make way for land spirits tied to crops, vegetation and harvest.

During Zielone Świątki, as the name of the holiday itself suggests, all the churches, homes and farmsteads were adorned with greenery. People would drape both the interiors and exteriors of their houses in various flowers and boughs of birch, willow, spruce, oak, ash and other trees, each chosen for their powerful protective qualities against witchcraft and evil forces, or their association with strength and vitality.

Indoors, it was common to dress the floors with calamus, and place boughs of birch behind holy icons. Outside, branches would be inserted in the thatch of the roof, fixed around beams and windows, or sometimes even planted in the ground at the front door. In some regions, folks would also take the Green Festivities outside of their property, dressing their fences, or taking green boughs to their fields, to protect them and ensure abundant crops.

Those who had larger homesteads and farm animals would make sure to decorate the farm buildings and even adorn their animals in flowers, for it was believed that the fresh greenery would protect them from evil spirits, witchcraft and illness, promoting their vitality and making them more resilient.

Other than dressing the animals and their buildings, folks would also take the time to fumigate them with the smoke of blessed herb bundles. Such bundles could be the willow "palms" consecrated for Easter, wreaths of flowers and boughs blessed at Corpus Christi, or bouquets of herbs from Our Lady of Herbs.

CHAPTER TWENTY-THREE

SUMMER

CZERWIEC: JUNE

The name of the month comes from *czerwiec polski* (Polish, cochineal; Latin, *Porphyrophora polonica, Margarodes polonicus).* It is also known as Polish carmine scales—a scale insect traditionally used to produce a crimson dye with the same name, colloquially known as "Saint John's blood." Alternative, older names for June include *ugornik* (coming from *ugory,* fallow fields that were plowed during this month), as well as *zok,* which is an old Polish word for grasshoppers whose numbers skyrocketed this time of year.

In the agrarian cycle and thus in folk tradition, czerwiec was a busy month of field and farm work. Days visibly peaking in their duration and the sun reaching its highest point in the sky lent themselves to tales of *południce* demons haunting farmers in the fields, and temptations of the flesh arising during the warm, short nights of bonfires under cloudless skies.

The symbolism of this month's folk traditions is rooted in much older, pre-Christian customs and rites. Much of it is related to the cult of fire and water (see: "Living Fire" and "Sacred Waters" chapters), which culminates during summer solstice celebrations.

June Calendarium

- **Second Thursday after Pentecost:** *Boże Ciało,* Feast of Corpus Christi (movable)
- **June 8:** *Świętej Jadwigi,* St. Jadwiga Feast Day
- **June 8:** *Świętego Medarda,* St. Medardus Feast Day
- **June 13:** *Świętego Antoniego,* St. Anthony Feast Day

- **June 20–21:** *Noc Kupały,* Summer Solstice (Movable)
- **June 24:** *Świętego Jana Chrzciciela,* St. John the Baptist Feast Day
- **June 29:** *Świętych Piotra i Pawła,* St. Peter and Paul Feast Day

Boże Ciało/Feast of Corpus Christi

Boże Ciało is a movable holiday, occurring sixty days after Easter, or on the second Thursday after Pentecost. The most important celebrations of this day are rooted in folk Catholicism. Traditionally, the day before the celebrations, folks create four altars around the village, richly decorated in elaborate mandala-like flower carpets, as well as young birch trees and other green boughs. During Boże Ciało, a procession carrying Corpus Christi visits all four altars to pray and sing. At the front of the procession, children sprinkle handfuls of flower petals, creating a beautiful flower carpet for the community. Each altar is consecrated by the priest, offering a rich supply of consecrated boughs, flowers, and herbs collected by the people for later use in healing and protection magic.

As soon as the official part comes to an end, people take boughs and flowers from the altars and carry them home, to stick behind holy icons or hang them from the ceiling, which is a common practice to this day. For a perceptive reader, this custom may appear very familiar with the aforementioned Green Festivities, where folks would dress their homes in a similar manner.

The consecrated plants were believed to hold strong apotropaic properties. They were also commonly used for fumigation in folk healing or even exorcisms. Folks would sometimes weave wreaths from the gathered blessed herbs and burn them whenever a family member was in need of aid in dealing with an evil spirit or persistent illness. An example historical formula for such an exorcism goes as follows:

"Idź, czorcie!
Idź w ogień wiechy
Z tego niewinnego ciała!
Idź za lasy, za góry,
Na bagna, na rozstajne drogi!
Nie wracaj tu nigdy,
Połom sobie nogi!
Niech to kadzenie wyjdzie na pożytek,
Że ustanie ten płac wszytek.

W imię Ojca i Syna, i Ducha Świętego!
Niech się stanie wolo Bożo!"

"Go, devil!
Go into the wreath fire
From this innocent body!
Go beyond the forests, beyond the mountains,
To the swamps, to the crossroads!
Never return here,
Break your legs!
May this fumigation be beneficial,
So that all this wretchedness ceases.
In the name of the Father, and of the Son, and of the Holy Spirit!
May God's will be done!"

Świętej Jadwigi/St. Jadwiga Feast Day (June 8)

Jadwiga Andegaweńska was the first female monarch in the Kingdom of Poland. Despite her short life (1374–1399), she was beloved by the people and known for her empathy and generosity. She founded many hospitals, shelters, and even restored the first university in Poland (Uniwersytet Jagielloński). Tales of Jadwiga portray her as a very spiritual person, a visionary, and a mature and wise ruler. In folkloric legends, she is often equated with Mary, even having her own sacred rock with foot imprints, similar to those of folkloric Marys. Her abilities include raising the dead and healing ailments. In her generosity, she was known for taking care of the poor and giving back to the community in every way she could. St. Jadwiga is petitioned for aid in everyday matters, taking special care of the poor, disadvantaged, ill, and dying.

Świętego Medarda/St. Medardus Feast Day (June 8)

June 8 also happens to be the feast day of *Święty Medard* (St. Medardus), whose cult was more popular in the medieval period than it is today. As a patron saint of farmers, gardeners, brewers, and reapers, people prayed to him for a good harvest. His feast day was observed for signs that would predict the rest of the season.

Here is a selection of agrarian folk sayings that indicate how this saint's feast day predicted the following several weeks in terms of weather:

- *"Gdy się Medard rozpłacze, a Jaś nie utuli, popłacze pewnie aż do Urszuli."*
  "If Medard starts crying [raining] and [St.] John doesn't comfort him, he'll probably cry all the way until Ursula's [feast day]."
- *"Jaki w Medarda dzień, taka będzie cała żeń."*
  "The kind of weather we get on Medardus' day, it will be the same all reaping season."
- *"Święty Medard w sobie mieści słót lub pogód dni czterdzieści."*
  "St. Medardus' day predicts the next forty days of rainy or sunny weather."

Świętego Antoniego/St. Anthony Feast Day (June 13)

St. Anthony is a patron saint of those who have lost things, as well as matters of marriage, relationships, fertility, and more. In Polish folk tradition, he would most commonly be petitioned to find lost objects and to find a partner; he never disappoints in finding exactly what you're looking for. Interestingly, in folk cults, he is also known to be petitioned by thieves for protection against being discovered.

Hornbeam tree has been traditionally associated with St. Anthony, and his apparitions would often take place in a hornbeam, making it a suitable place for petitioning him and leaving offerings for him.

There is a peculiar folk cure for warts using the aid of St. Anthony. The troublesome wart should be smeared with an onion three times, making the sign of a cross, when the church bells are ringing for "Angelus" (midday). While smearing the warts with onion, one should repeat the formula, *"Świynty Antoni brodowki góni"* ("St. Anthony chases away warts!"), three times. Then, one should tie one's finger (the one with warts) with linen thread and then put the thread under the gutter "so that it rots." As the thread rots, so does the wart disappear.

Noc Kupały/Summer Solstice

Noc Kupały (Kupała Night), also known as *Kupałnocka* or *Sobótki*, is the shortest night of the year. Heavily celebrated to this day across Poland—albeit interchangeably with the night of St. John's Eve—it announces the culmination of the reign of the sun. Kupałnocka is a celebration of the sun reaching the zenith of its potency, as well as the union of water and fire. It marks the beginning of the summer season.

Noc Kupały celebrates fertility and love. During this shortest night, lovers sneak into the forest to seek the mythical fern flower. This magical flower is believed to grant abundance and happiness to whoever finds it. This night is also considered to be the best time to procreate. Children conceived under the sun at its strongest point are granted its protection, strength, and a good *Dola* (fate).

The three most important parts of summer Sobótki celebrations, rooted in the older folkloric traditions, consist of jumping through bonfires to strengthen both body and soul, weaving wreaths and releasing them upon the waters to find love, and taking ritual baths in lakes or rivers. One should not fall asleep too early during this shortest night of the year as this is the time when we celebrate, drink, procreate, sing, and dance until dawn—to witness and greet the rising sun in its full glory.

Świętego Jana Chrzciciela/St. John the Baptist Feast Day (June 24)

Folklore surrounding John the Baptist is quite rich in Polish tradition. The saint became the central figure syncretized with the celebrations of Noc Kupały, which gave rise to the popularity of *Noc Świętojańska* (St. John's Night) celebrated in place of the older summer solstice celebrations. Contemporarily, St. John's Night is a popular and relatively mainstream festival, celebrated interchangeably with the summer solstice. Thus, a lot of the folklore of these two dates is applied to both.

St. John the Baptist also happens to be associated with quite a few plants, mostly St. John's wort *(dziurawiec)* and mugwort *(bylica)*, both playing an important role in summer solstice traditions. St. John's wort happens to bloom around the summer solstice and St. John's Feast Day, hence the association with this saint. It is most known for its apotropaic properties, protecting against witches, devils, demons, and other spirits who might wish us harm. When used in this way, it's often referred to as *fuga daemonum.* It was believed that witches traveled to the Bald Mountain on St. John's Eve, specifically to gather St. John's wort, as it was thought to possess potent magical qualities on this night. The herb was placed under the pillow for protection against mares, as well as placed inside babies' diapers so that they wouldn't get kidnapped by *boginki* (a type of female demon). It was also used for *okadzanie* (fumigation) as an effective exorcism, as well as for ease of labor while giving birth. Naturally, because of the red "blood" that the fresh plant produces when squished, it was related to life force and blood in sympathetic folk magic.

Mugwort's association with St. John the Baptist originates from a folk story of the saint's death. He was sentenced to beheading. And upon execution, the head fell to the ground between mugwort and St. John's wort (or burdock, depending on the version of the story). Similar to St. John's wort, mugwort is an important apotropaic plant with dual correspondences. It is the "mother of herbs" in Polish folk medicine and magic, helpful for a long list of ailments. However, it is also used for witchcraft. During the summer solstice specifically, it is traditional to wear a wreath of mugwort on one's head to protect from witchcraft and to be free from headaches in the coming year. Wearing mugwort around one's waist as a belt also brings protection from enchantments and grants good gut health in the year ahead. Mugwort okadzanie (fumigation) is the default in every magically inclined Polish household, for cleansing and protecting the house from unwanted influences and evil forces.

It was believed that witches harvested herbs for magic on St. John's Eve because they possessed the most concentrated magical powers during this shortest night of the year.

A Polish folk saying goes: *"Już Jan ochrzcił wszystkie wody, umyjcie się dla ochłody"* ("Saint John baptized all the waters, wash yourself to cool down"). This is no coincidence, as it was believed that the summer solstice or St. John's Feast Day is the time it finally becomes safe to swim and bathe in open waters. Before this date, water spirits were believed to be still too strong and vengeful and thus would often drown people. This time of year, when the sun (fire) is at its strongest, the chthonic powers of waters become less overwhelming and hostile.

St. John the Baptist is the patron saint of weather, especially rain, storms, and hail, as well as the patron of blacksmiths, people sentenced to death, and merchants. Weather correspondences and folk sayings related to this saint remain especially relevant for farmers who rely on weather for predictions of when it's best to plan a harvest, whether wheat will grow properly, and other work in the field. One such indicator is *deszcze świętojańskie* (St. John's rains). Warm rainy weather occurring for several days before St. John's Feast Day would predict a good season, especially if paired with relatively dry July and August.

Świętych Piotra i Pawła/St. Peter and Paul Feast Day (June 29)

According to Polish folklore, the feast day of St. Peter and Paul was considered an unlucky, if not dangerous, day. While it was believed that past St. John the Baptist's feast day, it was safe to swim and bathe in open waters, June 29 was an exception to the rule. Water spirits seemed to be especially hungry for human sacrifice on this day; therefore, it was safer to steer clear of water for the day.

A folk saying goes: *"Gdy Święci Piotr z Pawłem płaczą, ludzie przez tydzień słońca nie zobaczą"* ("When St. Peter and St. Paul weep, people will not see the sun for a week").

According to agrarian folk tradition, St. Peter and Paul's feast day foretells rain and the drying of rye, as is reflected in the following examples of folk sayings:

- *"Piotr i Paweł suszą korzenie żyta."*
  "Peter and Paul, dry the roots of rye."
- *"Pytoł się drukorz pisorza, co nadrukować do kalendorza? Drukuj co chcesz, ale w Piotra i Pawła musi być deszcz."*
  "A printer asked a writer, what to print in the calendar? -Print whatever you want, but on Peter and Paul's day, there must be rain."
- *"Po świętym Pawle i Pietrze muchy tłuste jak wieprze."*
  "After St. Paul and Peter's day, flies become fat like pigs."

LIPIEC: JULY

July is filled with farm chores, regular storms, and rains intertwined with periods of drought, as well as early harvest of forest berries and other fruits, vegetables, and plant materia. With climate changes, however, some harvest dates now come earlier than in the past. For example, wheat and other grains used to be traditionally harvested in August, but nowadays they're harvested in the second half of July.

In Polish, the name of the month is *lipiec*, coming from *lipa*—the linden tree—abundantly blooming this time of year. The scent of linden flowers is sweet and intoxicating, alluring one to lie in the tree's shade for a nap. In fact, linden trees made their appearance in countless Polish epigrams, poems, folk stories, as well as the folkloric cult of Mary and the land spirits.

July Calendarium

- **July 2:** *Matki Boskiej Jagodnej,* Our Lady of Blueberries
- **July 24:** *Świętej Kingi,* St. Kinga Feast Day
- **July 25:** *Świętego Jakuba,* St. Jacob Feast Day
- **July 25:** *Świętego Krzysztofa,* St. Christopher Feast Day
- **July 26:** *Świętej Anny,* St. Anne Feast Day

Matki Boskiej Jagodnej/Our Lady of Blueberries (July 2)

At the end of June and the beginning of July, forest berries such as blueberries, blackberries, and wild strawberries become ripe for harvest. However, folk beliefs indicated that it was taboo to pick these fruits until after July 2. Village folk would also include fruits such as cherries, raspberries, black and red currants, and gooseberries among the "forbidden fruit" that were supposed to be saved until after July 2—and for good reason.

On this day, mothers who miscarried or who suffered the loss of a child were especially looked after by Mary. It was believed that Mary knew of and understood their grief and despair, and that is why she was feeding and taking care of the souls of deceased children in their mothers' stead. Women who had trouble conceiving would pray to Our Lady of Berries for aid. In exchange for regular prayers to Our Lady, they would be blessed with a safe pregnancy and a healthy child.

Świętej Kingi/St. Kinga Feast Day (July 24)

St. Kinga was a Hungarian princess of the Árpád dynasty, and the wife of Polish king Bolesław Wstydliwy (Boleslaw the Chaste). She's a patron saint of the poor and of salt miners. Kinga was a rather intriguing figure in her lifetime, known for being very modest, rejecting wealth, and performing miracles. Some examples of miracles include healing incurable illnesses and disabilities, as well as possessing necromantic abilities, which appear to be a standard list of saintly special powers. There is a wealth of folkloric stories describing her many adventures and achievements, complete with how Kinga miraculously created the legendary salt mine in Wieliczka by pointing miners to a place where they should dig to find salt. Once widowed, she chose monastic life and began to engage in pilgrimages, which expanded her saintly powers. Similarly to St. Jadwiga, many of Kinga's qualities as a saint bear similarities to those of Mother Mary herself. Folk stories describe how each step she took on her pilgrimages would transform the land. A rock formation known as "the seat of St. Kinga" can be found in Beskid Sądecki mountain range. According to legend, she would rest there with fellow nuns while fleeing from a Tatar invasion. Miraculous springs can also be found in places where she was known to spend time, one of which is still believed to possess healing powers of curing eye illnesses. Kinga can be petitioned as the protectress of women and a miracle worker in tough cases.

Świętego Jakuba/St. Jacob Feast Day (July 25)

St. Jacob is a patron saint of fishermen, apothecaries, pilgrims, workers, and beggars. In old legends, he is known for aiding fishermen in their work, and once even cursing a greedy lord who abused his fishermen, thus turning him into a Fish King. Since then, local folks would often see a giant catfish wearing an ember crown, swimming in the waters of the lake, and causing dangerous waves. Only during the eve of St. Jacob's feast day, the waters would calm down as the lord was believed to be back on his island, feasting with the ghosts.

The Fish King is originally a benevolent guardian spirit of Mazury, the region where this folk tale takes place. He is indeed believed to be a catfish wearing an ember crown; however, he has nothing in common with the greedy and cruel lord. He is known as King Sielaw, possessing magical powers, protecting the inhabitants of the region, both human and non-human, as well as teaching certain people skills, such as understanding the speech of animals. It is possible that in the process of syncretization of older stories of King Sielaw with the Christian stories of St. Jacob, the benevolent Fish King was villainized, and Jacob took up the Fish King's good qualities instead.

Świętego Krzysztofa/St. Christopher Feast Day (July 25)

While there aren't as many elaborate folk tales of St. Christopher, he remains one of the most popular saints to pray to, and is petitioned among the Fourteen Holy Helpers. As a patron saint of travelers, the saint protects from all danger and evil spirits that one might encounter on their journeys. In the past, it was quite popular in Poland to place reliefs of this saint on buildings and houses. Travelers would always bow before the relief and say a little prayer to the saint to ensure safe travel. Nowadays, it is still very popular to carry medallions depicting St. Christopher attached to one's car keys or hung by one's car rearview mirror. Some carry the medallions in their wallet for protection while traveling.

Świętej Anny/St. Anne Feast Day (July 26)

There is a folk saying that goes: *"Od świętej Anki zimne wieczory i ranki"* ("St. Anne's day marks the beginning of cold evenings and mornings"). St. Anne, the mother of Mary and grandmother of Jesus, bears the role of a grandmother saint, a patroness of housewives, marriages, widows, servants, and those who help raise children. In folk customs, on St. Anne's feast day, women weave and consecrate wreaths of herbs to chase away all evil. In legends, she is known for apparitions in pine trees, often saving someone from assault by men or predatory animals.

SIERPIEŃ: AUGUST

August is the month of harvest—in the fields, orchards, gardens, forests and meadows. It is a busy month, filled with laborious gathering of the bounty of harvest that everyone's been working so hard for since spring. The name of the month—*sierpień*—comes from *sierp* (sickle), the primary tool of harvest.

August can be a capricious month. Some years it is extremely dry, which makes harvest work easier but also rougher on the body. In contrast, other years, it becomes cold really fast, reminding us of the inevitably approaching autumn. For our ancestors, it was a month of giving thanks to farm animals for their work, as well as gathering food supplies; this tradition can still be observed among our people today, even among those who aren't farmers. People still share freshly gathered fruits and vegetables and focus on making preserves, such as jams, syrups, jellies, kompot, pickles, and more.

Due to the month's intense focus on harvest activities, most of the celebrations of this month directly stem from specific types of harvest—wheat, fruits, honey, herbs, etc. However, plenty of traditional beliefs, taboos, and initiatory activities have been observed alongside the harvest.

August Calendarium

- **Observed in August:** *Wyzwoliny Kosiarza,* Liberation of the Reaper
- **August 6:** *Spas Jabłkowy/Przemienienie Pańskie,* Apple Spas/Transfiguration
- **August 10:** *Świętego Wawrzyńca,* St. Lawrence Feast Day
- **August 15:** *Matki Boskiej Zielnej,* Our Lady of Herbs
- **August 16:** *Spas Chlebowy/Świętego Rocha,* Bread Spas/St. Roch Feast Day
- **August 17:** *Świętego Jacka,* St. Hyacinth Feast Day

Wyzwoliny Kosiarza/Liberation of the Reaper

Under the ominous name of *wyzwoliny kosiarza,* we find a traditional rite of passage observed this time of year, meant to initiate boys into serious work in the field. Boys were tasked with numerous trials that involved proving their skill with the scythe or sickle, such as reaping with a blunt blade. Should the tasks be completed successfully, the young reapers would be announced as "liberated" and thus officially allowed to partake in the field harvest. Naturally, a successful trial was followed by a feast.

Spas Jabłkowy i Przemienienie Pańskie/Apple Spas and Transfiguration (August 6)

Apple Spas celebrates the gifts of orchards and forests—apples, pears, berries, and other fruits. August 6 marks the end of harvesting forest fruits and the beginning of harvesting apples and other orchard fruits. On this day, we bless our fruit-bearing trees, eat fruits, and thank the gods for the sweetness that Mother Nature bestows upon us.

In addition to Spas Jabłkowy, August 6 marks the celebration of *Przemienienie Pańskie* (Transfiguration of Jesus). In folk tradition, it isn't as much about Jesus as it is about celebrating and thanking the farm animals that aid us in field labor and feed us. On this day, folk would create handmade offerings of miniature beeswax animals, such as tiny cows, horses, pigs, sheep, and other animals. Such votives would be traditionally taken to church on this day and offered at the altar, accompanied by prayers for the animals. Prayers would also be spoken in the name of bees and beekeepers; tiny beeswax beehives would be given as offerings in their intention. In some regions, folk would also bring body parts made of beeswax, representing what needs healing. As they offer the miniature body parts, they would pray to regain health and strength. Such beeswax offerings and votives are known as *osiary*.

Świętego Wawrzyńca/St. Lawrence Feast Day (August 10)

St. Wawrzyniec Feast was the day when folk traditionally acquired a new Living Fire for their hearth. The head of the family would kindle a new flame for the hearth in a traditional manner. While there are several ways that this could be done, here's an example related to the harvest period specifically. First, the old flame at the hearth had to be extinguished, and the hearth prepared for the new flame. Then, the head of the family would grab flint and tinder, or two pieces of alder wood and rub them to create fire. The sparks needed to be transferred onto a ball of straw or flax fibers and carried into the stove, thus kindling a new flame. Whenever the flame was tucked away for the night, a prayer to St. Wawrzyniec would be said: *"Święty Wawrzyńcze przebłogosławiony, tobie oddaję ogieniaszek sławiony, pod najświętszą twoją opiekę."* ("Saint Laurentius, o blessed one, to you I give the blessed flame, under your saintly protection.")

Matki Boskiej Zielnej/Our Lady of Herbs (August 15)

Matki Boskiej Zielnej (Our Lady of Herbs) is the day of gathering bouquets of medicinal herbs and plants to consecrate for use in healing and magic. Some sources date this celebration (in its Christian form) back to the fifth century, which makes it one of the older traditions and hints at its pre-Christian origin.

August 15 marks the moment when all of the vegetation begins to prepare for the descent into the dark half of the year. As we harvest the herbs, their spirit is harvested with them and brought back from the fields and meadows into our households to protect us during the dark half of the year. This is directly linked to the traditions of the Last Sheaf, also known as Diduch, which is the last bunch of wheat harvested from the fields. Back in the day, this harvest used to occur around mid-August; however, in present times, due to climate change, wheat harvest occurs a month earlier. The harvesting of the plant spirit is meant to signify their symbolic departure from the earth, which can be associated with a symbolic death, slipping into the dream world and preparing for hibernation.

In the morning of August 15 (and sometimes the day before), women harvest bouquets of well-known medicinal herbs, as well as plants that grow in their gardens and fields, to consecrate them. The consecration of herbs is believed to boost their medicinal properties, as well as makes them potent for protection magic, removing curses, banishing magically induced illnesses, and such.

Each region has its own traditions regarding the herbs and plants chosen for the bouquet, depending on what is locally available and what herbs were considered to be most powerful according to local herbal lore.

Sources mention plants such as mugwort, thyme, mint, wormwood, cornflower, hazelwort, and yarrow. Others add poppy, sage, peony, tansy, dill, cumin, St. John's wort, henbane, southernwood, rosemary, lemon balm, mullein, hyssop, rue, and clover. In some regions, people would also add wheat, apples on sticks, late cherries, and flowers from their gardens.

The consecration is usually conducted in churches during a mass dedicated to Our Lady of Herbs. However, witches and healers bless the herbs themselves. After the consecration—be it during a mass or in a personal rite—the bouquets are taken home and handled in accordance with tradition. Farmers would leave their bouquets in the fields for a few days to ensure the protection of potatoes and cabbage from pests. After a few days (or in the case of non-farmers, right away), the bouquet would then be taken home and kept on a home altar, behind holy icons, on window sills, or hung from the ceiling beams.

Once brought home, farmers would take a handful of the herbs and boil them in a pot of water, adding wheat bran, oats, and barley. Such a mixture would then be given to cows to eat for a few days, especially cows who have just given birth, to help them cleanse.

The bouquets would be used throughout the year to help heal and protect both humans and animals from various dangers and ailments. Some of the folk uses of the bouquets include:

- **Fumigating with the bouquet:** Used for healing inflammation of cow udders. Fumigating the household would protect against storms, fires, and epidemics of dangerous infectious diseases (called *zaraza* or *morowe powietrze)*. Fumigating a person was always performed when it was suspected that they might've been cursed or hexed. The power of the bouquet would banish the curse.
- **Eating and drinking the herbs:** Specific herbs would be taken from the bouquets and ingested to cure illnesses of both humans and animals by adding them to food and fodder or steeping in herbal teas.
- **Other uses:** During storms, the bouquet would be placed on the windowsill next to a burning *Gromnica* (Thunder candle) to grant additional protection from storms. Sometimes, crushed herbs from the bouquet would be added to the fireplace so that the smoke coming through the chimney chases away thunder. Herbs from the bouquets would be used for healing baths/soaks for people suffering from lung illnesses such as consumption. Placed under the pillow of a dying person, the herbs would help ease the suffering. Placed under the head of a dead person to help them cross over in peace.

Traditional folk sayings for Our Lady of Herbs:

- *"Po co te wiązki i wianki z mięty wrotyczu, rumianku? Niesiemy je na znak hołdu Maryi Pannie przed ołtarz."*
  "What are these bouquets and wreaths of mint, tansy, and chamomile for? We carry them as our tribute to the altars of Our Lady."
- *"Hyzop, lawenda, jałowiec? Wszak to potrzebne chorobie? Mamy je, chcemy dziewanną ucieszyć Maryję Pannę"*

"Hyssop, lavender, juniper? They're needed to help with disease. We carry them with mullein to please Our Lady."

Spas Chlebowy i Świętego Rocha/Bread Spas and St. Roch Feast Day (August 16)

Bread Spas celebrates the harvest of grain and marks the beginning of the end of the summer harvest season. On this day, we bless our bread baked from fresh grain and give thanks for the abundance of crops. When sharing bread, we're asked to put all quarrels aside and only wish for each other's good fortune and health. Bread is considered sacred and should be treated with respect—even stepping on breadcrumbs is a sign of disrespect. It is, after all, a symbol of the most important basic needs of the community: abundance, good harvest, fertility, peace, and safety.

Spas Chlebowy coincides with the Feast Day of St. Roch, the patron saint of cattle, apothecaries, doctors, gardeners, and grave diggers. He is often portrayed with a dog cuddling at his feet. Roch is also the patron saint of protection from *morowa zaraza* (a folk name for epidemics), protecting both humans and animals from all contagious diseases. On this day, upon returning from pastures, folk would lead their cattle through bonfires kindled traditionally, with herbs from wreaths and bouquets consecrated during *Boże Ciało* (Corpus Christi) and *Matki Boskiej Zielnej* (Our Lady of Herbs). Such herbs were believed to possess powerful magical qualities of protection, healing, and cleansing. The procession of the cattle would often be accompanied by loud drumming, believed to chase away all pestilence and witchcraft.

Traditional prayer to St. Roch:

"Rochu, który masz moc z Boskiego daru,
Lud z morowego wybawić pożaru
Rozpędź te chmury, uzdrów zarażone."

"Roch, you who possess the power of divine gift,
Save our folk from the flames of pestilence
Disperse these clouds, heal that which is infected."

Świętego Jacka/St. Hyacinth Feast Day (August 17)

There is a fun folk saying that goes: *"Święty Jacku z pierogami, módl się za nami!"* ("Saint Hyacinth with pierogi, pray for us!") He is the patron saint of the Silesia region, as well as all those impoverished and starving. The folkloric legends of St. Jacek portray him as a savior of the common folk. He found sources of drinking water, saved people from starvation by praying over their destroyed crops, thus miraculously restoring them, as well as instructed people on how to make pierogi, which could feed many people with little food. As is often the case with saints, many miracles were recorded around the saint's resting place as well. Folks say that near his grave, the sick regain their health, the possessed are free from demonic oppression, and even the dead come back to life.

When eating baked pierogi, a prayer is said:

"Św. Jacku z pierogami, módl się do Boga za nami, żeby te pierogi cały rok na stole były i nas od głodu broniły."

"St. Jacek with dumplings, pray for us to God that pierogi may be on our table year-round and spare us from hunger."

CHAPTER TWENTY-FOUR

AUTUMN

WRZESIEŃ: SEPTEMBER

September marks the end of harvest and the beginning of preparations for the dark half of the year. By this point, all the grain has been harvested from the fields, and folks begin to turn towards the gathering of root vegetables. Parts of the fields are being sown with overwinter grains and plants. The weather, while still gracing us with sunny afternoons, visibly turns towards autumn - days are now increasingly shorter, the winds are moist and cold, and fog frequently descends upon meadows and hills. September is also the beginning of mushroom gathering season, with most edible species having had enough sustained moisture to bear fruit. In the forest, one may encounter fellow mushroom gatherers walking in silent contemplation, attentively hunting for mushrooms in the early morning fog, filling their baskets with autumnal goodness.

The name of this month—*wrzesień*—comes from blooming heathers (wrzosy). However, older Polish names for September include:

- *Pajęcznik (pająk* = spider) named after the *babie lato* gossamer threads floating around (in English this is known as ballooning or kiting);
- *Jesiennik (jesień* = autumn) due to autumn beginning this month.

September Calendarium

- **September 1:** *Świętego Idziego,* St. Giles the Hermit Feast Day
- **September:** *Dożynki,* End of Harvest (movable)

- **September 8:** *Matki Boskiej Siewnej,* Our Lady of Sowing
- **Mid-September:** *Wykopki,* Potato Harvest
- **September 29:** *Michała Archanioła,* Michaelmas

Świętego Idziego/St. Giles the Hermit Feast Day (September 1)

A folk saying goes: *"Święty Idzi w polu nic nie widzi"* ("St. Giles sees nothing in the fields"), which hints that by September 1, the harvest in the fields has been completed. St. Idzi belongs among the Fourteen Holy Helpers, and he is prayed to for aid with infertility and mental illness. He is the patron saint of nursing mothers, fishermen, hunters, shepherds, horse traders, castaways, epileptics, the sick, the wounded, sinners, archers, beggars, the stray, and good confession.

The saint is known for his miraculous powers of curing illnesses, as well as his ability to appear in people's dreams and warning them of imminent death, or appearing to folks in spirit and curing their ailments completely.

Some agrarian folk sayings related to St. Idzi:

- *"Dzień świętego Idziego gdy się wypogodzi, cztery niedziele potem pogodą dogodzi."*
  "If on St. Idzi's day it is sunny, then the next four Sundays will please with good weather."
- *"Święty Idzi—pszczółka w polu nic nie widzi."*
  "On St. Idzi's [day], bees see nothing left in the fields."

Dożynki/End of Harvest

Every community chooses its own date for this celebration each year, depending on when the end of harvest occurs locally. It is usually on a Saturday or Sunday during the first half of September, up until around the autumn equinox. *Dożynki* marks the end of summer and, therefore, the beginning of autumn and the dark half of the year. As days become shorter, the sun grows old, to eventually die and be reborn at the winter solstice. To this day, Dożynki is celebrated in Polish villages, preserving some of the most important pre-Christian agrarian symbolism of the autumnal equinox.

In Polish folkloric tradition, Dożynki is a time of celebrating the labor of local farmers and giving thanks for the harvest that will sustain the community during the dark half of the year. In villages and smaller towns, it is celebrated with a public event organized for the community as a whole, where local *koła godpodyń wiejskich* (rural housewives' circles) perform traditional harvest songs and sell their preserves, and the local craftspeople, farmers, and hunters are acknowledged for their accomplishments and given prizes or marks of quality for regional products and initiatives promoting local culture.

An important traditional aspect of Dożynki celebrations includes weaving oversized wreaths and crowns, symbolizing the generosity of nature. These wreaths and crowns are to be woven out of the most prominent harvest of the year, usually ears of wheat, apples, corn, flowers, and herbs. Each village or group makes its own wreath or crown, and during the Dożynki celebrations, they are all displayed and the most beautiful crown or wreath is awarded. Such wreaths echo much older, pre-Christian traditions of offering wreaths of harvest to the land spirits and local agrarian deities in thanks for the bounty, and in pleas for it being enough to feed the community through the winter.

Another crucial part of the celebrations—one with much older roots—revolves around the Diduch. It is the last (or first, depending on region) harvested sheaf of wheat, or the spirit of the fields itself, which will be kept indoors throughout winter celebrations to become the source of the first grain that gets sown in the fields in spring. Diduch symbolizes the continuity of the cycles of nature; it becomes the carrier of life from one season to the next. While this tradition is not as broadly cultivated anymore, due to fewer people working as farmers, some folks still keep it alive. The bundle is taken care of throughout the dark half of the year and participates in all major celebrations between Dożynki and the first sowing of the seed in spring. It is present during Dziady (Forefathers) celebrations of the ancestors; it lends its straw to be placed under the tablecloth during Wigilia (Christmas Eve); and during the winter Kolęda period, it is passed around the circle for everybody to dance with the Diduch.

Matki Boskiej Siewnej/Our Lady of Sowing (September 8)

September 8 is Our Lady's birthday, also known as The Nativity of the Blessed Virgin Mary. In Polish folk tradition, however, we celebrate *Matki Boskiej Siewnej*, Our Lady of Sowing.

Our Lady of Sowing's feast day is a celebration of hope. It could be seen as the end of the agrarian cycle, bearing the promise of bountiful harvests into the future. In some parts of Poland, people would wash their hands in holy water before sowing the seeds. The first handful of grain would often be sown in the sign of the cross, saying, *"W imię Boże"* ("In the name of God"). The sower always blessed the grain as it was sown into the Earth, thus merging them into one and ensuring a good harvest to come.

It was quite common to add some of the grain consecrated on Matki Boskiej Zielnej (Our Lady of Herbs, August 15) to the winter grains, to make them grow more potent.

A folk saying goes: *"Najświętsza Panna się rodzi, jaskółka odchodzi"* ("The Holy Virgin is born, swallows fly away"), which indicates that around this time of year, swallows migrate to overwinter in warmer parts of the world. Folks would often look up into the sky to bid them farewell.

Prayer to Our Lady of Sowing:

"Okryj nas swym płaszczem, dobra matko ziemio, a my cię na wiosnę okryjemy wspaniałą zielenią, łanem szumiącego zboża i złotymi kłosami, w których się przegląda cała dobroć Boża."

"Cover us with your cloak, good mother earth, and in the spring, we will cover you with wonderful greenery, with a field of rustling grain and golden ears, in which all divine goodness is reflected."

Wykopki/Potato Harvest (Mid-September)

Wykopki could be roughly translated as "digging up." Alternatively, it is also known as *święto ziemniaka* ("potato festival"). Starting in mid-September, people start digging up potatoes and other root vegetables, such as turnips, beetroots, and carrots. Potatoes are traditionally dug with hand tools or special potato harvesters.

After a day's work, folks traditionally gather by the fields in the evening to feast together. Bonfires are lit for baking some of the potatoes, people chat and tell stories by the fire, sing traditional songs, dance, eat, and laugh. While it may not seem like much in terms of tradition, it is truly one of the coziest and most enjoyable times. People can simply rest, eat, laugh, and be themselves by the fire.

Michała Archanioła/Michaelmas (September 29)

In folk beliefs, Michael is the patron of professions such as swordsmiths, goldsmiths, merchants, pharmacists, and bakers. However, St. Michael remains especially important in folk traditions of the countryside, particularly with autumnal chores and celebrations.

On this day, natural phenomena were observed and given special attention as a means of predicting the upcoming season. For example, a storm was to herald the harvest: *"Grzmot na świętego Michała. Żywność przyszła, Bogu chwała"* ("Thunder on St. Michael's day. The food has arrived, thank God").

The Feast Day of St. Archangel Michael was the day that predicted the winter. If it rained, the winter would be relatively bearable. If the night was bright, winter would be harsh. If birds haven't migrated away yet, winter would be late, and so on.

With autumnal chores, there's a folk saying that I find hilarious: *"Święty Michał do beczki kapustę wpychał"* ("St. Michael pushes cabbages into kegs"). It indicates the opening of pickle-making season. The end of September was a time when most of the other harvest-related chores were largely complete. Thus, it was time to start pickling everything— cabbages, cucumbers, beetroots, peppers, mushrooms, and so many other foods—for the winter.

In the old calendars, it was written: *"Siać po świętym Michale to już troszkę niedbale"* ("Sowing after St. Michael is a bit careless"), which suggests that the sowing of winter grain had to be done between September 8 (Matki Boskiej Siewnej) and September 29.

After September 29, shepherds began the autumn *redyk,* closing the season and returning with their flocks to the village until spring. The proverb said: *"Kto pasie po Michale, nie wróci na hale"* ("Whoever herds after St. Michael's day will not return to the pastures").

Outside of the agrarian context, Archangel Michael's presence is called upon when protection from all evil is needed. Michael is known as a fierce warrior with a flaming sword, smiting all devils, demons, and wrongdoers.

Other weather-related folk sayings of this day include:

- *"Gdy noc jasna na Michała, to nastąpi zima trwała."*
  "When the night is bright on St. Michael's, long winter will come."
- *"Ptaszki do Michała, gdzieś zima została."*
  "Birds remain till Michael's, somewhere winter is stuck."
- *"Zbytek na świętego Michała żołędzi wiele śniegu w Boże Narodzenie napędzi."*
  "If on St. Michael's there's an abundance of acorns, there will be a lot of snow for Christmas."
- *"Gdy w Michała deszcz upadnie, lekka zima będzie snadnie."*
  "If it rains on Michaelmas, the winter will be light."

PAŹDZIERNIK: OCTOBER

October is the longest month of the year due to daylight saving time, which prolongs it by one hour in comparison to other 31-day months. In terms of Polish folk traditions, it's one of the quietest and slowest months, with barely a couple of celebrations. Compared to other autumnal months, October offers a deep pause in between the seasons, with all of nature enjoying its last moments of sunlight before the pre-winter months.

The Polish name of October, *październik*, comes from dried-up stalks of flax and hemp (paździerze). Older variations of the name include *paździerzec, paździerzeń*, and *pościernik*. An alternative old Polish name for the month is *winnik*, derived from *winogrona* (grapes) and *wino* (wine) as the last harvest of grapes occurs during this month, and homemade wine is produced.

October Calendarium

- **October 2:** *Świętych Aniołów Stróżów*, Memorial of the Holy Guardian Angels
- **October 16:** *Świętej Jadwigi Śląskiej*, St. Hedwig of Silesia Feast Day

Świętych Aniołów Stróżów/Memorial of the Holy Guardian Angels (October 2)

There is a folk saying connected to this date: *"Jak anioły w słońcu ciepłym chadzają, to potem w zimie mrozy się trzymają"* ("If the angels walk in warm sunlight, then in the wintertime frost will hold for a long time").

Polish demonology is extremely rich with all kinds of devils, spirits, demons, and various other supernatural creatures, each of them serving a specific function in their domain of influence. Similarly, folk angelology not only exists but is also rich in lore and serves an important role in the overall folk understanding of the world. These heavenly beings have been subject to interesting syncretisms, similar to figures of folk saints. A good example of this is the folklore associated with Archangel Michael explored in the September calendarium.

It is believed that angels are present both at birth and death of each human being. When a child is born, angels can hear the screams of the mother, and they arrive on Earth to assist in the process. They sit by the windows of the household where the birth is taking place, and they pray for it to go well. Once the child is born, angels remain by the crib for three days, guarding the newborn child. Before they leave, they light a new star in the sky. This star will be the child's fate, guiding them for the rest of their life, and it will be thrown down from the sky when they die. This belief alone bears a close resemblance to the pre-Christian lore of the fates, or *Rodzanice.* The three sisters, also equated with the three *Zorze* (Aurorae, representing Venus as the morning and evening star), appear by the crib on the third day after birth, and they weave the fate (Dola) for the newborn. One of them measures the length of the child's life with a thread, another measures out their luck, and the third one their *niedola* (misery). Dola is not only our fate but also a living spirit who can be contacted and prayed to for aid and guidance, similarly to a guardian angel.

In folk beliefs, each evening as we go to bed, an angel and a devil are present with us. The angel writes down all our good deeds of the day, while the devil jots down all the evil deeds. Then, all the deeds are weighed on dragonflies (*ważyć,* weighing; *ważka,* dragonfly; *waga,* scales). Whichever deeds are heavier signify our judgment after death. It was believed that hosts of angels and devils are always present at our deathbed, fighting for the soul to try and drag it to their respective sides. If the soul was won over by the devils, it ended up in hell. However, the angels were responsible both for transporting the soul to heaven and to purgatory.

Guardian angels are believed to remain guardians of the chosen person even after death, which suggests their role as psychopomps. It is believed that guardian angels are often present at the graves of their pupils, especially children. Out of all children, orphans were believed to be the most taken care of. If you ever see a will-o'-the-wisp by a child's grave, that is their guardian angel holding vigil over their soul. There's also a belief that guardian angels, together with Mary, sometimes take the soul of the child from their grave and move it to the grave of their mother, so that they are reunited once more, and the child doesn't suffer from orphanhood any longer.

Growing up, we were taught to always say a prayer to the guardian angel in the evening before sleep. I remember how my grandmother would explain that the guardian angel always wants all the best for me and that they are always by our side. Should we be in danger or scared, we should call out for their aid. When compared with older spirits recognized in Polish tradition, it appears that guardian angels have taken on the role that used to be fulfilled by family spirits and the dola, spirit of individual fate.

Polish prayer to the Guardian Angel:

"Aniele Boży, stróżu mój,
Ty zawsze przy mnie stój.
Rano, wieczór, we dnie, w nocy
Bądź mi zawsze ku pomocy,
Broń mnie od wszelkiego złego
I zaprowadź mnie do żywota wiecznego.
Amen."

"Angel of god, my guardian,
Always be by my side.
In the morning, evening, day and night
Always be there to aid me,
Guard me from all evil
And guide me to eternal life.
Amen."

Świętej Jadwigi Śląskiej/St. Hedwig of Silesia Feast Day (October 16)

St. Jadwiga of Silesia is a patron saint of marriage, refugees, international reconciliation, and the region of Silesia. Originally from Bavaria, she married a Silesian prince, Henry I the Bearded, when she was only 12 years old. After giving birth to seven of their children, Hedwig and Henry took vows of chastity and devoted themselves to matters of faith. Jadwiga was known for living a very modest life. She always walked barefoot and wore a religious habit instead of dresses worthy of nobility. She took care of the poor, the widows, and the orphans, especially. There are many places in Silesia where we can witness traces of her presence to this day—holy stones with imprints of her feet, or sacred springs and rivers that emerged because of her prayers. This paints a strikingly similar picture to that of other female folk saints, such as St. Kinga and St. Jadwiga Andegaweńska—all of whom share traits equating them with folkloric Marys.

The unique abilities attributed to St. Jadwiga include creating healing springs, stopping floods, and being highly skilled in prayer and meditation (even being whipped by devils would not break her concentration). Additionally, Jadwiga is known for saving troops of knights from death in battle by putting them to sleep. According to legends, such armies of sleeping knights reside in several grottos and beneath mountains across Silesia, believed to be capable of waking and aiding the living in a time of dire need.

St. Jadwiga is petitioned for safe refuge, international peace, and a good marriage.

Agrarian sayings for St. Jadwiga Day:

- *"Po świętej Jadwidze są dojrzałe grzyby i rydze."*
  "After St. Jadwiga Day, there are ripe mushrooms and saffron milk caps."
- *"Święta Jadwiga bydło z pola ściga."*
  "St. Jadwiga chases cattle from the fields."
- *"Kto sieje na Jadwigę ten zbiera figę."*
  "Who sows on St. Jadwiga's Day, will reap figs [nothing]."

LISTOPAD: NOVEMBER

November is the month of first frosts, thick fogs, and naked trees. Days are significantly shorter at this point, and overnight frosts occur more frequently. This time of year, the sun sets around 4 p.m., meaning we spend a lot more time in darkness. This lends itself to the pensive, melancholic atmosphere present throughout the month, as if our minds and hearts were slowly becoming enveloped in the cold fogs and the fallen leaves.

The Polish name of the month—*listopad*—means "the falling of leaves". In Old Polish leaves shared the same word with letters (list), hence the name of the month being listopad and not *liściopad.* I like to think that fallen leaves are like love letters exchanged between the living and the dead—as they fall, we are prompted to contemplate our own mortality and think fondly of our beloved ancestors.

November Calendarium

- **November 1:** *Wszystkich Świętych.* All Hallows' Day
- **November 2:** *Zaduszki.* All Souls' Day
- **November 11:** *Świętego Marcina,* St. Martin Feast Day
- **November 24:** *Katarzynki,* St. Catherine's Eve
- **November 29:** *Andrzejki,* St. Andrew's Eve

Wszystkich Świętych i Zaduszki/All Hallows' Day and All Souls' Day (November 1 and November 2)

November 1 and 2 are dedicated to the dead and became a forced replacement for the original pre-Christian celebrations known as Dziady. Despite Christianization and the cultural transformations that occurred, Poles never gave up their deep-rooted reverence for the beloved dead and the ancestors. While our pagan predecessors were used to celebrating their dead up to six times a year, the new religion slowly enforced cramming all the ancestor veneration into a mere two November days. As a result, we continue to incorporate ancestor work into other celebrations around the year, always inviting the dead to our Christmas Eve dinner or visiting the graves with egg-shaped grave candles for Easter. Yet the most outright commemoration of the dead is still celebrated during the first two days of November.

Before we continue to dive deeper into the folk customs, it is important to explain the background of these celebrations. Originally, this time of year, our pre-Christian ancestors celebrated *Dziady Jesienne,* the Autumnal Forefathers. The date of Dziady Jesienne was movable and tied to the lunar cycles. Since the dead are believed to avoid light (including moonlight), Dziady was commonly celebrated during the second dark moon after the autumnal equinox, which happens to occur close to today's Zaduszki. The date got later, permanently tied to November 2, and is still recognized as such. According to official Catholic doctrine, November 1 is the day we celebrate all the dead who are baptized Christians, who received the state of grace, and who went to heaven after death. Zaduszki, however, celebrates all the dead, no matter their state of "grace" or where they went after death. In practice, who's to proclaim themselves the judge on Earth of where the dead go and how blessed they are in the eyes of god(s)? Church officials certainly try, with poor results. While the church says one thing, the people do another. Nobody truly heeds the religious doctrine where the ancestors are concerned. In our eyes, they all deserve equal love and attention.

It usually starts during the last few days of October; more and more people begin to visit the graves of their families, scrubbing the tombstones clean, and adorning them with flowers (chrysantemums, carnations, dahlias, and lilies) and grave candles in a plethora of shapes and sizes—some made of stained glass, some resembling beautiful tombstones and monuments, others being heart-shaped, or even Mary-shaped. All the visitations culminate on November 1 and 2, leaving no grave bare. It is customary to take care of old, abandoned graves, so that those who have no living family left to care for their grave still receive the blessing of fire from a grave candle lit in their honor by a stranger. Nobody is left in darkness.

In the village where I grew up, we had an interesting custom: A few days before All Souls' Day, children from elementary school would go to the cemetery together to clean and care for old, abandoned graves of children in our local graveyard. I always loved this tradition and had my favorite grave that I tended to each year. Such a simple custom, yet so deep and precious, familiarizing us with death from a young age.

It was believed that on the eve of All Souls' Day (during the night between November 1 and 2), the souls of the dead were granted the ability to visit their family homes and dine with the living. Such beliefs were consistent with older customs of welcoming the spirits of one's beloved dead at home for supper. People would kindle torches or even bonfires to guide the dead, and leave their gates open that night. Some would even set up a bath for the dead to wash themselves. At home, supper would be consumed and the leftovers of the meal would be left on the table overnight, allowing the spirits to nourish themselves. The next day, the offerings would be taken to the cemetery.

In some regions of Poland, folks believed that the eve of All Souls' was when the local dead would wake up from their graves and make their journey to the nearest church, to partake in a midnight mass, led by the spirit of a dead priest. One may encounter faint echoes of similar remnants of the cult of the dead existing in places such as the *Kaplica Czaszek* (Skull Chapel) ossuary in Kudowa-Zdrój, where a midnight mass takes place once a year to honour the countless dead who rest there. The priest himself may not belong among the dead, and the date of the mass itself may differ, but the sentiment remains consistent.

Back in the day, the fear of the dead who died violent deaths was very prominent. As Polish demonology explains, those whose life was cut short in unnatural ways, would turn into a plethora of demonic spirits *post mortem*. For this reason, folks would kindle flames on the graves of such individuals, as well as bonfires near cemeteries and at the crossroads, so that the troubled souls may warm themselves by the fire, and hopefully find their way back to the otherworlds without wreaking havoc on the local community. In addition to serving as a guide for the spirits, such bonfires were also believed to protect the living from harm. Fire served as an apotropaic agent, as well as a preventative. Beliefs like these directly reflect the older traditions of Dziady, where folks would gather around the sacred fire, dressed in *kraboszki* (simple masks made of bark or leather), and feast with the dead, passing on messages, asking for advice from the Ród, or helping the souls of those who were stuck move on into the otherworlds.

Today, bonfires and summoning the dead may not be as popular as it was back then, but traditions are still cultivated in more covert forms. One such tradition is known as *wypominki*, which can be translated as "reminiscences." The priest collects names of the dead (along with donations) from the local community and then calls out each name during mass dedicated to the dead, as a form of prayer for their souls and an act of remembrance.

Świętego Marcina/St. Martin Feast Day (November 11)

Saint Martin is the patron saint of soldiers, millers, blacksmiths, tailors, as well as other military and crafts people. His attributes include: goose, horse, two dogs, and book, among others. His feast day falls around the time when folks would be knee deep into the process of gathering supplies for winter. Particularly, now was the time to sacrifice some of the farm animals, such as geese and cattle, to prepare a supply of meat for the dark months ahead. The meat would often be preserved to last longer by drying or smoking. During this saint's feast day, it was taboo to work at the mill—all millers considered St. Martin's feast to be a day of celebration and rest.

Some say that even our worst vices have their own patron saints. Such is the case with St. Martin, whose feast day was an opportunity for unlimited eating and drinking in many regions of Poland. This may have been related to the slaughter and treatment of meat. After all, if you're cooking and treating food for supplies, one might as well eat some extra pieces.

In accordance with a folk saying, *"Dzień św. Marcina dużo gęsi zarzyna"* ("St. Martin's feast day slaughters many geese"), one of the main dishes traditionally cooked on this day was *gąska świętomarcińska* ("St. Martin's goose"). After it was eaten, the leftover bones were then used for fortune telling. It is said that if the bones (especially the breastbone) are white, then winter will be white. If the bones are red, winter will be frosty. If the bones are dark, it will be rainy.

Other than the goose dishes, pastries were also very popular. Especially *rogale świętomarcińskie* ("St. Martin's croissants") with poppy seed filling, which are commonly served across Poland on this day.

St. Martin's feast day most likely has much older, pre-Christian roots. In folk belief, farmers weren't allowed to do any more field work past this date. Working past November 11 meant bad luck and poor crops in the forthcoming season, as it was believed that the soil needed proper rest and should not be disturbed. In pre-Christian times, the saint's feast day most likely had a different original name that got syncretized and associated with Martin later on. The name Martin has Latin origins and stems from Mars, the god of war. As we know from the chronicles of Marcin Bielski (1551): *"Marsá zwali Marzá / tę potym náaszy Marze albo Márzáne"* ("They called Mars Marza, which is our Marza or Marzana"). The goddess Marzanna was often compared to or even equated with Mars by Polish and foreign chroniclers alike, and was considered to be his Slavic corresponding deity, primarily because of the root word *"mar"* shared by both deities. This aligns with the sacrificial killings of farm animals, likely performed initially as offerings to the gods of harvest, household spirits, and the ancestors. A lesser-known fact about the god Mars is that, before he evolved into the god of war, he was a patron god of agriculture. Similarly, Marzanna was the goddess of agriculture before her primary function evolved into that of a death goddess. Such transformations are not unusual and have happened in all pantheons over the centuries, to accommodate the societal and cultural transformations of their peoples. However, even if we consider both older and newer functions of these two deities, they both seem to fit equally well within the scope of St. Martin's feast day: the sacrifice of geese and cattle (death, war), the baking of traditional pastries, and millers being especially celebrated on this day (grain, agriculture) all point toward a much older festival dedicated to the goddess Marzanna in her Grain Mother and Death Goddess aspects. (Not to mention her deep associations with herding geese, guiding the souls of the dead.)

Katarzynki i Andrzejki/St. Catherine's Eve and St. Andrew's Eve (November 24 and November 29)

November 29, St. Andrew's Eve, is the most well-known night dedicated to fortune-telling and divination in Polish folk tradition—and still celebrated to this day. It is traditionally one of the five days of the year when mortals are allowed to safely peek beyond the veil to see their future. Other dates include November 24 (St. Catherine's Eve), Christmas Eve, New Year's Eve, and St. John's Eve.

As St. Andrew is the patron saint of lovers and marriage, *Andrzejki* celebrations were originally dedicated to women's fortune-telling and divination related to matters of love and relationships, sometimes even fertility. This does not mean that men weren't interested in love spells and fortune-telling about matters of love. The night of November 24 (St. Catherine's Eve) was originally the "manly" equivalent of Andrzejki, known as *Katarzynki.* Men and women preferred to do this type of fortune-telling and divination work separately, which likely stems from the fact that folks were used to doing various farm chores and homesteading works separately or in groups of same-sex people. Over time, this lent itself to ritualizing certain aspects of the work, thus making them taboo and reserved for "insiders" only.

Nowadays, everyone celebrates Andrzejki together. As the separation between men and women dissipated in the twentieth century, the significance of Katarzynki had faded over time in favor of Andrzejki celebrations, now evolved into dress-up parties, similar to Western Halloween or New Year's carnival parties.

Let us examine some of the most well-documented methods of fortune-telling and divination used in Poland from the sixteenth century onward. Many of them are still practiced today.

Fortune-Telling With the Help of Animals

Some methods of fortune-telling included animals. Don't worry, no animals are hurt in the process.

One such method includes going outside the house in the evening and listening for dogs barking. The direction from which the first bark could be heard would foretell the direction from which the future partner arrives.

Another one that included dogs was performed in a circle. Each participant would carry either a bovine bone or a piece of bread with lard. They would call a dog inside the circle and then lay their bones or bread on the ground. The order in which the dog would eat these offerings would foretell the order in which the participants would get married.

A similar method included a rooster. The bird would be let inside the circle, and each participant would lay some grain on the ground. The order in which the cock eats the grains would predict the order in which they get married.

Fortune-Telling With the Aid of Saint Magic

On the eve of St. Andrew's Day, one must collect and bring wood and kindling home and kindle the fire in the fireside alone. Then, one must cook three vegetable dishes and dress the dining table for two. There can be no knives or forks, or other sharp tools on the table to avoid hurting the one performing this spell, or the spirit of the future spouse. Nobody must see this, nobody must touch anything, otherwise the spell will not work. Then, one must stand in the middle of the room and say: "In the name of the Father, the Son, and the Holy Spirit, I invite you to dine with me. Amen." Upon reciting these words, one's future spouse shall appear in spirit and walk around the table three times, then disappear.

An important part of Andrzejki divination includes dreamwork. One should pray to St. Andrew multiple times during the day of the eve of St. Andrew's to meet their future love in dreams or otherwise receive prophetic dreams. Some ways to aid prophetic dreamwork included:

- Placing a piece of male clothing under the sheets to meet a future partner in dreams
- Placing a bowl of water near the bed and building a little bridge of twigs over the bowl (so that a future beloved's spirit can walk over the bridge right into one's dreams)
- To make sure no demons or evil spirits make their way into one's dreams, it was advised to rub garlic over the bedroom's thresholds, door handles, and windowsills
- Burning "St. Andrew's bonfires" in the backyard to protect the household from demons and evil spirits, as well as inhaling the bonfire's smoke to aid in prophetic dreaming (especially if consecrated herbs were added to the fire)
- "Sowing" seeds of oats in bed or around it while praying to St. Andrew for prophetic dreams

Popular Ways of Fortune-Telling That Survived Today

Wax pouring divination, known as carromancy, is one of the most popular methods that is still broadly practiced. One should melt wax in a pot and then pour it through a keyhole into a bowl of cold water. Once the wax hardens, one should pick it up and try to decipher the meaning of its shape. To make it easier, people would traditionally hold the wax blob against a wall and direct candlelight at it to cast its shadow upon the wall, similarly to how you make shadow puppets with your hands. Then, one should turn the wax blob around in their hands until they see a shape that makes sense to them—this shape will predict their future.

Another popular fortune-telling method can be performed with a group of friends. Everyone takes off one shoe, and all the shoes are arranged in a line, starting at the wall of the room that's the farthest from the door. Then, people replace their shoes, taking the one that's at the end of the line and placing it in front of the line, until one of the shoes steps on the threshold of the door. The owner of the shoe that stepped on the threshold will get married first.

Apples also play an important role in fortune-telling this time of year. One such method requires an apple, a small knife, and some basic skill in peeling apples. The idea is to peel the skin of the apple in such a way that the peel becomes as long as possible without tearing. Once it tears, that's it. Then, one should take the peel and throw it behind them. If it resembles a letter, this will be the first letter of one's future spouse's name. If it resembles something else, it shall predict the future in ways unrelated to love.

A method of fortune-telling that pairs well with dream divination includes writing possible names of future partners on little pieces of paper and placing them under one's pillow before going to sleep on the eve of St. Andrew's. The next morning, one is supposed to draw one piece of paper from under the pillow. The name written on it foretells the name of a future partner.

To divine one's future love life, a wedding ring, a rosary, and a branch of myrtle should be placed under three mugs. The wedding ring symbolizes getting married, the rosary predicts becoming a monk/nun, and the myrtle branch suggests staying single (and a virgin) forever. The mugs are mixed around on the table, and then one turns a chosen mug to reveal which object foretells their fate.

Finally, a rather adorable method of foretelling the future of an existing relationship required two tiny candles that could be placed in two halves of a walnut shell, then placed in a bowl of water. If the two candles on their tiny shell boats end up swimming toward one another and touching, it is interpreted as a sign of a happy, long-term relationship.

There are plenty more variations of the traditional fortune-telling games and practices mentioned above. Oftentimes, adults pair Andrzejki celebrations with having the last proper party before Advent. Nowadays, it's also popular to invite tarot readers, mediums, psychics, and astrologers to such parties. Of course, kids have fun as well. Andrzejki are often organized in schools and kindergartens, where kids get to learn and try some of the folk methods of fortune-telling.

CHAPTER TWENTY-FIVE

WINTER

GRUDZIEŃ: DECEMBER

December, the last month of the year, greets us with thick snow, sub-zero temperatures and days now getting rapidly shorter. This is naturally reflected in the celebrations of this month, largely focusing on spending time with family, celebrating community, eating hearty foods, praying by candle light, exchanging gifts, sharing songs and stories by the fire, and indulging in fun activities like *kulig* sleigh rides, or folks dressing up as *kolędnicy* (carolers) and play-acting little shows as a way of bringing joy and blessings to the households of their neighbors.

The name of the month itself comes from the word *gruda,* meaning a lump of frozen soil.

December Calendarium

- **December:** *Przedgody/Adwent,* Advent (movable)
- **December 4:** *Barbórka/Świętej Barbary,* St. Barbara Feast Day
- **December 6:** *Mikołajki,* St. Nicholas Feast Day
- **December 13:** *Świętej Łucji,* St. Lucia Feast Day
- **December 24–25:** *Wigilia and Boże Narodzenie,* Christmas Eve and Christmas
- **December 25–January 6:** *Koladka/Szczodre Gody,* Caroling/Generous Festivities
- **December 26:** *Świętego Szczepana,* St. Stephen Feast Day
- **December 31:** *Sylwester,* St. Sylvester Feast Day

Przedgody/Advent

Advent, also known as *przedgody* (pre-festivities), used to begin in November, right after St. Martin's Feast Day, and lasted for 40 days, all the way to Christmas Eve. This was later changed so that Advent begins on the fourth Sunday before Christmas, thus making its inauguration movable and its length anywhere between 23 and 28 days. In Catholicism, Advent marks the beginning of a new liturgical year.

Once Advent was announced, folk would generally cease to engage in parties, socialising, and pleasures until Christmas and turn to contemplation and prayer. From this point on, every day before sunrise, people would participate in a traditional mass known as *jutrznia* (matins) or *roraty* (rorates) dedicated to Mother Mary, present in Polish culture since at least the thirteenth century. This would go on for the Advent period, until Christmas. This pre-dawn mass is traditionally observed in relative darkness, lit only by dim candlelight, with one big altar candle known as *roratnica,* and all the participants hold smaller candles and lanterns known as *roratki.* This results in a beautiful spectacle of light, resembling a dreamy night sky filled with stars. The name of the mass comes from the beginning of a traditional song beginning with the words, *"Rorate coeli desuper"* ("Drop down, ye heavens," although the Polish version could be translated as "Release dew from heavens above"). The symbolism of dew and pre-dawn darkness illuminated by countless little lanterns bears old associations with Jutrzenka, the goddess of dawn, Venus as *Gwiazda Poranna* (Morning Star), who later got syncretized with Mother Mary as Stella Matutina.

Around Advent, days become very short, which meant that folks used to spend a lot of time in darkness, or by candle light, indoors. It was a time of rest, slowing down, and tending to the hearth. These long, quiet evenings lent themselves to partaking in simple repetitive chores, such as mending clothes, embroidering shirts or tablecloths, sorting through food supplies and such. In rural communities, women enjoyed coming together during this time and engaging in traditional activities, such as feather tearing, or spinning yarn. While they worked, they would sing traditional songs, share about their feelings and troubles to receive community support, or engage in innocent gossip.

This time of year was also considered the best time for matrimonial consultations. While doing their tasks, women would exchange information about the men available in their local community, thus finding the best possible matches for their daughters. Young men knew this practice and would often sneak around outside the windows and try to eavesdrop on what was being said about them.

In Northern Poland, folk would begin to dress up as *kolędnicy* since the beginning of Advent, much earlier than in the other regions. The groups of kolędnicy consisted of people dressed up as various animals, or traditional figures of folklore such as bears, storks, devils, "starmen", or old hags. Some of them would carry accessories, such as a whip, a drum, and other primitive instruments, as well as dried fruits and candy, for the kids. They would visit people's homes throughout Advent, until Christmas Eve. However, in other regions of Poland, groups of kolędnicy would usually begin making their rounds after Christmas, more of which will be explained below.

Barbórka or Świętej Barbary/St. Barbara Feast Day (December 4)

St. Barbara, the patron saint of coal miners, has always been especially revered in Silesia, where most of our coal mines are, and where coal mining is a prominent part of the local culture. However, she also belongs among the Fourteen Holy Helpers, and is the patron saint of builders, architects, masons, raftsmen, and all folk whose jobs are considered dangerous and potentially deadly. It is believed that if she cannot spare them, at least she can offer them a good death.

Growing up in Silesia, I witnessed my fair share of *Barbórka* celebrations. It was—and still is—a big deal for the local communities. Miners dressed in their festive uniforms and feathered hats, carrying a hand-embroidered banner with St, Barbara, would be present during mass dedicated to the saint, and then parade the town or village, often culminating in some kind of local party. Interestingly, during this day, miners would also host their own traditional rites of initiation for new miners, known as *wyzwoliny na rębacza* (liberation of a hewer). The aspiring new miners had to jump through a special piece of leather known as *łata* and then enjoy a meal of *Silesian krupniok* (a traditional type of lunch meat) and beer with the rest of the miners.

While St. Barbara's cult is especially prominent among miners, she's also a patron saint of families and good death. Back in war times, she would often be petitioned to spare a man from the military draft.

Lastly, on St. Barbara's feast day, folks would pay special attention to the weather to predict the winter. While a variety of folk sayings exist regarding weather on this day, they all boil down to this: *"Kiedy w świętą Barbarę błoto, Będzie zima jak złoto, A jeśli mróz, to sanie na górę włóż, a szykuj wóz"* ("If St. Barbara's is muddy, winter will be golden [perfect], but if there's frost, put up your sleighs and prepare your cart"). Ideally, we would expect warmer days and mud around St. Barbara's feast day, so that Christmas may be beautiful and snow-covered.

Mikołajki/St. Nicholas Feast Day (December 6)

The tradition of receiving gifts from *Święty Mikołaj* on the night between December 5 and December 6 is relatively new in Poland, dating back about 200 years. It was believed that on this night, St. Nicholas descended from the heavens on his golden ladder. He'd then mount his white horse and ride with a big sack of gifts. Those who were kind to others would receive gifts, while those who were mean would experience a not-so-pleasant whipping from the Devil instead. As it turns out, Mikołaj never rode alone but was accompanied by the Devil, who held a *rózga* (rod) and used it to whip bad people. The accompanying Devil would sometimes be referred to as Nikołaj. Some suggest that Mikołaj/Nikołaj may be both the saint and the Devil simultaneously.

For our ancestors, St. Nicholas was a patron saint of shepherds, sailors, prisoners, merchants, bakers, and poor children. The shepherd aspect of Mikołaj seems to have played an especially important role. Many legends of this saint portray him as a shepherd of wolves. It was believed that St. Nicholas could control wolves, and therefore, shepherds often prayed to him for protection from wolves and other wild animals.

"Święty Mikołaju,
Weź klucze idź do raju.
Zamknij pysk psu wściekłemu,
I wilkowi borowemu."

"Saint Nicholas,
Take your keys to the paradise and go.
Close shut the mouths of the rabid dog,
and the forest wolf."

According to legend, on the night of December 6, there was a large forest meeting hosted by St. Nicholas and all of the wolf kin were invited. The wolves had to attend this meeting to receive instructions from Mikołaj regarding their tasks and orders for the upcoming year. Each wolf would come forth to Mikołaj and he would whisper instructions into their ear. Should any human witness such a gathering, they would never be seen again. But for those who respected St. Nicholas and prayed to him with regularity, he would become a fierce protector and savior from wolf attacks and even werewolves.

Scholars often point out that post-Christianization Święty Mikołaj took over the functions and attributes previously attributed to Weles, the chthonic god commonly syncretized with the Devil, and known for his domain over wolves and other wild beasts.

Świętej Łucji/St. Lucia Feast Day (December 13)

Originally, the celebrations of this day most likely took place on the winter solstice. The difference of almost ten days between St. Lucia's Feast Day and the winter solstice comes from the reformation of the calendar from Julian to Gregorian in the 1500s, thus shifting the reformed date to December 13. Some old folk sayings from before the calendar reformation still confirm the original meaning of this day in folk tradition: *"Święta Łuca dnia przyrzuca. Święto Łucy noc króci"* ("St. Lucia adds the day. Lucia's Day shortens the night").

According to folk beliefs, on the night of St. Lucia's feast day, witches become especially active and dangerous—their magic became much more potent than usual. They might cast a curse on one's cows, steal a child, and replace it with an *odmieniec* (changeling), or otherwise make the common folks' life harder. It was believed that the eve of St. Lucia's was when witches would apply a flying ointment and fly to the sabbat on Babia Góra (Hag Mountain) to feast and cast curses. Therefore, to protect themselves, folk would avoid leaving the house after dark, pay special attention to their kids so that they don't get swapped with an odmieniec, as well as say protective charms and prayers both over the household and the barns to protect their families and farm animals. The best ways to chase away witches were to hang or burn consecrated herbs around the place or spill poppy seeds at the front door so that the witch will be too busy counting the seeds and thus cannot perform her malicious magic before the night is over.

For witches, this is the night of intensified magical workings, as well as engaging in practices such as dream work, spirit flight, and entering trance states for purposes of divination or serving justice to those who deserve it.

Wigilia and *Boże Narodzenie*/Christmas Eve and Christmas (December 24–25)

In Polish folk tradition, unlike in Western cultures, Christmas Eve is the main celebration. This isn't an isolated occurrence; we seem to prefer celebrating the eves of important dates rather than the dates themselves. Other than Christmas Eve, some more prominent examples include St. Wojciech's Eve, St. John's Eve, St. Andrew's Eve, St. Lucia's Eve, and New Year's Eve. Incidentally, these eves are also regarded as times when witches are especially powerful and active; many miracles and magical occurrences can be witnessed in the wild on these nights.

Christmas Eve, however, was the most important of them all, marking the beginning of a new solar year, with a plethora of winter solstice and old folkloric traditions still preserved and cultivated.

According to a Polish folk saying, *"Jaka wigilia, taki cały rok"* ("Same Christmas Eve, same all year round"), which means that the way one behaves on Christmas Eve is how one will act in the entire year ahead. Thus, people try to pay special attention and put more effort into being kind, patient, and perhaps trying to restrain themselves from addictions or unwanted behaviors. It was forbidden to argue and encouraged to resolve conflicts and forgive one another. It was also believed that one shouldn't lend anything to the neighbors on this day, or else abundance would leave the household in the coming year. However, little acts of theft were commonly performed as pranks on the neighbors, with everything returned after. A thief who was successful in their acts would be granted the blessing of all financial matters going well for them in the coming year. Throughout the whole day and night, animals would be treated like family, with love and respect, receiving better food and sharing the wafer with their human caretakers.

The dead and ancestors are not to be forgotten either. They receive a special empty seat at the dining table and are regarded as being present in the household throughout the day and night. Because of their presence, some works were considered taboo during this day, to avoid accidentally hurting the spirits. People would blow on a chair before sitting in it, to ensure they don't accidentally sit on their deceased grandpa. They would also avoid weaving, spinning, and shaking pots with hot foods, so they would not harm the invisible guests.

Because the entire day was believed to be filled with miracles and magic of all kinds, folks believed flowers could bloom on this day (even the mythical fern flower), waters in springs and wells acquired magical or healing properties, treasures could be uncovered from the depths of the Earth, and animals could speak human language (and could tell the future). All creation rejoices and is closer with each other than usual, allowing for all sorts of miracles to happen.

Kolacja wigilijna (eve dinner) is a serious matter. Everyone in the household participates in preparations for this evening from early in the morning, if not days prior. Traditionally, everyone was required to get up early and wash themselves in cold water to preserve good health. Afterwards, men would hunt for fish or game for dinner, while women would cook traditional dishes and decorate the space. All the traditional decorations were primarily valued for their symbolic and magical functions rather than their aesthetic value. Examples of traditional decorations include: *pająki* (hanging decorations made of straw and paper), *podłaźniczka* (evergreen boughs decorated and hanged from the ceiling, the original precursor of the Christmas tree), *szopka* (a miniature setup of the nativity scene), *gwiazda* (stars made of wafer, paper, straw, or other craft materials), sheafs of grains stood in the corners of the room, and grains were spilled on the tablecloth with straw hidden beneath the cloth. All the agrarian decorations of straw and grains come from much older traditions of Diduch—the spirit of grain is invited into the household to overwinter.

There also had to be twelve traditional dishes. The dishes would vary depending on the region or what was accessible, but some of the most popular ones include:

- *Barszcz wigilijny z uszkami* (beetroot soup with miniature dumplings)
- *Zupa grzybowa* (mushroom soup)
- *Pierogi z kapustą i grzybami/Pierogi ruskie* (dumplings with cabbage and mushrooms/dumplings with potatoes and cottage cheese)
- *Kapusta z grochem lub z grzybami* (cabbage with peas and mushrooms)
- *Karp smażony lub w galarecie* (carp fish—fried or in jelly)
- *Ryba po grecku* (it's called Greek-style fish, but it is a traditional Polish dish—a fish cooked or baked with vegetables)
- *Śledź w śmietanie lub oleju* (herring with cream or oil)
- *Kluski z makiem* (a type of "lazy dumpling" with no filling, served with poppy seeds)
- *Makowiec* (poppy seed cake)
- *Piernik staropolski* (Old Polish gingerbread cake)
- *Kompot z suszu* (infusion of smoked and dried fruits)

- *Kutia* (dessert made with poppy seeds, nuts, almonds, raisins, grains, and honey)

The dining table is the biggest deal of all—set up in a specific way—with straw placed underneath the cloth, and plates set up for all the living participants, as well as for the dead. Depending on the region, folks would generally look for the first evening star to appear in the sky, which would be the sign that it is time to gather at the table and begin the festivities. Before sitting at the table, folk would officially invite the dead to the table:

"Pójdźże dziadku do obiadku."

"Come, grandfather, to dinner.".

Animals weren't left behind either. The head of the family would open the front door wide and call to them:

"Wróblęta, ptasięta, chodźcie ku nam obiadować
A jak nie przyjdziecie, nie przychodźcie przez cały rok"

"Sparrows, birds, come dine with us
And if you don't come, do not come all year round"

"Wilczku, wilczku, chodź do groszku,
Chodźże z nami wieczerzać,
A jak nie pójdziesz, żebym cię przez cały rok nie widział!"

"Wolf, wolf, come for the peas,
Come dine with us,
And if you don't come, may I not see you at all in the year ahead!"

It is believed that the calling and invitation of both the dead and the animals is one of the oldest animistic remnants of the celebrations of the winter solstice, still so perfectly preserved to this day.

After calling in the dead and the animals, people would share the wafer with each other. Everyone would hold a little piece in their hand and allow the other person to break off and consume little pieces of it as they wish them all the best. Once everyone had the chance to exchange wishes and wafers, it was finally time to sit at the table and eat. Eating would often be accompanied by speaking traditional formulas to the food so that it may be abundant in the coming year, and so that all the plants would grow well. While people were eating, it was forbidden to get up from the table until everyone was finished. It was believed that getting up could cause misfortune, illness, and a lack of abundance to those present. Once everyone was finished, the setup was left as it was—nothing was removed from the table and left overnight for the spirits to feast upon. The only thing that was allowed to be taken was a scale from the carp fish. People would clean it and place it in their wallet as a talisman that would attract money.

Lastly, after dinner, people would exchange presents and sing traditional carols, while digesting all the food and patiently waiting for *Pasterka,* a midnight mass in honor of the birth of Christ (or the rebirth of the sun, originally). This mass has always been very popular, especially in rural areas. Everyone would meet their neighbors, sneak in a shot of vodka outside the church, and share the jolly mood.

The next morning, on Christmas Day, there wasn't much to do in terms of traditional celebrations. People would either visit extended family or simply clean up after the previous night's dinner, relax, and continue to devour the foods and desserts in a relaxed atmosphere. It is generally a day reserved for resting with the family, no working, cooking, or sorting things around the household is allowed.

Koladka i Szczodre Gody/Caroling or Generous Festivities (December 25–January 6)

Christmas Day marks the beginning of the *Gody* or *Koladka* period, which lasts until January 6, known as the Three Magi Day (Epiphany). The term Gody can be translated as "festivities," but it also has an additional meaning, coming from the word *godnie,* meaning proudly or with dignity. During these twelve days, there wasn't much work to do, and everyone could finally rest and relax, continue to feast on good food, sing traditional carols, and truly, fully enjoy all the good things in their life—with dignity, pride, and joy. The alternative name Koladka comes from *kolędy* and *kolędnicy,* carols and the carolers dressed up as traditional folkloric figures. Each region had its own version of the figures that were present. Earlier on, we mentioned the star man from Northern Poland. However, some of the most iconic regional variations include *turoń* (a type of Polish auroch), *koza* (goat), and *konik* (horse). During this time of Gody, in most regions of Poland, kolędnicy would walk from house to house, singing carols and blessing each household with abundance and joy. The people who participated in the caroling groups usually came from the poorest families in the community. As they entered the household, they would bless the family, act out a little scene, sing traditional songs, and ask for a donation. The donation or gift was also called *kolęda* and usually consisted of *szczodraki* (coming from *szczodry*, meaning generous)—a type of bread baked for kolędnicy—gifted along with apples, sausages, nuts, and cakes. Kolędnicy were always received with joy and openness, and generously showered with donations in each household, believed to be the bringers of abundance and good luck.

Świętego Szczepana/St. Stephen Feast Day (December 26)

St. Stephen's feast day was the day of blessing oats and other grains. In folk Catholicism, the grains were first blessed by the priest during mass, and then taken home. At home, the folk festivities would continue in ways truer to older traditions. Once at home, all the family members present would exchange wishes for a plentiful harvest in the coming year. Then, they would throw the grains at each other, exclaiming:

> *"Na szczęście na zdrowie, na ten święty Szczepan! Żeby wam się rodziła kapusta i rzepa, żyto jak koryto, pszenica jak rękawica, owiesek jak pański piesek."*
>
> *"For luck, for health, for St. Stephen! May your cabbages and turnips grow, may your rye be abundant like a trough, may your wheat be like a glove, may your oats be like a noble's dog."*

After the fun of throwing grains at each other, folks would then go out in groups of *podłaźnicy*, usually consisting of young men. They would walk from household to household, similarly to kolędnicy—singing songs and bestowing blessings—but their intentions weren't to receive a donation, but to present themselves as men ready for the taking. They paraded to households where they had an eye on someone in a romantic sense. This was the boys' opportunity to make a good impression on the parents and gain their favor.

Sylwester/St. Sylvester Feast Day (December 31)

The joyous festivities of *Sylwester*—New Year's Eve—seem to have inherited many of the original traditions and customs practiced around Christmas Eve, stemming from the perception of the winter solstice as a new beginning and rebirth of the sun. Similarly to Christmas Eve, Sylwester was perceived as one of the most magical nights of the year, with witches being especially active and powerful. While many of the original winter solstice practices can be applied to this celebration, several ways of folk divination seem to have been practiced exclusively around this time of year:

- **Night sky divination:** On the night of New Year's Eve, one can divine the future in the coming year by looking up at the night sky. If the stars shine brightly, that means good luck and prosperity in the coming year.
- **Eavesdropping fortune telling:** Single women attending Sylwester parties should carefully listen to conversations around them at midnight. The first name they hear will be the name of their future partner.
- **Champagne glass fortune telling:** Big chaotic bubbles of champagne in the glass foretell significant changes and a romance. Tiny bubbles forming little strings foretell good health and happy family life. Strings of bubbles crossing each other foretell health issues and warn against spending money frivolously.
- **Mirror gazing:** Those who wish to see the face of their future partner should light two candles and gaze into a mirror at midnight.
- **Sky gazing:** The first 12 days of the new year were especially important in terms of sky gazing to divine the weather in the coming months. The most important, however, was January 1, which would reveal the future harvest. Some of these observations were recorded as folk sayings:

    - *"Jak Nowy Rok jasny i chłodny, cały roczek pogodny i płodny."*
      "If the New Year is bright and cold, the whole year will be sunny and fertile."
    - *"Na Nowy Rok pogoda, będzie w polu uroda."*
      "Good weather on the New Year, there will be an abundance of crops in the fields."
    - *"Nowy Rok pochmurny, zbiór będzie durny."*
      "If the New Year is cloudy, the harvest will be weak."

STYCZEŃ: JANUARY

In the Polish language, January is known as *styczeń*. The word is directly related to the word *styk*, which could be translated to mean a point of connection or a link—a time in which two things touch, meet, or are otherwise joined together. This beautifully unveils the meaning of this time as experienced by our ancestors; a period that mediates between the old and new year, a liminal time of transition. An alternative etymology that linguists point toward is the archaic Old Polish word, *tyczeń*, relating to *tyki*, which are long pieces of wood chopped this time of year to grow flax and legumes in the coming farming season, or—in case of emergency—could also double as firewood.

An older name for this period was *sieczeń*, which is sometimes ascribed to January, but other times to February; therefore, it isn't fully clear which month it originally belonged to. However, the meaning of sieczeń is related to a verb *siec*, which means "to hack," "to slash," or otherwise cut into things. This is specifically descriptive of the harsh weather of this time of year, especially the violent, cold, and icy snow that cuts into your skin mercilessly.

January Calendarium

- **Until January 6:** *Koladka i Szczodre Gody*, Caroling or Generous Festivities
- **January 6:** *Trzech Króli*, Epiphany
- **January 6 until Ash Wednesday:** *Zapusty*, Polish Carnival

Trzech Króli/Epiphany (January 6)

In Polish tradition, ordinary folk weren't as much concerned with the Kings (or Mages) from faraway lands as they were with using this opportunity to consecrate certain objects and ingredients used in folk magic. The most important items to consecrate on this day were chalk, juniper (instead of incense), conifer resin (instead of myrrh), any gold (and sometimes silver) objects that one possessed, and water.

Consecrated water was used for blessing the house and farm buildings, cleaning wounds, and blessing children when one needed to leave them unattended during the day or for the night. It was also used for washing the sick, dying, and deceased.

Consecrated gold was used for healing sicknesses by touching or rubbing the ill body parts. This tradition of using gold for healing is widespread in Slavic folk medicine. It is related to old beliefs surrounding the god Weles as the guardian of riches in the underworld.

Consecrated juniper incense and conifer resins were used for *okadzanie* (smoke cleansing) of humans and animals.

As for the consecrated chalk, it was used for healing (added to concoctions or baths), for drawing protective circles on the ground, as well as specifically used to write the "K + M + B" sign above the main entrance door as a way of blessing the home. It was believed to represent the three initials of the Three Magi. Interestingly, this was never intended by the Church - the letters were supposed to be "C + M + B" to stand for Latin *"Christus Mansionem Benedicat"* ("Christ, bless this home"), but our folk wouldn't have it and continued to use the "incorrect" inscription with the "K" until the 1960s when a new custom was introduced. Priests would visit people in their homes and write the "correct" inscriptions on their doors themselves while also blessing the house with holy water.

Zapusty/Polish Carnival (January 6 until Ash Wednesday)

January 6 marks the final transition from Christmas and New Year celebrations to *Zapusty* (Polish Carnival), which would last until Ash Wednesday and the beginning of Lent. This tradition dates to at least the sixteenth century, and each region has a unique way of celebrating. Folks would organize street parades with groups of people dressed in traditional costumes that they used during *kolędowanie*, as well as unique carnival costumes of devils, monsters, colorful animals, reapers, ghosts, and other strange creatures. The parades are accompanied by dancing, singing traditional songs, and creating effigies of animals to parade around the streets. Drinking lots of alcohol and eating fatty foods, such as *placki ziemniaczane* (potato pancakes), was a staple around this time of year. Folks wanted to stock up on fat reserves before the fasting period of Lent.

LUTY: FEBRUARY

The name of February, *luty*, is an old term meaning harsh, frosty, and sharp. This stems from the fact that February used to be the coldest month of the year in this part of Europe. In Old Polish, this adjective was used to describe the harsh winter conditions and the behavior of animals.

One of the most well-known folk sayings about February is *"Luty, podkuj buty"* ("In February, shoe your shoes"). It's a funny metaphor for ensuring you mend your shoes well to keep yourself warm in the harsh winter conditions.

February Calendarium

- **February 2:** *Gromnica/Matki Boskiej Gromnicznej,* Our Lady of Gromnica
- **February 3:** *Świętego Błażeja,* St. Blaise Feast Day
- **February 5:** *Świętej Agaty,* St. Agatha Feast Day
- **February 14:** *Walentynki,* St. Valentine Feast Day
- **52 days before Easter:** *Tłusty Czwartek,* Fat Thursday (movable)
- **Last three days before Ash Wednesday:** *Ostatki,* Culmination of Zapusty Carnival

Gromnica/Matki Boskiej Gromnicznej (February 2)

The word *Gromnica* comes from *grom* (thunder), and it is both the name of the celebration as well as the traditional "thunder candles" that are the key element of this festival. On February 2, folk would traditionally go to church to consecrate their long beeswax Gromnica candles for later use in protection and healing magic.

As the candles burned during mass, people would observe the dripping wax and tell fortunes from its shapes. If the wax was dripping heavily, it signified a long and harsh winter ahead. If the candle burned with a tall flame or made crackling sounds, it meant that the summer would be stormy and rainy.

On the way home from church, it was important to try and carry the candle still burning. This is a symbolic remnant of the significance of Living Fire in Polish folk magic—a flame that was kindled from a consecrated source of fire (Living Fire) had to be protected at all costs as it carries the spirits, the blessings, or the magic that was worked during the rite. (Catholic mass is also considered a rite in this context.) The protection of the Living Flame was one of the reasons why many Gromnica candles were traditionally dressed in a protective dome made of white cardboard or paper and tied with a blue ribbon.

If the candle made it home still lit, the head of the family would carry it through the threshold and then mark the sign of the solar cross on the ceiling and above windows and doors. This was done to protect the household from misfortune, especially from storms and other harsh natural phenomena. Once that was done, folk would transfer the flame from the candle onto the central hearth of the home, transferring the Living Fire in this way, which blessed the household with love, unity, and good fortune.

Gromnica candles were then used throughout the year, until next year's consecration of a new candle. One of the most common uses included lighting a Gromnica candle in the window to ward off lightning during storms. Gromnica was also believed to possess healing properties. Its flame and smoke were used in folk medicine to cure ear infections, skin conditions, and even throat inflammation. Lastly, Gromnica was also placed in the hands of a dying person to help them transition from this life to the next.

Świętego Błażeja/St. Blaise Feast Day (February 3)

St. Blaise is a saint who belongs among the "Fourteen Holy Helpers." He is most known for being the patron saint of doctors, protector of animals, and the saint to turn to for aid with throat infections. On February 3, folk would consecrate apples, which were then believed to possess healing properties for the throat. Other than apples, people would also consecrate *błażejki* (blaisies), which were small candles, sometimes tied in a cross shape, that would be lit and held under the chin as throat infection prevention.

Świętej Agaty/St. Agatha Feast Day (February 5)

St. Agatha is a patron saint of chimney sweepers, bell-founders, casters, and others who work in fire-related professions. She protects from fires and fire-related natural disasters.

On St. Agatha's feast day, people would consecrate bread, salt, and water for use in protection against fire. In the event of a fire, folk would take the consecrated items and literally throw them into the flames to extinguish them. Z. Gloger attests this tradition in *Encyklopedia staropolska* (Old Polish Encyclopedia), describing a fire that took place in Łomża on February 5, 1864, during which local folk would throw their "St. Agatha's salt" into the flames and miraculously kept the fire from spreading that way.

Salt consecrated on this day also had an additional use related to well magic, which was most likely the original reason for its consecration in the first place. One could use "St. Agatha's salt" to purify their old well or to dig a new well on St. John's Eve.

Walentynki/St., Valentine Feast Day (February 14)

The cult of St. Valentine blossomed in medieval Europe when it became trendy to travel to holy places that displayed reliquaries of saints and to work with saints in folk magic. Even before the cult of St. Valentine arrived in Poland, this saint was best known for his patronage over those who suffer from illnesses of the nervous system, such as epilepsy or migraines, and mental illness. Folk also petitioned to him for help during plagues and epidemics. Once his cult became prominent in Poland, folk traditions followed. One such fascinating tradition comes from the Kurpie region, where people would make votive offerings of beeswax in the shapes of a human figure, leg, ear, hand, jaws, hearts, and other body parts or, alternatively, flat discs or balls of wax. These wax offerings for the saint are called *osiarki.* Folk would bring their osiarki to church with the intention of infusing them with blessings and healing powers from St. Valentine. Naturally, the shapes weren't random; they resembled the body parts that needed healing. Participants would walk around the main altar three times, each time wiping their osiarki in the dust gathered on the wooden pieces of the altar. Once back home, they would rub these dusty beeswax votives onto the sick body parts to heal them.

Tłusty Czwartek/Fat Thursday

Fat Thursday is the last Thursday before Lent. As the name would suggest, it is a day of feasting on fatty foods. Back in the day, nobility would indulge in roasted game, hares, partridge, *pasztet* (pate), and poultry. The food would be covered in fatty sauces and washed down with homemade alcohol. Village folk would be eating groats with fat, cabbage with greaves, and bacon, while those who were wealthier would also include *kiełbasa* (sausage) and *rosół* (chicken broth). Fatty foods symbolized abundance, prosperity, and protection from hunger and malnutrition in the year ahead.

Since around the sixteenth century, Poles prefer to eat fatty sweets such as *pączki* (donuts, minus the hole), *faworki*, or *chrust*. Originally, pączki would be filled with meat, but over time, the filling was changed to sweet jams and marmalades. It is believed that eating pączki on Fat Thursday grants good luck and prosperity in the year ahead and is widely celebrated to this day.

Ostatki/Last Days of Zapusty Carnival

Ostatki ("leftovers") are the three last days of Zapusty Carnival. This is the last Sunday, Monday, and Tuesday before Ash Wednesday, which marks the beginning of the Lenten period. While carnival Zapusty activities usually took place from January 6 until Lent, these last three days were truly the culmination of all the carnival activities. Folks would feast on fatty foods, drink alcohol, dance, and parade in the streets. Because of the wild character of these festivities, they would also be referred to as *diabelskie dni* (devilish days).

BIBLIOGRAPHY

Baranowski, Bohdan. *Pożegnanie z Diabłem i Czarownicą. Wierzenia ludowe.* Wydawnictwo Replika, 2020.

—. *Procesy Czarownic w Polsce w XVII i XVIII wieku.* Wydawnictwo Replika, 2021.

Bartmiński, Jerzy. *Słownik stereotypów i symboli ludowych. Tom I: Kosmos. Zeszyt 1: niebo, światła niebieskie, ogień, kamienie.* Lublin: Wydawnictwo Uniwersytetu Marii Curie-Skłodowskiej, 1996.

—. *Słownik stereotypów i symboli ludowych. Tom I: Kosmos. Zeszyt 2: ziemia, woda, podziemie.* Lublin: Wydawnictwo Uniwersytetu Marii Curie-Skłodowskiej, 1999.

—. *Słownik stereotypów i symboli ludowych. Tom II: Rośliny. Zeszyt 4: zioła.* Lublin: Wydawnictwo Uniwersytetu Marii Curie-Skłodowskiej, 2022

Basiura, Tadeusz. *W Ogrodzie Maryi: Atlas roślin maryjnych.* Wydawnictwo M, 2018.

Berwiński, Ryszard. *Studia o gusłach i czarach.* Sandomierz: Armoryka, 2019.

Biegeleisen, Henryk. *Lecznictwo ludu polskiego.* Polska Akademia Umiejętności, 1929.

Bugaj, Roman. *Nauki tajemne w dawnej Polsce. Mistrz Twardowski.* Poznań: Wydawnictwo Replika, 2022.

Ciołek, Tadeusz, Jacek Olędzki, and Anna Zadrożyńska. *Wyrzeczysko: O świętowaniu w Polsce.* Białystok: Białostockie Zakłady Graficzne, 1976.

Chmiel, Sylwia. *Polskie tradycje i obyczaje.* Wydawnictwo Dragon, 2019.

Czernik, Stanisław. *Trzy Zorze Dziewicze. Wśród Zamawiań i Zaklęć.* Wydawnictwo Łódzkie, 1968.

Ceklarz, Katarzyna, and Urszula Janicka-Krzywda. *Góralskie Czary: Leksykon magii Podtatrza i Beskidów zachodnich.* Tatrzański Park Narodowy, 2024.

Frazer, James George. *The Golden Bough: A Study of Magic and Religion. The Floating Press*, 2009.

Gawalewicz, Marian. *Królowa Niebios: Legendy o Matce Boskiej.* Instytut Wydawniczy Pax, 1985.

Gieysztor, Aleksander. *Mitologia Słowian.* Wydawnictwo Artystyczne i Filmowe, 1985.

Gloger, Zygmunt. *Rok Polski w życiu, tradycji i pieśni.* Warszawa: Jan Fiszer Nowy Świat, 1900.

Gocół, Damian, and Joanna Szadura. *Przed ołtarzem pól: Święci w kulturze ludowej.* Wydawnictwo UMCS, 2021.

Grąbczewski, Wiktoryn. *Diabeł Polski w rzeźbie i legendzie.* Warszawa: Ludowa Spółdzielnia Wydawnicza, 1990.

Hryń-Kuśmierek, Renata, Zuzanna Śliwa, et al. *Wielka Księga Tradycji Polskich.* Wydawnictwo Publicat, 2009.

Jaguś, Jacek. "Uwagi na temat wymowy magicznej średniowiecznych amuletów i ozdób na ziemiach polskich." *Annales Universitatis Mariae Curie-Skłodowska. Sectio F, Historia,* vol. 58, 2003, pp. 7–24.

Janicki, Kamil. *Cywilizacja Słowian: Prawdziwa historia największego ludu Europy.* Poznań: Wydawnictwo Poznańskie, 2023.

—. *Pańszczyzna: Prawdziwa historia Polskiego niewolnictwa.* Poznań: Wydawnictwo Poznańskie, 2021.

Jóźwik, Zbigniew. *Madonny.* Self-published, 2018.

Karwot, Edward. *Katalog magii Rudolfa. Źródło etnograficzne XIII wieku.* Zakład Imienia Ossolińskich, 1955.

Kochan, Anna. *Postępek prawa czartowskiego przeciw narodowi ludzkiemu.* Oficyna Wydawnicza Atut, 2015.

Koprowska-Głowacka, Anna. *Magia Ludowa z Pomorza i Kujaw.* Wydawnictwo Region, 2016.

Kowalenko, Władysław, et al. *Słownik starożytności słowiańskich. t. I, cz. I.* Zakład Narodowy im. Ossolińskich. Ossolineum, 1961.

Kowalski, Piotr. *Kultura magiczna: Omen przesąd znaczenie.* Warszawa: Wydawnictwo Naukowe PWN, 2007.

Kubiak, Irena, and Krzysztof Kubiak. *Chleb w tradycji ludowej.* Ludowa Spółdzielnia Wydawnicza, 1981.

Kujawska, Monika, et al. *Rośliny w wierzeniach i zwyczajach ludowych. Słownik Adama Fischera.* Polskie Towarzystwo Ludoznawcze, 2016.

Leciejewicz, Lech. *Mały słownik kultury dawnych Słowian.* Wiedza Powszechna, 1988.

Lecouteux, Claude. *Demons and Spirits of the Land: Ancestral Lore and Practices.* Inner Traditions, 2015.

Litwinow, Siergiej. *Zdejmowanie uroków jajem.* Wydawnictwo Akasha, 2012.

Merski, Rafał. *Modlitwy Słowiańskie.* Wydawnictwo Watra, 2016.

—. *Obrzędy Rodzinne Słowian.* Self-published, 2023.

Miechowicz, Łukasz. *Święte i przeklęte: Kamienie w religijności ludowej.* Instytut Archeologii i Etnologii PAN, 2023.

Niedźwiedź, Anna. *Na granicy światów. Aniołowie w tradycyjnych wyobrażeniach ludowych.* Czasopismo Topos, 2004.

Niedzielski, Grzegorz. *Drzewo Świata. Struktura symboliczna słupa ze Zbrucza.* Wydawnictwo ARMORYKA, 2011.

Nordblom, Carl. *Historiola: The Power of Narrative Charms.* Hadean Press, 2021.

Ogrodowska, Barbara. *Polskie obrzędy i zwyczaje doroczne.* Wydawnictwo MUZA SA, 2010.

—. *Polskie tradycje i obyczaje rodzinne.* Wydawnictwo MUZA SA, 2012.

Ostling, Michael. *Between the Devil and the Host: Imagining Witchcraft in Early Modern Poland.* Oxford University Press, 2011.

Pilaszek, Małgorzata. *Procesy o czary w Polsce w wiekach XV-XVIII.* Kraków: Wydawnictwo Prac Naukowych Universitas, 2008.

Pełka, Leonard. *Polska demonologia ludowa. Wierzenia dawnych Słowian.* Wydawnictwo Replika, 2020.

Podgórscy, Barbara and Adam Podgórski. *Wielka Księga Demonów Polskich. Leksykon i antologia demonologii ludowej.* Wydawnictwo KOS, 2005.

Rożek, Michał. *Diabeł w kulturze polskiej.* Wydawnictwo Replika, 2021.

Simonides, Dorota. *Kumotry diobła: Opowieści ludowe Śląska Opolskiego.* Warszawa: Ludowa Spółdzielnia Wydawnicza, 1977.

—. *Dlaczego drzewa przestały mówić? Ludowa wizja świata.* Wydawnictwo NOWIK, 2010.

Szczepanik, Paweł. *Słowiańskie Zaświaty: wierzenia, wizje, mity.* Wydawnictwo Triglav, 2018.

Szczypka, Józef. *Kalendarz Polski.* Instytut Wydawniczy Pax, 1980.

Świerzbieński, Romuald. *Wiara Słowian z obrzędów, klechd, pieśni ludu, guseł, kronik i mowy słowiańskiej wskrzeszona.* DRUKIEM S. ORGELBRANDA SYNÓW, 1880.

Świrko, Stanisław. *Rok płaci - rok traci: Kalendarz przysłów i prognostyków rolniczych.* Wydawnictwo Poznańskie, 1990.

Szyjewski, Andrzej. *Religia Słowian.* Wydawnictwo WAM, 2003.

Tomiccy, Joanna, and Ryszard. *Drzewo życia: Ludowa wizja świata i człowieka.*

Ludowa Spółdzielnia Wydawnicza, 1975.

Tuwim, Julian. *Czary i czarty polskie oraz wypisy czarnoksięskie i czarna msza.* Warszawa: Wydawnictwo Iskry, 2010.

Tylkowa, Danuta. *Medycyna ludowa w kulturze wsi Karpat polskich.* Wrocław: Zakład Narodowy Imienia Ossolińskich, 1989.

Uryga, Jan. *Rok Polski w życiu, tradycji i obyczajach ludu.* Włocławek: Wydawnictwo Duszpasterstwa Rolników, 1998.

Vargas, Witold, and Paweł Zych. *Święci i Biesy.* Wydawnictwo BOSZ, 2017.

Wijaczka, Jacek. *Magia i Czary. Polowanie na czarownice i czarowników w Prusach Książęcych w czasach wczesnonowożytnych.* Wydawnictwo Adam Marszałek, 2020.

Wilby, Emma. *The Visions of Isobel Gowdie: Magic, Witchcraft and Dark Shamanism in Seventeenth-Century Scotland.* Academic Press, 2011.

Wisła. Miesięcznik Geograficzno-Etnograficzny. vol. 17, no. 3, 1903. Wielkopolska Biblioteka Cyfrowa, wbc.poznan.pl.

Wójtowicz, Magdalena. "Etnografia Lubelszczyzny – ludowe wierzenia o wodzie." *Ośrodek „Brama Grodzka - Teatr NN,* 2010, https://teatrnn.pl/leksykon/artykuly/etnografia-lubelszczyzny-ludowe-wierzenia-o-wodzie/.

Wyporska, Wanda. *Czary w nowożytnej Polsce w latach* 1500–1800. Wydawnictwo Naukowe UMK, 2021.

Zacharek, Natalia. *Udział zwierząt gospodarskich w ludowych obrzędach dorocznych.* Wrocław: „Zoophilologica. Polish Journal of Animal Studies", 2017.

Ziółkowska, Maria. *Gawędy o drzewach.* Wydawnictwo Triglav, 2024.